THE COLONIAL IMPACT ON SOUTHEAST ASIA

THE
COLONIAL IMPACT
ON
SOUTHEAST ASIA

Donald A. Carlson
University of Missouri - Kansas City

K|H

KENDALL/HUNT PUBLISHING COMPANY
DUBUQUE, IOWA

Printed in the United States of America

Contents

Introduction

On November 19, 1869, the French vessel L'Aigle sailed from the eastern end of the Mediterranean Sea through the Suez Canal into the Red Sea and ultimately reached the Indian Ocean, thus formally opening the Suez Canal to world traffic. This magnificent accomplishment of nineteenth century science and technology, combined with the vision of the French engineer, M. de Lesseps, symbolized the beginning of a new age in European colonial activity and initiated a renewed interest in Southeast Asia. The importance of the Suez Canal in terms of world trade, communications between East and West, and colonial expansion by the European world cannot be overstated. China, India, and the Indies could now be reached in a relatively short period of time and at far less cost than the long and expensive trip around the African horn. (By using the Canal and steam navigation, the trip between London and the East was reduced from six months to three weeks.) As a result of the reduced transportation costs and travel time the resources of the East could be more readily exploited for European consumption and the European could market manufactured items at a substantially cheaper cost in the Orient. As an indication of the importance of the Canal, within a relatively short period of time, the Suez area emerged as one of the most active shipping centers in the entire world. A second factor to affect the importance of the Canal and to increase the potential for world trade came with the rise of steam navigation. A steamer, by using the facilities of the Canal, reduced the travel size of the world and added a considerable safety factor to ocean travel. The combined advantages of the Suez Canal and the steamer produced a revolution in trade and communications which can literally be compared with the revolutio produced by the growth of transoceanic air flights in the twentieth century.

The opening of the Suez Canal symbolized the dawn of the nev age of imperialism. Associated with this event were many factors within European society which fostered the acceptance of the new imperial drive. By 1870, Europeans had reached a level of economic and political development whereby they could easily justify colonialism on the basis of economic and cultural expansion, national growth, and military necessity. Though no single cause determined the rise of imperialism, the following factors, working as a whole, brought forth the colonial drive which characterized the last decades of the nineteenth century and the first decades of the present century.

(1) The motive most frequently mentioned in association with the new age of colonialism was economic imperialism. In itself the economic motive played a considerable role in colonialism but this was only one cause for the rise of new empires, and must share with other concepts of nineteenth century Western culture the rejuvenation of interest in imperialism. Beginning in 1815, Western Europe slowly fell under the dramatic influence of the Industrial Revolution. Within a matter of two generations the changes initiated by the Industrial Revolution reached almost every level of society, and by 1870 most states in Western Europe had reached a full scale level of industrial development. Competition between nations for new markets reached the point where some statesmen believed that national survival demanded new outlets for industrial overproduction or for continued economic expansion. The initial search for new markets began in Central and Eastern Europe and later in the United States. But, as industrialization reached these traditional markets, they soon proved to be inadequate as dumping grounds. In some cases, particularly in the United States, with industrial growth, we began to compete with the Europeans for world markets. As a result, additional outlets or markets had to be acquired. With this changing economic atmosphere, many European economists and statesmen publicly demanded that world markets be established to replace the reduced importance of traditional outlets. Though the above argument for expanded trade might be questioned, the more important factor remained that many believed in the necessity of finding new world markets. By 1870, society openly advocated spending time and money, and where necessary, lives, to cultivate new trade areas and extend imperial holdings. (Empire and the search for new markets complemented one another in that with empire, foreign trade could be excluded and safe markets established.) Associated with the search for trade, there emerged other arguments favoring colonialism which can also be classified as economic. With advancing industrialism, Europeans found that tropical raw materials such as vegetable oils, cotton and later rubber, were absolutely necessary for continued economic growth and development. Furthermore, as the demand for these products grew, the cry arose that "safe" areas for exploitation of these products be readily available. This generally meant that physical control over areas capable of exporting these valuable materials had to be found,

controlled, and then cultivated or developed. This particular aspect of colonial theory involved considerable amounts of money and only a safe area for investment would attract the investor class. Cotton serves as an example of the importance of empire and industrial economic development in the nineteenth century. During the American Civil War era, England suffered considerably in that the supply of raw cotton almost ended. The effects of the American Civil War disaster on the English economy proved to most all classes in British society that self-sufficiency in tropical products had to be developed in order to preserve domestic prosperity. Events such as this helped to produce an acceptance of the imperial drive among all classes, even the working class. Another factor associated with economic imperialism involved the constant search for safe places to invest surplus capital. By the end of the nineteenth century, few areas in Europe offered attractive opportunities for profitable investment. For the speculator, the non-European world offered many opportunities for investment, but the element of risk remained exceedingly high. To invest in nations or areas with independent governments might result in excessive regulations which would limit profits or there remained the potentially dangerous situation where foreign investments and foreign industrial developments would be seized by independent and hostile governments. In less developed areas the natives had to be controlled in order to ensure a constant supply of workers and a good environment for expansion. However, in colonial areas, the government could be counted on to be protective and co-operative and ensure the safety of the monies spent in the growth of a colonial area. Generally, Europeans found it far more profitable and secure to build a railroad in a colony than in an independent area where they remained subject to alien governments and peoples. Markets, highly prized valued raw materials, and a safe area for investment grew to be the dominant theme in the economic factor for the drive to extend and build empires in the twilight years of the nineteenth century. It is important to recognize that the above philosophy or justification for colonial expansion was not limited to the wealthy class alone, but shared by all classes. By 1870, both employers and employees recognized the importance of expanded world markets and a constant supply of raw materials.

(2) Nationalism as a force for empire building can hardly be classified as a strictly nineteenth century phenomenon behind the imperial drive. From the time of the ancients down to the nineteenth century, greatness and empire went hand in hand. The arguments associated with the building of the Roman Empire differed little from those presented in the nineteenth century. However, during the nineteenth century, nationalism developed into a highly important factor both in the creation of public opinion and in government action. The reason for the importance given to

nationalism in the nineteenth century can be partially explained by the rapid growth of the reading public and the popularization of nationalism by politicians, statesmen of the age and the popular press. During this period, the theme of nationalism touched on most every major political movement, and in the area of imperialism, nationalism became a vital factor in the acceptance of building empires. For many, national greatness and empires came to be one and the same thing. A nation, to be truly great, both for the present and for the future, had to have an empire to pass on its accomplishments and achievements. To the avowed nationalist, empire differed little from having sons and grandsons to continue the family tradition. The appeal of national greatness and empire served the politician well in that public support could always be rallied behind the man who stood for national greatness and the excitement of empire. For example, the German people demanded from their political leaders that every effort be expended for the creation of a German empire so that they might secure a "place in the sun." Again suggesting that national greatness and empire were one and the same. A second group to echo the nationalist appeal were the militarists. By the mid-nineteenth century, European military strategy embraced the entire world. For example, to defeat the English, a nation had to meet England wherever the English held power, and to accomplish this, a strategically located empire emerged as a military necessity. Naval authorities also considered the importance of coaling stations and naval facilities on a world basis in order to ensure the strength of their capacity to strike against the enemy. Generally, military strategy, nationalism, and imperialism remained closely tied together. A further side to imperial nationalism came with the general excitement associated with empire. No English school child failed to thrill over the extent of the empire and no proper thinking Englishman failed to appreciate that the "sun never set on the British Empire." The British statesman and nationalist, Benjamin Disraeli, noted the importance of colonialism in that he made Victoria not only the symbol of the British Empire, but brought to mind the image of the great Indian Mongols by making Victoria Empress of India. It is perhaps this very image which Disraeli created for the royal family that ensured its survival down to the present. Thus, as the age of imperialism progressed, the sentiment of empire and the nationalistic spirit merged into a single national consciousness among the leaders and the people of the western world. An additional element to be added to the nationalist drive came with the union of economic thought and nationalism. Economic nationalism quickly became a very real factor in the acceptance of colonialism. An undeveloped area that promised rich economic reward symbolized national strength for the nation fortunate enough to acquire this type of valuable imperial holdings. Furthermore, to prevent a rival nation from acquiring valuable colonies created an additional feeling of national importance for the acquiring nation and suggested defeat for the nation deprived from achieving colonial advancement. Finally, economic self-sufficiency came to be considered a source of strength in the nineteenth century. Colonies which encouraged self-sufficiency enhanced national power. Thus, by the beginning of the Suez era, national pride and national power came to the aid of the imperialist and greatly assisted in forming a public opinion favorable to the creation and expansion of empire.

(3) A third general justification for empire came with the growth of humanitarianism in the nineteenth century. This defense of colonialism provided excellent window dressing for imperial expansion, yet at the same time it frequently meant a highly sincere attempt to bestow the benefits of Western civilization on the savage or uncivilized. In Africa, this proved to be far more intellectually defensible than in Southeast Asia, for, in general, Southeast Asia was neither as savage nor as uncivilized as Africa. The European had a considerable number of achievements to contribute to the outside world, and many Europeans felt obligated to transmit these advantages and accomplishments to Southeast Asia and to Africa. Perhaps the most outstanding contribution to the colonial world came with the growth of modern medicine. However, in order for the benefits of European medicine to be transmitted to the peoples of the East, a form of government control over a given area was required. Medical persons, without the force of knowledgeable governments behind them, could accomplish little in native acceptance of Western medical practices.

A second source of humanitarian involvement in Southeast Asia came with the activity of the missionary. In the pre-nineteenth century era, the only major missionary activity came from the Catholic Church. Protestant sects generally ignored this aspect of religion. Early in the history of European interest in Southeast Asia, Catholic missionaries established strongholds in Vietnam and the Philippines. However, these missions could hardly be classified as humanitarian in their orientation, since conversion remained their principle goal. During the latter half of the eighteenth century, public opinion moved against mission work. The general argument against missionaries stated that they bore the responsibility of corrupting the environment. Interestingly enough, both the church and the secular society echoed this argument. By the mid-nineteenth century, European Christianity became increasingly oriented toward the evangelical aspect of religion and they found that by condemning mission work, colonies developed without benefit of Christian influence. Also, religious groups, like most elements in European society, gradually showed a strong interest in introducing Western values into the non-Western world. The improvement of the standard of life, of which conversion was only a part, became the new goal of the missionary and the religious societies. Thus, the humanitarian factor gradually merged with the religious motive to reinforce Western interest in colonialism.

As the acceptance of colonialism grew among the various peoples of Western Europe, the concept of social responsibility contributed to the growth of humanitarianism as applied to imperialism. In the English speaking world, the words of Rudyard Kipling suggest the importance of this social humanitarianism. Kipling urged the Britisher to "take up the White man's burden." These words of Kipling inspired many Victorians to justify colonialism as a moral responsibility to pass on the spectacular accomplishments of their age to the unfortunates in Asia and Africa. At times, this justification for empire took on a rather nationalistic orientation, in that the French sought to transmit their civilization to the native and the German longed to see his culture established in the non-Western world. Whether the humanitarian motive is viewed as a nationalistic front for colony grabbing, or a genuine expression of social responsibility, humanitarianism, like economics and nationalism, must assume part of the responsibility for the colonial race of the latter years of the nineteenth century.

(4) The final factor to influence the acceptance of empire is that of the individual. Whether in Africa or Asia, individuals sought to create empires for their motherland. The spirit might be economic, political, social, or entirely personal, but these individuals, whether they received official government sanction or acted on a purely individual basis, must share with the more broad justifications of imperialism the responsibility for the growth of empire. However, the individuals did not have to accomplish this goal by residing in some exotic place. The newspaperman, the statesman, the writer, or religious leader who could mold public and government opinion, offered considerable support to the colonial drive. The force of their personality, either in the words they spoke or the letters they wrote, frequently began the building of important colonies in both Asia and Africa.

As indicated above, the Europeans pieced together a number of basic philosophies or ideas existing in the nineteenth century to form what has been called the new imperialism. However, imperialism and colonialism existed long before the latter half of the nineteenth century. What made the new imperialism so important to the contemporary age was the extent of its popular appeal and the enormous energy poured into the colonial race after 1870. Turning back to the first age of European penetration into Southeast Asia, the Portuguese began the movement into the Orient by the discovery of a navigation route from Europe to Asia via the Cape of Good Hope. This initiated the first age of European exploration and discovery. Within a matter of a generation the African, Asian and American continents were frequented by explorers flying the flags of all Western maritime nations. However, the sixteenth century can best be described as the age of Iberian exploration and colonization. The Spanish ruled the Americas and the Philippines while the Portuguese dominated the trade routes along the African coasts and the sea routes to the Indies. At the end of the century, the Portuguese monopoly of the Asia trade routes ended with the arrival of both British and Dutch traders. By the mid-seventeenth century, the Dutch had replaced the Portuguese in the Indies and the British had begun the conquest of India. Toward the end of the century the French tried to supplant British influence in India and attempted to gain supremacy in the area of Indo-China (Vietnam). The French failed to gain a lasting foothold on India and acquired only limited influence in Indo-China.

The Spanish kept control of the Philippines, but their principle area of interest remained with the Americas. As for the Portuguese, they controlled a few eastern islands and dominated a few small trading centers on the Asian continent. While the previous century can be labeled the age of Iberian supremacy in the East, the seventeenth and eighteenth centuries remained the province of the Anglo-Dutch community.

European rule in Southeast Asia, up to the mid-nineteenth century, remained under the control of large trading companies which assumed pseudo-government responsibilities. The various East Indies Companies basically concerned themselves with trade and protecting their factories (trading centers) from native uprisings and other European military and trading activities. During this era, the welfare of the native, the introduction of the arts of European civilization, the moral responsibilities of foreign domination of alien territories, and the general disruption of native life seldom concerned the trading company magnates. Trade and the protection of company interests remained the dual responsibilities of the East Indies Companies.

The importance of the various Southeast Asian empires in general European development remained limited. The spice trade, though considered to be one of the major reasons for original European interest in this area, gradually declined in importance by the end of the sixteenth century. Though spices remained a lucrative source of trade, both the traffic and the profits gradually declined. As for other aspects of trade between Europe and Southeast Asia, the European had to face a rather strange dilemma. Items which the Westerner offered for trade had little value in Southeast Asia. Clothing, basically wool, had no appeal in the tropics, and European manufactured goods were frequently both more expensive and inferior, or similar to items already available in this area. As a result, gold tended to flow from Europe to the market places in the Indies where it was exchanged for spices and luxury items. Criticism of European involvement in the East came from mercantilists who insisted that the Oriental trade violated the spirit of bullionism and the prevailing economic theory of the age, mercantilism. Critics argued that too much gold flowed to the East to justify continued trade with that area. Yet, the critics of the Eastern trade never gained sufficient strength to bring the Europeans to abandon the Indies. The Westerners remained in the East, and rather than reduce the contact with that area, they gradually expanded their spheres of influence. However, the growth of European power in the Indies remained slow during the eighteenth and the early part of the nineteenth centuries. The empires that existed reflected the traditional orientation of trading centers and lack of specific government supervision. (The major exception to this was the extensive Indian empire ruled by Great Britain.) After the passing of the mid-century era, interest in colonialism revived and with the dawn of the new imperialism, traditional empires were quickly converted from confederations of trading centers into the modern concept of colonies with full governmental control and responsibilities.

The European trader and missionary provided only part of the foreign influence to reach the peoples of Southeast Asia between the fifteenth and nineteenth centuries. Traditionally there have been two major sources of civilization and culture in the Orient, Indian and Chinese. Both peoples transmitted part of their culture to the peoples of Southeast Asia. The transmission of their cultures came with the tradesmen, the missionaries and occasionally with the invasion of the territory by military force. Perhaps the best illustration of the impact of these two cultures is the present day Indo-China. Here, more than anywhere else in Southeast Asia, the transition between Chinese and Indian cultures is readily identifiable in the culture and society of the people of this region. Cambodia and Laos reflect Indian cultural traits, while Annam and the Eastern regions reflect Chinese civilization. Indian influence touched, in varying degrees, most areas of Southeast Asia, but in the region from Burma to Cambodia, traditional Indian values proved to be the strongest cultural force. For example, the Burmans are Oriental in origin, but their culture came primarily from India. Through trade, prestige, and religious activity, Indian culture, both institutional and intellectual, furnished the roots for many cultural developments in Southeast Asia. Chinese influence, like Indian influence, extends far into the distant past. Chinese prestige, however, remained far less direct than Indian and, as a result, had less direct influence on the cultural development of this region. In terms of areas of greatest impact, the Eastern side of Indo-China has traditionally been the area of greatest Chinese influence. An additional area to acquire Chinese culture was the island of Java in Indonesia. This came during the thirteenth century when the Mongol conquerors of China extended their influence into Indonesia. After the decline of the Mongols, direct Chinese power in this area quickly declined. Though direct interest in Southeast Asia declined, Chinese trade with this area continued, thus maintaining sufficient cultural and economic ties with mainland China to justify the concept that the Chinese have maintained a long history of influencing the development of Southeast Asia. Owing to the economic contact between the two areas, events in China generally have had a strong influence on Southeast Asia.

Another source of influence to reach Southeast Asia came from the Near East. This was the rise of Islam in the Malaya-Indonesian area. Islam reached this region both from Arab traders and missionaries sent from India. Once Islam swept through portions of India, the Sword of Allah rapidly became an important religious movement in both Malaya and Indonesia. The reason for Islamic success in this region might be ascribed to the Indianized nature of the new religion or merely because the Indian-oriented cultural pattern of the natives suggested a certain submission to Indian leadership in intellectual activity. In both Malay and Indonesia, Islam established roots which have enabled it to survive down to the present. Islam did not succeed east of these areas because of the interruption created by the arrival of the Portuguese and the Westerner with their deep anti-Islamic orientation. Islam made no inroads into areas of Burma, Siam, and Cambodia because of the deep penetration of Buddhism.

When the European arrived in Southeast Asia, he found conditions particularly favorable for conquest and colonization. These two major powers, China and India, had retreated from direct involvement in Southeast Asian affairs and in addition, the European found the peoples deeply divided into small and unimportant governmental units. It generally proved to be easy to establish small but important ports of entry into the world of Southeast Asia. From these early beginnings the Southeast Asians began to experience Western colonialism.

The purpose of this study is to provide the reader with an introduction into the field of colonial history in Southeast Asia. It will also afford the reader the opportunity to combine the pressures in Western Europe for empire with the results of these pressures in the areas they colonized. In general, it is quite safe to speak of the Western impact on Southeast Asia. British, French, Dutch, Portuguese, Spanish and American colonials and colonial policies reflect a common Western influence. Though they might differ in direction and emphasis, what holds true for one colonial power tends to hold true for all areas affected by Western colonialism. On this basis, a collection of readings are provided which illustrate the dual aspect of colonialism in Southeast Asia. The impact of each particular system and the general nature of Western imperialism are viewed together. Colonial government in one region faced many of the same problems that colonial governments had to face in regions as different as Burma and the Philippines. Emphasis, rather than innate differences becomes the dominant theme in the study of colonial Southeast Asia. Therefore, though the readings are presented on the basis of national developments, as a matter of reality they are either problems or results of the entire colonial system in Southeast Asia.

The order of presentation does not reflect relative importance in terms of colonial rule in Southeast Asia, but rather historical development within the area. The Portuguese and the Dutch were the first to arrive in significant numbers while the Americans were the last of the great Western Imperialists to arrive. Thus the Americans are presented at the end while the Portuguese and Dutch are presented at the beginning.

THE COLONIAL IMPACT ON SOUTHEAST ASIA

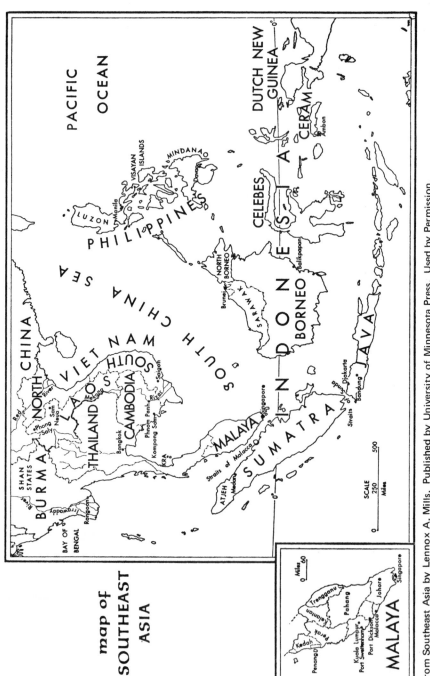

map of
SOUTHEAST
ASIA

PACIFIC
OCEAN

DUTCH NEW
GUINEA

CERAM
Ambon

CELEBES

INDONESIA

Balikpapan

NORTH
BORNEO
Brunei
SARAWAK

BORNEO

VISAYAN
ISLANDS

MINDANAO

LUZON
Manila

PHILIPPINES

SOUTH CHINA SEA

CHINA

NORTH

VIET NAM

LAOS

SOUTH

Red River
Sam Neua
Phong Saly

SHAN
STATES

BURMA

Irrawaddy River

BAY OF
BENGAL

Rangoon

THAILAND

Bangkok

CAMBODIA

Mekong
Phnom Penh
Kompong Sohm

Saigon

KRA

MALAYA

Singapore

Straits of Malacca

ATJEH
Medan

SUMATRA

JAVA

Djakarta

Bandung
Tjilatjap

Sunda Straits

SCALE
0   250   500
Miles

MALAYA

Kedah
Penang
Perak
Port Swettenham
Kuala Lumpur
Selangor
Trengganu
Pahang
Port Dickson
Malacca
Johore
Singapore

Miles
0   60

From Southeast Asia by Lennox A. Mills. Published by University of Minnesota Press. Used by Permission.

CHAPTER 1

The Dutch East Indies

Prior to the age of European exploration and discovery, the areas or regions known as the Indies, Cathay, and the land of the Great Khans remained a mystery to most men of the European world. Men, such as Marco Polo, had visited this area, but their accounts of the East included many half-truths, which combined Christian mythology with unscientific observations and oriental mystery. A second source of information concerning the East came from Arab trading centers along the Mediterranean Sea. By the time of the Renaissance, Islam had reached India and had made inroads into Malaya and the Indies. Arab traders and apostles of the Islamic faith frequented the Orient and returned with accounts of their travels and observations. From the Arab cities along the Mediterranean Sea these accounts gradually reached most trading centers in Christian Europe. The combined sources of information from both Arab and Christian travelers in the East began the gradual process of expanding the horizons of the European world. However, prior to the age of European exploration and discovery, European ideas concerning the East remained exceedingly vague and based on a considerable foundation of misinformation.

Beginning with the age of the Renaissance, the pace of European society began to quicken. Associated with this revival of activity, the discovery of the non-European world began. Prince Henry of Portugal initiated the age of expansion during the mid-fifteenth century. He began by establishing an academy at Cape St. Vincent where experts on navigation and astronomy gathered together to examine the problems of sea travel and to pool their information concerning the non-European world. These men pieced together knowledge about Africa and the Indies from both Arab and Christian sources in what might be considered the first European school of navigation and geography. Associated with the academy were a series of explorations along the western coastline of Africa which proved to be of exceptional value to the future of navigation and expansion of the European world. In addition,

1

many of the fears associated with sea travel ended, since sailors and captains gradually abandoned their dread of the uncharted sea. In place of their previous concern for prolonged sea voyages, sailors now would attempt prolonged voyages without unnecessary fear. After Prince Henry's death, interest in additional exploration declined, but revived during the reign of John II, and a new series of explorations along the African coast began. John, like Prince Henry, sought through explorations of this kind, to acquire greater knowledge of the unexplored, to make a profit, and to find the home of Prester John. (Prester John was a mythical Christian prince supposedly ruling the East. Europeans identified his empire with that of the great Khans described by Marco Polo and other explorers of the Orient. Mythology held that the empire of Cathay had been converted to Christianity by Prester John, but communications between his empire and the Christian world had been lost owing to Arab-Christian hostility. Hopefully, relations could be established between the two Christian worlds and a united effort could be made to crush the power of Islam. In general, the desire to find Prester John involved the whole concept of the crusading zeal which typified both Portuguese and Spanish thought during this period.) The first major geographic success in the Portuguese drama of explorations came in the later years of the 1480's, when two Portuguese explorers reached the East via an overland route and by the accomplishments of Bartholomew Dias, whose expedition reached the southern tip of Africa, or the Cape of Good Hope. Once the southern tip of Africa had been reached, a sea route to India would soon be accomplished.

The last decade of the fifteenth century produced two major voyages of exploration, both of which produced lasting changes in the orientation of European life and economic development. The first occurred in 1492, when Christopher Columbus, sailing under the flag of Castille (Spain) attempted to reach the Indies via a westward voyage. Columbus failed in his original purpose, but he did begin the astonishing age of Spanish, and later, European colonization of the Americas. The second expedition, this time under the Portuguese flag, sailed in 1497, under the command of Vasco da Gama. After rounding the Cape of Good Hope, da Gama traveled along the African coast and then, with the aid of an Arab navigator, sailed eastward to India. He received a cool reception in India. Moslems were not pleased to see the Christian invader and his gifts were viewed as poorly as compared to the riches of India. However, the great mission was accomplished. A workable trade route to the East had been discovered, the Arab monopoly of the Eastern trade had been broken, and soon the combined riches of the African coast and the Indies would make Portugal one of the richest and most important trading nations in Europe. Other voyages quickly followed. By 1500, the Portuguese reached South

2

America and laid claim to the Brazilian coast and in 1512, they established contact with the Spice Islands. As for the Spanish, they concentrated on the discoveries made by Columbus. Within a generation, settlements along the coast line of the Americas began to take shape, and with the discovery by Balboa of the Pacific Ocean, the Spanish realized that they had begun the colonization of a new world. Perhaps the last of the early and amazing expeditions came with the return of the <u>Victoria</u> to Spain in 1522. The voyage of the <u>Victoria</u>, under the command of Magellan, a Portuguese subject in the service of Spain, became the first vessel to circumnavigate the world. His voyage proved to those who needed proof that Columbus had discovered a new world and that da Gama had laid the foundation for a practical sea route to the Indies.

Portugal based her monopoly of the Orient during the 16th century on two major factors. From a religious point of view, they had been granted exclusive title to the "Indies" by the Popes of the last half of the fifteenth century. This grant of power to subjugate all the countries of the infidel, to seize their property, and to govern them accordingly was reaffirmed several times prior to 1492. However, with the discoveries made by Columbus, and official concern by the Portuguese that he had sailed into their territory, a restatement of authority was necessary. In 1493, both Spain and Portugal appealed to Pope Alexander VI to settle the problems raised by Columbus' discoveries. Alexander VI divided the world into two parts: land lying west of the Line of Demarcation would be Spanish while land east of the Line would remain Portuguese. The Papal Line of Demarcation proved unsatisfactory to both nations and was moved westward by the Treaty of Tordesillas. This treaty became the final statement between the two nations as to the division of the infidel world. A second factor that assisted Portugal's claim to the East was the weakness of the non-Iberian states. Those nations which normally might challenge the Treaty of Tordesillas and aspire to participate in the exploration of the East and the Americas were not capable of challenging Portugal's monopoly at this time. Internal conditions in France, England, and what was to be Holland prevented their intervention into the East. As for the division of the world by the Papacy, no European state other than Spain and Portugal accepted this division and they simply ignored the Treaty of Tordesillas. Thus, owing to the right of discovery, Papal sanction, and Europe's internal weaknesses Portugal maintained her monopoly of the East for over a century.

For approximately a century (1500 to 1600) the Portuguese dominated European influence of the Orient. Portuguese seamen, traders, and missionaries traveled both land and sea routes to the East seeking riches and converts. During the sixteenth century, Portuguese men of God and of trade established regular contact in all areas of Southeast Asia, India, and China. Factories or forts as well as missions were established in port cities from which European items of trade and religious values were exchanged for oriental knowledge, spices and luxuries. As a result of this activity on the part of the followers of da Gama, the East first learned of the European world on a regular basis, and the European learned of the mystery and enchantment of the exciting East. As for the impact of the Portuguese in Southeast Asia, aside from her presence in this region, Portuguese influence tended to be highly negative. The greedy nature of her traders more than offset the spiritual and cultural influence of Portuguese missionaries.

By 1600, Portuguese power in the East began to weaken. Many factors, both Asian and European, contributed to this decline. In the East, native hostility toward the avaricious Christian traders and her intolerant missionaries weakened Portuguese control. Secondly, Portugal had overextended herself. This tiny country dominated the African coast, Brazil, and the East. Physically, it proved impossible for her to maintain such a vast empire. On the domestic scene, the Portuguese misused the wealth they acquired from their eastern trade. Only a small percentage of the profits were used to maintain the empire, while vast amounts were spent on non-productive activities, such as an elaborate living standard, by those fortunate enough to profit from the empire. On the foreign scene, Europe began to challenge Portugal for the spice trade. For example, by 1600, English and Dutch traders had reached the East. Finally, the death blow to the empire occurred when Spain, under the powerful hand of Philip II, took the Portuguese crown in 1580. Spain did not deliberately dissipate the Portuguese empire, she merely became the catalyst for the inevitable to occur.

During the years when Spain ruled Portugal, government policy required that the two empires remain separate. However, the Spanish remained far more concerned with their American interests than with the Portuguese East. As a result, a marked decay descended over the far-flung Portuguese empire. Furthermore, dynastic union also resulted in Portugal inheriting Spain's enemies, namely the British and the Dutch. The Spanish wars against England and Holland required the use of the Portuguese Navy. In 1588, England defeated a combined Spanish-Portuguese naval armada. A decade and a half later, a Dutch fleet defeated a combined Iberian squadron off the coast of South America. In both of these naval engagements, Portugal lost a substantial portion of her fleet. This loss in naval power further reduced Portugal's ability to control her trade monopoly in the East. Thus, owing to Portugal's domestic and imperial problems and to the growing interest of both England and Holland in foreign trade, the Portuguese empire fell under attack from both the English and the Dutch. In particular, the Dutch became the more aggressive in their attack on Iberian interests in the East. Hollanders, eager to destroy anything that could be associated with Spain and anxious to participate in the spice trade, soon destroyed the Portuguese Eastern empire. Furthermore, commerce had become the life blood of the Dutch state, and to gain control of the eastern trade added untold riches to their economy. In the East, the determined Hollanders succeeded. By 1610, the Portuguese monopoly had come to an end and Holland soon became the new dominant European force in the Indies.

During the years when Portugal gradually lost her control over the East, England and Holland underwent dramatic changes which enabled both nations to seek empire and involvement in the Americas and the Indies. By 1600, both nations had experienced a national vitality quite similar to the enthusiasm displayed by the Portuguese and Spanish a century earlier. England and Holland, as young and aggressive nations, sought power, glory, trade, empire, and, if possible, the destruction of the power of Catholicism. Finally, they had acquired adequate navigational knowledge and skill to engage effectively in sea travel between the East and the West. This last factor is illustrated by the highly successful voyage of Sir Francis Drake in the 1570's and by the early activities of Dutch and English trading vessels in the East, following the age of Drake. Armed clashes between the invaders and the Portuguese began to occur and, from these small encounters the Protestant invaders soon realized that the Portuguese lacked sufficient power to repel the newcomers to the Indies. Interest in the East increased, owing to the huge profits secured by the invaders either through trade in spices or the plundering of Portuguese forts and vessels. Recognizing the potential of the eastern trade, in 1600, English merchants secured from the crown a charter to permit interested persons to participate in the Indies trade. Thus, beginning in 1600, the first of a series of charters were granted which eventually formed the basis of the British East India Company. Though interest in the Company remained strong, the Company's financial strength proved to be highly limited. Englishmen, though now free to trade in the East, lacked financial resources to exploit their favored position.

News of the founding of the British Company produced immediate concern by the Dutch for their future in the Eastern trade. To protect their interests, the Dutch Estates General organized a similar Company to exploit the East. However, the Dutch Company received far greated government and financial support than the English organization. In effect, the resources of the entire

Dutch state were placed behind the newly created trading organization. Holland had now officially entered the race for the spice trade. Not only her merchant class entered the struggle, but the future of the Dutch nation came to be closely tied to the success of her sea captains in distant Java, Malaya, and the islands to the east. Furthermore, the Dutch, almost from the beginning, showed no interest in sharing the trade with their English bretheren. Holland, like Portugal, sought to build a monopoly of the eastern trade.

During the first two decades of the seventeenth century, competition between the English and the Dutch for control of the spice trade gradually resulted in armed conflict. Holland had put her entire national economy behind the success of the Indies venture. British competition resulted in oversupply and reduced profits from the spice trade, a factor which hurt Holland's economy. Furthermore, in Europe, the English attempted to reconcile their differences with Spain, which, to the Dutch, was second only to treason. Thus, as a result of both fear of competition and England's abandonment of the crusade against Spain, increasing numbers of conflicts between the two powers occurred, first in Asia and later in Europe.

The most dramatic Anglo-Dutch struggle came in 1623, the year of the Amboina affair. The Dutch seized a British expedition on the island of Amboina, composed of eighteen English subjects and a number of Asian and European adventurers. After confinement, the prisoners confessed that they intended to seize the Dutch fort on the island. Having obtained these questionable admissions, they executed the prisoners. The British called this a massacre; the Dutch justified their act as a defense of their holdings in the Indies. The effect of the Amboina incident changed the entire course of Anglo-Dutch colonization of the East. The English gradually retired from the Spice Islands and devoted their efforts to expansion in India, leaving the Dutch free to apply their efforts to expansion in the Indies without excessive competition. However, the Dutch victory was not without its negative aspects. England would eventually punish Holland for the Amboina affair in a series of commercial wars later in the century. In addition, during the long years of struggle between the two powers, the Dutch had to invest in forts and naval squadrons capable of defending her self-imposed monopoly of the spice trade. The cost of protection seriously dipped into the profits secured from the eastern trade. Moreover, after the Amboina affair, the demand for spices declined; partly because of over-supply, and partly because the Dutch could never fully enforce their monopoly over the trade.

As the seventeenth century progressed, the Dutch view of her eastern interests expanded beyond the spice trade. Batavia, founded by the Dutch on the island of Java, was to serve as a trade center for a vast commercial empire which eventually included the smaller islands of the Indies, Malaya, Indo-China, Siam, Burma, parts of India and China, and Japan. Ultimately, this plan succeeded. By the end of the century, the spice trade, combined with their general commercial activities in the Orient and by the Dutch monopoly of the Japanese trade, made Batavia and the island of Java the center of most eastern trading activities. A second aspect of the changing nature of Dutch rule in the East came with the decision to more effectively control the spice trade. Limitations on spice production were imposed on the natives to prevent over-production and punitive wars were fought against native princes who assisted smugglers. In general, by the end of the seventeenth century, the Dutch became far more rigid in their control over their empire in Southeast Asia, and with this a more mature concept of empire began to develop. The Dutch gradually moved from a purely commercial orientation to a territorial and economic power in the East.

The eighteenth century proved to be an age of territorial expansion. Both Java and the surrounding islands fell under more complete Dutch domination and Ceylon and the Cape of Good Hope were consolidated into the empire to ensure safe trading relations between the East and Holland. Economically, during the early years of the century the empire appeared to prosper, but the Dutch policy of squeezing the maximum amount of profit from her various enterprises in the East soon destroyed the lucrative trade between the Indies and Holland. In addition, colonial corruption and smuggling rapidly increased during this age. To overcome the economic plight of the empire, the Dutch tried several methods to rebuild their faltering economy. Improved methods of cultivation of high profit items combined with the introduction of coffee as a new cash crop plus stern efforts to end corruption and smuggling quickly brought prosperity. Coffee, in particular, produced immediate rewards to both the government and the native population. With prosperity, the native farmer soon devoted too much land to coffee production and the world market was quickly flooded with excess coffee. To reduce the amount of coffee yield, Holland cut the price paid for coffee beans which eventually resulted in tremendous losses and eventual depression for the native producer. As a final solution to the economic problems of the empire, the Dutch turned to tribute and forced labor. The evils associated with this semi-slave system were legion. Corruption, exploitation, and poverty became the dominant traits of the Dutch East Indies.

In the later years of the eighteenth century the Dutch system of controlled production and native semi-slavery bore bitter fruit. The natives, impoverished by the system, resented Dutch rule, and as a means to undermine Dutch economic policy, willingly assisted the pirate, the smuggler, and the corrupt colonial officials. By the end of the century, the Dutch East India Company found itself hope-lessly in debt and close to losing control of the Indies. In 1799, the home government assumed control of the Company. With this dis-solution, two hundred years of Company rule came to an end. The Dutch government now assumed responsibility for a large but very bankrupt empire.

Between 1789 and 1815, the French Revolution and the age of Napoleon dominated European history and produced lasting results in most areas where European influence reigned supreme. During this period, Holland eventually fell under complete French control and with French occupation, the relationship between the Dutch and their empire became a serious problem for all peoples involved. The French dreamed of an expanded empire, and the Indies offered a valuable addition to this dream. On the other hand, England would never permit the French to occupy such valuable territory. The English concern for India forced the London government to re-act to any French move in the direction of this territory by ordering the Royal Navy and the Indian Colonial Army to prepare to occupy the Dutch colony in the event of possible French aggression. In the past, Britain had tolerated Dutch rule in the Indies, Ceylon and South Africa because Holland remained weak and offered no threat to British India. However, France was another matter. French influence in any of these areas might well be a disaster for British India. In the Indies and in particular Java, the policy established by the Dutch colonial officials was to remain relatively independent of all European events and to strengthen the defenses of the islands against possible outside attack. As for the Dutch government in exile, England promised that if occupation should happen, a fair adjustment in colonial affairs would take place after the final defeat of the French. By 1810, the cost of securing the Batavian defenses had ruined the already faltering economy. Finally, in that same year Britain began to prepare for the occupation of the Dutch em-pire.

In 1811, the expected British invasion occurred. The Dutch colonies in the Orient, in South Africa, and Ceylon fell under British control. Stanford Raffles, a British colonial official with experience in Malaya, became the administrator of Java and the outer islands. Raffles, deeply committed to a liberal approach to colonialism, believed that British imperialism reflected a certain genius not found in other colonial systems and that British imperial expansion was absolutely imperative to the future of Britain herself. As the administrator of Java, Raffles did much to consolidate for-eign rule over the Indies and to reform the existing system of government. In terms of administrative reforms, he abolished the forced labor system which had served to partially enslave the na-tive population and replaced it by a land tax based on land productiv-ity or land values, and finally he revised and liberalized the legal

8

system of the islands. Under his rule, the Indies began to experience the effects of early nineteenth century liberal thought. Though Raffles tried to humanize colonial rule in the Indies he did not solve the complex financial crisis which continued to plague the islands and Batavia.

Raffles intended to add the Indies to the British empire. However, the English government decided to return the islands to the Netherlands at the conclusion of the French wars, and, in 1815, Holland regained control of part of her lost empire. Though the islands were returned to the Netherlands, the impact of Raffles' administration remained. His reforms continued to influence Dutch policy long after the age of Napoleon and British occupation ended.

In the early years after Dutch restoration, the situation in Java and the islands was critical. Dutch prestige remained low, and both the home and colonial governments faced serious economic problems. Attempts to initiate colonial reforms failed as long as the economic life of the colony continued to be depressed. However, one important act did occur during this period which assisted in the eventual restoration of effective Dutch rule and helped to solve the pressing economic problems in both Holland and the Indies. This came with the formation of a national trading company which would, in effect, control the economic relationship between Holland and her empire. Control of the company resided in the royal family, the government, and the wealthy Dutch merchant class. The new company pooled the power of the entire Dutch economy into one national effort, since it controlled almost every phase of trade and economic activity between Holland and the Indies.

To assist the company, beginning in the 1830's, a new economic policy was established for the colonies which, if successful, would restore the economy of the islands and provide handsome returns for the royal trading company. The new system, known as the "culture policy," required that each native cultivate a specific portion of his land for exportable products. In lieu of taxes, the harvest from this government land had to be turned over to the administration, handled by Dutch merchants, and shipped to Holland in Dutch vessels for further distribution. Under the new system of forced culture all economic activities were controlled and supervised by and for the benefit of the Dutch. The new system provided many benefits for Holland. If the Dutch government controlled a substantial part of the native's crops, foreign trade or piracy would by necessity end and Holland would once again be a major center for tropical commerce, and with all foreign competition removed, the native market would, by necessity, consume more Dutch manufactured goods. The system achieved all the expected economic rewards. Holland, assured of a constant supply of tropical exports at a favorable price sold these items at huge profits on the European markets, and with her import monopoly,

9

Dutch imports into the Indies increased many fold. Owing to the success of the culture system, almost every tropical product of value fell under the new economic policy.

The culture system proved to be an economic success for Holland, and in many respects solved some of the financial problems faced by the colonial administration and the native population. However, the system was not without its critics. From a liberal point of view, this new economic policy appeared to be merely a nineteenth century version of slavery. According to her critics, the abuses associated with the system were many. The best agricultural lands were used for the government crops while the poorer lands were left to the natives. Secondly, in areas where food crops and cash crops could both be grown at a profit, cash crops replaced food production. Finally, the richest of the islands, Java, bore the heaviest weight of the culture system while the less valuable islands were ignored. On the positive side, the Dutch attempted to introduce new products into the islands. Tea cultivation became a valuable export product and later, with the introduction of the rubber plant, rubber production became important to the Indonesian economy. Finally, under the culture system the population of Java increased substantially suggesting that conditions could not have been too severe for the native population. However, as the nineteenth century progressed, it became more and more obvious that the culture system was being abused, and that the Dutch now commanded an outmoded and highly conservative, if not reactionary, system of colonization.

Dutch liberals denounced the culture system in government circles, in the press, and in literature eventually producing a domestic reaction in favor of colonial reform. In place of the old government controlled economic system, the liberals advocated a more capitalistic or free enterprise orientation for Indonesia. The new philosophy known as the "ethical system," combined liberal economics with humanitarianism. The liberals argued that this would provide better government for the East Indies and greater profits for the business community. With the adoption of the ethical system, private business partially replaced government controlled production of Indonesian agriculture. Though private enterprise controlled most major aspects of imperial economics, the government did not forget the humanitarian side of the proposed reforms. One important reform that the liberals demanded was the separation of the colonial and Dutch national budget. In the past, revenue from the colonies had been used to enrich the treasury of the Dutch government. With separations of the two budgets, revenue from the Indies now could be used to finance humanitarian policies in the Islands. In particular, medicine and education facilities profited from this new system. In addition, the Dutch introduced land laws to protect the native against the expanding capitalistic spirit. Indonesians could not sell their land to aliens, including the Dutch. This policy forestalled many of the social problems which some colonial powers created during this period of foreign rule in Southeast Asia. For example, one of the greatest social evils in Burma under British rule was the right of the natives to mortgage or sell land to aliens. With the growth of the ethical policy, the Dutch slowly began to formulate a new policy of colonialism which combined humanitarianism and the free enterprise system with the traditional colonial policy.

Between 1870 and 1917, colonial policies in all European capitols underwent dramatic change. Part of this change came with a new race for empire. The Dutch reacted to this new development in Southeast Asia by extending their control over all of the Indies. By 1900, all the islands of the East Indies fell under firm Dutch supervision and authority. Secondly, the new interest in imperialism required that particular concern be paid to social welfare and social development. The combined impact of greater control over the Indies and increased social concern for empire resulted in far greater contact between the Dutch and the Indonesians.

In terms of governmental policy, after 1900 the Dutch began to alter the colonial administration of the Indies and devoted far more interest to social welfare projects and native welfare. Profit, though always remaining an important motive for empire, was now combined with a definite concern for the well-being of the native. Social service programs, the extension of political rights to the natives, and economic reorganization became part of Dutch policy in Indonesia.

One of the first reforms was the reorganization of the government. Prior to World War I, Dutch colonial officials and local native chiefs dominated the government of the islands. In effect, the local chiefs functioned as the tools through which colonial officials ruled the land. Native chiefs who rebelled against the Hollander or refused to co-operate with the cultural and ethical systems were replaced by men willing to support Dutch policy. In the past, the policy of indirect control via the native chiefs kept Holland in complete control of Indonesian affairs. By 1914, this indirect system of control showed signs of decay, and world opinion demanded that traditional arbitrary colonial government be replaced by more democratic institutions. Bowing to world opinion, the Dutch introduced a representative legislature called the Volksraad. The Volksraad, though designed to appease the critics of Dutch policy, never exercised sufficient power to determine government policy. Rather, it perpetuated, in part, the indirect rule policy of the past. The Volksraad did not have the power to initiate legislation nor to control finance. It became merely a sounding board for public opinion and a partial solution to the alarming

11

growth of native nationalism. The Indonesian was told that the Volksraad would be a step toward self-government, but it never evolved toward a full governing body. Political power remained with the governor general and the Dutch home government. To maintain Dutch supremacy, the civil service remained basically Dutch rather than Indonesian. Generally when colonial governments are truly interested in extending self-government to the native population, the civil service is used as a training ground for future government leaders. Perhaps one of the reasons for the reluctance on the part of the Dutch to grant greater political freedom to the Indonesians involved a deep-seated concern by the home government that the enormous investment by Hollanders in the Indies would be upset by native rule. Furthermore, the Dutch believed that they had struck a happy medium between self-government and colonial rule, while in fact, they only scratched the surface in advancing domestic political responsibility. Had the Dutch been willing to move forward in the area of self-government during the pre-Second World War period, they might have achieved considerable native support. However, the Dutch remained cautious and reluctant to commit themselves to further reforms in government even in the face of Japanese occupation of the islands. After World War II, the Indonesians were not prepared to accept the return of the Dutch, particularly since the Dutch refused to promise additional reform. A native guerilla army, supplied by abandoned Japanese weapons, under the leadership of Sukarno, opposed all efforts by the Dutch to restore colonial rule. For three years civil war dominated Indonesian life. The Dutch failed to restore their lost power. World opinion, domestic weakness following World War II, and native determination forced the Dutch to the conference table in 1948. In that year, discussion began for the gradual dissolution of the Dutch empire in the East. Shortly thereafter, the Indonesian Republic was established.

The following selection by Amry Vanderbosch provides the reader with an examination of Dutch welfare policies in the latter years of colonial rule in Southeast Asia. His commentaries reflect not only the problems faced by the Dutch in Indonesia, but the problem of welfare faced by all colonial powers. In general, the Dutch followed a conservative but extensive social program for the Indies. The Dutch believed that they had struck a balance between humanitarian reform and conservative control. Their record in land ownership policy and rural credit suggests that perhaps they did evolve, in part, an enlightened social service program for the Indies.

WELFARE POLICY*

A liberal colonial welfare policy is highly dependent upon a Western industrial policy. The original requirements of the indigenous population can be met by the primitive methods of production, but the requirements of a civilized people cannot. Clothes, shoes, soap, churches, schools, police, law courts, hospitals, medicine, and all the other instruments and institutions of civilization require a much increased production for their support. Surplus goods must be produced by the economic system of the country to pay for these costly Western institutions. In the old civilized countries the supply of these utilities developed slowly in answer to the gradually increasing wants of the people. In a colony, however, these services and institutions are introduced not in answer to a gradually evolving demand of the population, but by the colonial government, largely in response to the demands of the humanitarian and liberal forces in the metropolitan country, and partly in response to the demands of the Western colonists. The indigenous community has not evolved an economic support for these services and institutions for the reason that it has not learned to demand them. The government is therefore compelled to provide them by means of taxation. This leads to a peculiar result. The more insistent is the demand at home for a liberal colonial welfare policy, the more necessary it becomes to encourage the introduction of Western enterprises, since Western methods of production produce so much more than the crude native economy. But Western enterprises can do nothing without native labor, and therefore the government must also by one means or another make a dependable labor supply available. All this raises a thousand and one problems.

The importance of Western economy in producing the surplus values necessary for the maintenance of a liberal welfare policy is evident from a few figures. It has been estimated that before the depression (1930's) 40 per cent of the public revenue in Java was contributed by the inhabitants, 40 per cent by Western industries, and 20 per cent by the Government industries.[1] The Europeans pay over half of the income tax alone. The East Coast of Sumatra, the center of the large European industries, before the depression yielded to the central treasury a surplus of 50,000,000 florins after deduction of local costs of administration.

Does the presence of Western capitalist enterprises aid or retard native welfare? About this there is much dispute. The Western agricultural enterprises have tremendously increased the social income, but they also stand in the way of the development of an independent farmer class. In the sugar districts of Java the

*Amry Vandenbosch, The Dutch East Indies Its Government, Problems, and Politics 3rd ed. (Berkeley; University of California Press, 1933) pp. 258–92.

13

native landowner rents his land to the sugar companies and becomes a laborer on his own land as well as in the factories. In the Outer Islands, as for instance on the East Coast of Sumatra, the soil alone has a purely native character. The land is acquired through long-term concessions from the Government; for the rest, everything is imported. Capital, the managers, and the assistants are all European. Even the laborers are imported, being "contract coolies" from China and Java. There are no gradations in this economic structure by means of which the native can climb to higher economic levels. Between the native small holders and the highly and technically organized Western industry there is nothing. The native finds it practically impossible to forge ahead in the presence of these powerful economic units with their highly developed technical organizations. Differentiation in native society takes place very slowly. There are also many complaints from the natives that the Government officials, Indonesian as well as Dutch, do not champion the rights of the natives against the sugar industry. The villages, so runs the frequent complaint, are under the control of the industry, which does not give the natives a fair deal in such matters as water division and land rent. If the official is pliant he is praised; if not, influences are brought to bear against his promotion or for his transfer.

The trade-balance figures indicate how largely the East Indies is an economic as well as political dependency. The great export surpluses are pointed to by Indonesian nationalists and European liberals as clear evidence of "drainage." The theory is true only if the export surplus comes out of and cuts down native income. But this is hardly the case, except probably with respect to minerals. Once the oil and tin have left the country they are irretrievably lost, and the future productivity of the country is that much impaired. Fortunately the Government itself is a large producer of both, so that a large part of the profits remains in the country. [2] Excessive profits have been made in good years and the Government might have kept a larger share of this in the country by higher profits taxes. [3] The Volksraad has demanded a tax on the export of petroleum, but this request has been rejected by the Minister of Colonies. Profits in the oil industry have in certain years been seven times as great as the amount paid out in wages in the East Indies. [4] In this economic structure the foreigner provides the capital, the native the land and labor. The natives are kept on a wage-earning basis and the new capital, accruing to the foreigner, is reinvested. [5] It is practically impossible for the natives to break through this circle and acquire a share in the profits. And because of the unproductivity of labor in the indigenous sphere the formation of native capital takes place very slowly.

The alien entrepreneur in all agricultural industries seeks to place the natives in a position of economic dependence, even where

14

he buys for export. He does this by advancing seed, by giving advice and instruction in production, or by advance payments or contracts. This happens in spite of efforts on the part of the Government to protect the native. Where the alien entrepreneur is unable to bind the native by advance credit or other means and where there is a free market and a consequent sharp competition in the purchase of the product, the natives have done very well in establishing a purely native industry, as in the native rubber culture in the Outer Islands.

There are evidences of a growing participation of the natives in the production of export articles on a large scale. This is especially true of the Outer Islands, where conditions are much more favorable than in Java.

Welfare Conditions

In its concern for the native welfare the Government has had two important surveys made. The first, begun in 1902, was not completed until 1914. As a result of this survey some twenty important monographs were published, giving an unusually valuable picture of the economic life of the country. A second inquiry, instituted in 1924, has also yielded valuable material. These inquiries provide the information upon which a realistic welfare policy can be based.

The average income is not over 200 florins per family. Income tax statistics indicate that of the income taxes paid by Indonesians, 54.44 per cent is paid by those receiving incomes of from 120 to 400 florins, and 85.5 per cent by those receiving incomes of from 120 to 1200 florins. (See Table 1) Among people of such low incomes little saving is possible. Whatever the farmers save they invest in houses, cattle, clothes, and ornaments—sometimes in gold, which is hidden in a secret place. In this way some formation of capital takes place. With the extension of money economy the Government had to consider the possibility and desirability of the creation of capital by natives. For this purpose the postal savings bank and the popular credit system were instituted. In 1913, Indonesians had nearly 2,000,000 florins on deposit in the Postal Savings Bank, in 1924 over 4,600,000 florins, and in 1932 Indonesian deposits had increased to 8,624,000 florins. The average number of Indonesian accounts increased from 56,134 in 1913 to 213,583 in 1928. In 1937 a total of over 28,000,000 florins was deposited in the Postal Savings Bank and nearly 23,000,000 florins withdrawn, leaving a total of deposits at the end of the year of over 42,000,000 florins. The number of depositors totaled 305,588, of whom 87,537 were Europeans, 32,572 nonindigenous Orientals, and 185,479 natives. Savings in this form are not made by farmers but by the new indigenous classes, such as functionaries, soldiers, clerks, and servants, who have lost contact with the soil and are completely taken up in the money economy. [6]

TABLE 1

Distribution of Income-Tax Payers

Class of Income (in Florins)	Europeans	Foreign Asiatics	Natives
120- 400.....	0. 04	7. 76	54. 44
400- 1, 200.....	0. 66	29. 29	31. 07
1, 200- 5, 000.....	13. 73	23. 71	11. 20
5, 000- 10, 000.....	21. 60	10. 11	1. 65
10, 000- 25, 000.....	27. 02	10. 67	1. 15
25, 000-200, 000.....	32. 65	17. 09	0. 49
200, 000-500, 000.....	4. 30	1. 37	......
	100. 00	100. 00	100. 00

*From the Departement van Landbouw, Nijverheid en Handel, Mededeelingen van het Centraal Kantow voor de Statistiek, No. 69, 1929.

The depression caused a very serious lowering of the stand-ards of native welfare. The annual national income, which was estimated at about three billion florins before the depression, sank to less than a billion. The native population withdrew from the Western money economy and returned to the closed economy of the native village. In some sections the population lived very near the starvation level. The tuberculosis rate went up alarmingly. To prevent actual starvation the Government had to distribute rice to districts in extreme need. As a result of these conditions the Government established in 1934 the Institute for Popular Food Consumption. The Institute investigates dietary conditions, foods, food shortages, trains dieticians, disseminates information, and engages in propaganda for better dietary habits.

The material condition of the indigenous population is char-acterized by very frugal food, scanty clothing, few durable dwell-ings, and little ability to withstand economic shocks. This is of course the condition among all Eastern tropical and semitropical peoples. In competition with more aggressive foreign population groups like the Europeans, Chinese, and Arabians, and the large-scale Western enterprises, the development of a native middle class takes place only slowly, but gradually some differentiation is taking place in native society. Recently middle-class societies have been organized in several of the leading urban centers. In the Outer Islands, where economic conditions are much favorable, owing to a far greater sparsity of population, the natives are sharing much more widely in the economic development of the country. Since the

16

East Indies do not yet constitute an economic unit, welfare standards differ from place to place. In many parts of the Outer Islands the closed village economy has not yet been broken down by trade, and economic conditions depend upon a large number of local factors, such as the density of population, the production possibilities of the locality, and the stage of economic development. While differences in the standard of living are greatest in the least penetrated Outer Islands, they are great even in Java.[7]

How the natives can be made to share more generously in the economic life and development of the country is the fundamental problem in all native welfare policy. One leading Dutch student[8] of this subject holds that no great advance may be expected until the Indonesian develops a much greater appreciation of the value of goods which will serve future needs. For the Indonesian, goods have a rapidly diminishing marginal utility. He will work hard if the reward is immediate; the offer of a far greater remuneration in the future fails to move him. Many factors may be singled out in explanation of this strong preference for immediate goods. The Indonesian has few needs; the climate is mild and nature bountiful. Money economy has not yet deeply penetrated all sections, and hence he has small conception of exchange except for immediate use. The arbitrariness and fiscal tyranny of the princes in the past and the general insecurity have developed a subjective preference for present goods. Poverty and the average short duration of life, which is only about twenty years as compared with fifty-five years in advanced countries, have an unconscious influence on his time preference. And lastly, the tribal, family, and village communism, which serves as a sort of old-age insurance, also has its effect. "The campaign of the popular credit system against usury and the native's inclination to borrow, and the efforts to develop in him a desire to save," concludes this writer, "will remain difficult so long as his value curves continue to drop rapidly because of the great future dis-agio. The same is equally true of the campaign against the practice of asking for advances, against the inclination of the native to mortgage his goods and against all forms of credit-taking."[9]

Another Dutch student has emphasized the necessity of self-activity as a means of improving native welfare. Unless the natives are brought to a point of greater energy, initiative, and self-reliance, all efforts at improving welfare must fail, for an increase in population will neutralize every gain made. Hygiene, irrigation, better methods of protection—all these merely enable a larger population to live at the same low level at which the smaller population lived before. Efforts must be directed at changing the mentality and attitude of the persons rather than at increasing production. Training should be personal rather than factual.[10] For this reason great importance is attached to cooperatives and the cooperative movement. If cooperation is to succeed, the initiative must come from the people; cooperation cannot be imposed from above. At best the Government can lend powerful support and provide necessary control, but the actual work must be left to the Indonesian individuals; cooperation must begin at home. It is held that cooperatives have a great educational value and can lead the way to economic independence. [11]

Java's Population Problem and Colonization

The starting rise of Java's population during the last one hundred years has already been discussed. [12] Careful analysts of the statistics conclude that a gradual decline in the rate of increase is noticeable. However that may be, the population of Java and Madura has reached an amazing density for a country which is about 96 per cent rural and it is increasing at the rate of about 400, 000 to 600, 000 a year. In contrast with the 314. 5 inhabitants per square kilometer (800 per square mile) of Java and Madura is the average of 10. 7 inhabitants per square kilometer for the Outer Islands. The limits of agricultural extension have been reached, both native and European, and a population crisis has developed. The average area of land at the disposal of the peasant has become so small as to form a barrier to national prosperity. Food products such as rice and soy beans already have to be imported. Though extensification is no longer possible, something can probably still be done by more intensive cultivation. The situation is indeed serious. A dutch colonial official a few years ago figured that Java's need of food supplies was increasing at 4.2 kilograms per second.

The solution of this problem is indeed a difficult one. Every advantage of nature and every advance in the means of production is quickly neutralized by an increase of population. Western hygiene has come in to destroy the old balance between population and native production technique; therefore Western technique must be brought in to restore the balance. However, the introduction of this technique from the outside merely enables a larger population to live at the former low level of existence. In Europe the social and intellectual revolution took place before the development of a dense population, and thereafter served as a check upon it, but in Java the conditions are just the reverse. The increase of population in Java came from an intense colonization and Western peace and hygiene, and the social awakening is only now taking place, after the population has already become very dense and the problem acute. [13] For this reason the economic outlook, and in consequence also the cultural future, of Java and Eastern and tropical countries in a similar position is extremely gloomy.

What has the Government done and what more can it do to solve this problem? As early as 1905 the Government began with colonizing the Javanese in the Outer Islands. The impetus to this movement was given by the general belief during the years from 1900 to 1905 that the welfare of Java was declining. The colonists were given free transportation and financial support during the first years of settlement. Government encouragement of colonization has been a settled policy ever since, but the policy has been costly and has yielded meager results. Including the contract labor emigrants, the total number of Javanese living in the Outer Islands did not exceed 800, 000 in 1930. Since then more than 150, 000 Javanese coolies have been sent back to Java by the Western culture enterprises in Sumatra. There has also been some emigration from Java to Surinam, the Straits Settlements, Indo-China, and New Caledonia.

In the last few years the Government has gone at the problem with more vigor. Part of the gift of 25, 000, 000 florins from the mother country has been used for this purpose. In 1937 a Central Commission for the Emigration and Colonization of Natives was set up. Increased amounts have been set aside in the budget to finance the work. The number of colonists has increased rapidly: 13, 152 in 1936, 19, 700 in 1937, 33, 399 in 1938, 45, 339 in 1939. Plans call for the transmigration of 55, 000 in 1940. The majority are settled in Sumatra, but an increasing number are now being sent to Celebes and some to Borneo. If the number of colonists can be increased to 100, 000 a year, transmigration may bring some relief to the population pressure of Java, but until then it can hardly be more than a minor factor. There has also been some colonization of Eurasians, but their colonies have not been very successful. A colony started in New Guinea in 1930 is almost completely a failure. . . .

It is thought by some that the abundant water power in Java may be utilized to produce electricity at such low rates as to make possible a revival of native industries. Native industries must, however, overcome the sharp competition of Western and Japanese factory-made articles. While the revival of native industries is not impossible, it waits upon a better domestic market, that is, upon an improvement in agricultural methods. Mr. Wellenstein of the Welfare Commission advocated encouragement of cottage industries. The people are only periodically employed in farm industry and have frequent and long idle periods. Men too old and feeble to work in the fields could also be profitably engaged in batik making, spinning, weaving, and carving. Cotton could be planted and the people taught to make their own clothes instead of importing them. Two important advantages are claimed for cottage industry: it would give the villager a greater income and it would

19

teach him to use his time profitably. It is significant that the nationalists have adopted swadesbi as one of their slogans.

The introduction of the Western factory system has also made some progress. Large-scale native industries are impossible, for the reason that there are no native capitalists and there is still very little native capital. It is also difficult to improve and extend the small native industries, for the industries cannot be improved without raising the price of the articles, and the moment prices are raised the native market vanishes.

Public Health

The problems of public health are great enough in any country, but in a tropical country with the masses still in a primitive stage of development these problems seem almost insuperable. The tremendous population of Java makes constant vigilance against epidemics doubly necessary. Since the number of private medical practitioners is necessarily small it becomes all the more necessary for the Government to maintain a large staff of doctors. The Government maintains a large corps of doctors, nurses, vaccinators, and other types of assistants. Many clinics are conducted throughout the country. Fortunately the Government receives some aid in this vast task from missions and private industry.

While mass inoculations and vaccinations have been successful in reducing deaths from epidemics, far more importance must in the long run be attached to positive measures. In this work the East Indian Public Health Service has achieved remarkable results through the use of ingenious methods.[14] The work of hygiene propaganda is entrusted to a separate department of the Public Health Service, called the Division of Public Health Education. The principle upon which the division works has been described by its directing genius, Dr. John Lee Hydrick, as follows:

The idea underlying the organization of this Division was the belief that if Publicity or Health Education could instill in the people an understanding of the fundamental rules of hygiene and a realization of the importance and necessity of healthful habits of life, many diseases and conditions might soon be brought under control and in time be eradicated.

Also it seemed most probable that if the interest of the people could be awakened and held long enough to establish an understanding of these elementary rules, the carrying out of further health measures would be far less difficult since the cooperation of the people would then have been secured.

However, the teaching of even the most simple
hygienic rules is not easy, because it means in most
cases that people must be asked to make changes in
their manner of living, and it is only too well known
how extremely difficult is the task of bringing about a
change in the habits of life. Also this teaching of hygiene must be planned to reach, after gradual extension, a population of about fifty million people. This
great group is made up of many different peoples who
speak many different dialects and have many different
manners and customs. Therefore the methods and
materials which are to be used in this health educational work must be carefully devised, accurately
tested, and frequently revised. [15]

It was learned from experience that general hygiene could not
be taught in the beginning, since it required the discussion of too
many subjects at the same time. While the teaching of rules for the
prevention of an acute disease receives a greater momentary interest, the educational effects are only temporary; for the moment
the epidemic passes, interest wanes. For this reason the Division
concentrated upon teaching the masses "the simple but fundamental
facts concerning some widespread disease, the cause, treatment
and prevention of which could be easily explained and demonstrated."
It was found that the most common diseases were intestinal diseases
such as typhoid fever, cholera, dysentery, and worm diseases,
diseases which are spread by the insanitary disposal of human ex-
crement. Of these diseases the worm diseases were most prevalent
throughout the country, and also the easiest to demonstrate and explain. The dangers of soil and water pollution are brought home to
the people and an interest in hygienic habits of life awakened. An
effort is made always to combine treatment with educational work,
for in that way only can permanent results be obtained. Coercion is
useless; it merely stirs up the people to a passive resistance.

The Division of Public Health Education is attempting mass
education in the general principles of hygiene. It seeks to stir up
an active interest by getting the people to do things themselves
rather than having them done for them. The motion picture had
been found to be one of the best mediums of instruction, for the
people like the action and life. People will go again and again to
see the same film, for it gives them a free moving picture show.
In addition to the motion picture there are other special and public
lectures. These are followed up by school lectures and demonstrations and house-to-house demonstrations by trained mantris
or nurses. Great emphasis is placed upon health-education work
in the schools.

In its war on the plague, emphasis has been placed upon the improvement of housing. In the plague centers of Java over a million new houses have been built at a cost of over 30,000,000 florins. The municipalities have also adopted a policy of the improvement of popular housing. Since this is also regarded as a general interest the Central Government supports the local government in this work. Corporations are formed for this purpose, three-fourths of the capital of which is subscribed by the Central Government and the other fourth by the municipality. The maximum dividend which the corporation may pay is 6 per cent. The housing corporations' building plans must be projected upon a basis of carrying their own costs. [16]

The annual death rate in the East Indies is only 20 per 1000, [17] which is very low for an Eastern and especially for a tropical country. Fortunately only one-half of one per cent of the people of the country live in large cities. Without in any way detracting from the excellent public health service of the country, this low percentage of urban population may in considerable part explain the low death rate. The native death rate in the cities fluctuates between 25 and 40 per thousand. The European death rate in the three large cities of Batavia, Semarang, and Surabaya, from 1923 to 1927, was 10.5, 12.3, and 11.9 per thousand, respectively. The expenditures of the Public Health Service increased from 3,500,000 florins in 1909 to about 17,000,000 florins in 1930.

The Opium Problem

The large Chinese population in the East Indies and the constant influx of Chinese immigrants make opium smoking a major problem of the East Indian Government. On the basis of Government statistics it has been estimated that in 1930 there were a total of 167,191 opium smokers in the country, and that of this number 80,762 were Chinese and the remainder Indonesians. An expert on the problem[18] concludes that this figure is much too low, probably by half. The Chinese, who constitute only one-fiftieth of the population, spend three times as much on opium as do the Indonesians, which means that the Chinese consume about 150 times as much opium per capita as the Indonesians. Until recently the problem was only one of smoking opium, but now the "drug" problem has made its appearance.

During the 19th century the sale of opium was farmed out by the Government. This system was found highly unsatisfactory. The objections to the system led in 1894 to an experiment in Madura of Government monopoly, and a Government opium factory was started in Batavia. From Madura the system was gradually extended; by 1904 all Java had been placed under the new system, and by 1920 the system had been extended to all parts of the country.

The system of Government monopoly as it has been developed is flexible and takes into account the diverse conditions in the different islands. There are first of all areas where the vice never took root and where there are few Chinese. Here the sale of opium is altogether prohibited. The prohibited areas contain about one-fifth of the population. As soon as an area becomes free of addicts it is made a prohibited area. Other areas, principally a few of the larger cities, are known as "free." Here the Chinese and Indonesians may purchase and possess opium—up to a certain amount at a time—and a record is kept of each purchase. The "free" areas embrace about one-twentieth of the population. Between these two types of areas are the areas under what is known as the "perfect license" system and the "imperfect license" system. Under the first, sales are permitted only to registered license holders, with no new names added to the list. [19] Under the second, there is also registration and rationing, but new names may be added to the list, which generally involves immigrant addicts and those moving from one area to another. A population of about 20,000,000 live within each of the latter two types of areas. The sale of derivatives or drugs except for medicinal purposes is prohibited.

The whole system stands under the "Opium Administration." There are altogether 1051 shops where opium is sold and 49 licensed "divans," or places where opium is used. The consumer brings his own opium to the "divan," as it may not be sold there. The only profit the divan keeper receives comes from the coffee he sells to smokers, rent from the use of pipes, and the dross left in the pipes. The dross, which contains a considerable amount of morphine, is sold to the opium factory. The Opium Administration has a difficult task. Its functions are threefold. It is meant to serve as a means of restricting the opium evil; as a sales organization, the profits of which go to the enrichment of the public treasury; and as a monopoly, which must guard against loss of income through smuggling. All authorities on the problem are not agreed that measures used by the administration for the purpose of restriction have been successful. Apparently there are many clandestine divans in the "license" areas and many smokers not in the possession of a "license." [20] As a Government industry the Opium Administration has served well, though the high prices which are asked for opium, with the object of restricting its use, put a premium upon smuggling. However, the Opium Administration yielded a net profit of 27,000,000 florins in 1930, or about 5 per cent of the total revenue of the Central Government for that year.

Mr. Herbert L. May, who a few years ago made a survey of opium-smoking conditions in the Far East and who is now a member of the League of Nations Permanent Central Opium Board, gives the following estimate and criticisms of the Dutch East Indian system:

Considering all the methods of control preparatory to prohibition, I should say that the Dutch system in the East Indies is at the head of the list for efficiency, practicability, and flexibility. It is not as complicated as it seems on paper, and it allows properly for all sorts of varying conditions. Existing government prices most everywhere, however, are too high, especially in the Netherlands Indies. Not only do they induce smuggling but they constitute a high penalty against the man who obeys the law by buying government opium and a high reward for the one who buys smuggled opium at the much lower price. Divans (public smoking establishments) apparently have a social feature which makes smoking more attractive. Therefore, since the object is to reduce or stamp out the vice, divans should not be permitted. [21]

Mr. May concluded that the improved form of government monopoly, accompanied by world drug control, is the only reasonable way of handling the problem of opium smoking today. [22] Prohibition he regarded as for the present unworkable and a source of corruption. These are in substance also the conclusions of the League of Nations Commission of Inquiry into Opium Smoking in the Far East, whose report appeared in January, 1931.

So long as the East Indies receives new Chinese opium-smoking immigrants and China[23] does not actually prohibit the production of opium, introduction of prohibition would be futile. Opium, and especially the derivatives, can too easily be smuggled into the country. Smuggling is especially difficult to combat in a country like the East Indies, which is composed actually of thousands of islands. Now that a plan for the international control of the manufacture of drugs has been agreed upon, the threat of the drug menace should be greatly lessened. The East Indian Government may be fairly criticized for not using more of the profits from the opium monopoly for the purpose of combating the evil by positive methods. It subsidizes in small amounts two antiopium societies, one of which maintains a hospital for opium addicts. Unfortunately the Chinese community, whose problem it is in a peculiar sense, has given little actual aid in combating the evil. But sentiment against the evil is growing in all the communities—European, Chinese, and Indonesian. An Opium Advisory Council of three Europeans, three Chinese, and four Indonesians assists the Government in planning measures to combat the evil.

Labor Legislation

In a country like the East Indies the protection of labor takes quite different forms from that in the West. Since industrialization is only in its infancy the problem of protecting the industrial worker is not yet acute. The chief problem comes from quite a different source. Western capital cannot exploit the backward regions without an assured labor supply, and since the indigenous labor supply is either inadequate, as in sparsely settled areas, or little disposed to regular labor, governmental intervention is sought. The Government, pressed to carry on a liberal policy by home and world public opinion, can hardly resist this call. Welfare measures cost money and, since native economy has so little productive power, the Government is largely dependent upon the European industries for the revenue needed to support a liberal welfare policy.

With the abolition of slavery and debt serfdom in the middle of the last century other methods of securing a dependable labor supply had to be resorted to. A regulation of 1838 had permitted collective labor agreements with village chiefs, but this system, which placed at the disposal of the employer all the sanctions of customary law, led to serious abuses and was abolished in 1863. Individual labor agreements were again introduced, but complaints about the uncertainty and irregularity of the laborers soon became numerous. With the abolition of state exploitation in 1870 and the opening of the country to Western private exploitation, the demand for sanctions against the violation of labor contracts became more insistent. A general police regulation of 1872 supplied the required sanction. Indonesians breaking a labor contract were subjected to punishment of fine or imprisonment. When the States General heard of this regulation it immediately demanded its repeal, even though the East Indian Government pleaded for retention on the ground that it was necessary for the security of business enterprises employing native labor. By a resolution passed in 1877 Parliament insisted upon the withdrawal of the police regulation, but indicated that it would accept regulations mutually protecting employers and workers should the latter be imported from other sections or other countries. [24]

As a result of this resolution the coolie ordinance of 1880 was passed. The ordinance therefore has its origin in the peculiar distribution of population in the East Indies. The Dutch Parliament would permit labor contracts with penal sanction only as an exception in districts where labor had to be imported. The labor contract with penal sanction was devised to furnish an adequate and certain labor supply for the development of the sparsely peopled Outer Islands as well as to protect the imported coolie laborer. With the rapid growth of the population of Java relief to the population pressure of that island has become an important factor in the policy. Unlike the one-sided regulation of 1872 the new ordinance made the sanction applicable to both parties. This ordinance, applicable only to the East Coast of Sumatra, contained a model agreement and register for these contracts. This model agreement, subsequently enlarged and improved, was later incorporated in similar ordinances for other districts. The conditions under which the Sumatra East Coast ordinance emerged ought not be lost sight of. They clearly prove that the object was primarily to protect the coolie against being capriciously turned loose far away from home and friends and in an inhospitable region.[25] Under these ordinances about 450,000 laborers had been brought into various sections of the Outer Islands and were there in 1930. Of these, 80,000 were Chinese; the rest were Javanese. The Government itself employed contract laborers in its tin mines. About 260,000 of the contract laborers were found in the East Coast of Sumatra, the great center of Western agricultural enterprises.

The obligations and rights of both parties must meet the requirements laid down by the coolie ordinances and must be drawn up in a contract which is invalid unless registered with the Government. The employer must pay wages regularly, provide proper housing, make proper food available, provide hospitals and free medical care, provide good drinking water, and give free transportation home after the expiration of the contract. For violation of contract, both parties are subject to punishment, either imprisonment or fines, but since the coolie has no money it generally means imprisonment for him. In addition, the contract coolie is forced to go back to the plantation from which he deserts to complete the term of his contract, which is generally two or three years. This use of governmental machinery to force a coolie to return to finish his contract against his wishes is undoubtedly the worst feature of the contract. It has been suggested that it would be better to punish a deserter more severely and then release him altogether from the contract.[26]

The term "indentured labor" is bitterly resented by the defenders of the system of the labor contract with penal sanction, and yet it is this aspect of it that is most frequently emphasized by them. The costs of recruiting and transporting average about 100 florins for an unmarried man and about 150 florins for a family. The imported coolie is unprofitable during the first few months of the contract period; he must become acclimated and accustomed to his work. The employer insists that he must have the assurance that these expenditures can be recovered, and the tobacco planter demands in addition a guarantee that the coolies will not abandon work in the midst of harvesting a perishable crop. The shortage of laborers in these districts would make it impossible to obtain substitute laborers in time to save the crop.

The defenders of the penal sanction have made out an elaborate case for the system. Without it, they contend, the Outer Islands could not be developed, as this is the only way Western enterprises can obtain a sufficient and regular labor supply. The system has brought about the development of a gigantic industry and its immediate abolition would bring about the industry's ruin and have a fatal influence on the development of the whole East Indies. The coolies come from the worst of their people and can be educated to regular work only by means of the penal sanction. Living conditions among the contract coolies are far better than among any other element of the native population; the coolies are well housed, well fed, have better medical attention, and a lower death rate prevails among them. Indeed the death rate has been lowered until it is now less than 7 per 1000. The contract coolies receive a greater measure of protection than other native laborers, for the contract coolie ordinances call for an elaborate government labor inspection. This special protection would fall with the abolition of the penal sanction. The employers, eager to win public opinion for the system, have exceeded even the high standards set by the coolie ordinances. Some plantations have provided exceptionally fine schools for the children of their coolies, and a few have instituted sickness and retirement pensions. The very large number of coolies who enter freely into reengagement contracts is further evidence that the system works well. Moreover, so the defenders of the system contend, it is utterly wrong to brand the labor contract with penal sanction as forced labor; it merely calls for the compulsory execution of a contract freely entered into. [27]

While all this is true, the system has more opponents than defenders. The Western world, and also the Westernized leaders of the Eastern world, no longer look with favor upon relations of this sort. Practically, contract coolies may be better off than other coolies; the world is inclined to look only at what it regards as the unequal relationship. There are also practical difficulties. Abuses have occurred in recruiting; immoral practices such as the use of opium, alcohol, prostitution, and misrepresentation have been employed in spite of the Government's careful supervision. Formerly, recruiting was carried on by professional recruiters, but this method necessarily led to abuse. Recruiting directly by the enterprises themselves is now in general use. A labor-inspection service, to be adequate, requires a very large number of inspectors and men carefully selected and trained for their work. Though the Government strives to attain these high standards they are difficult to obtain under the best of conditions and are seldom reached in practice. The numerous occurrences of violence on the contract coolie plantations point to some of the weaknesses of the system. The frequent attacks of coolies on the mandoers and European assistants occur as retaliation for abusive treatment or failure to understand native psychology. The new contract coolie, unused to regular and systematic labor, undergoes a psychological crisis in the first few months of his service, and he is then difficult to handle. The great disproportion between men and women and the absence of family life for thousands of coolies brings with it most of the evils inherent in a faulty social structure. The objection is also expressed that since the contract coolies are recruited only from the Javanese and Chinese the system creates racial hatred and may ultimately endanger international relations, for Chinese national pride will finally lead the Chinese Government to intervene.

The principal objection to the labor contract with penal sanction is, of course, the fact that it inevitably places the worker in a very inferior position with respect to the employer and his personnel. It is only natural that this power should be abused. Many abuses are reported every year to the labor inspectors, and not all the abuses come to light, since intimidation is resorted to. There is constant wrangling between the planters and the Labor Office over the manner of inspection. The planters hold as grievances the fact that the inspectors come without giving the planters previous notice, that they place themselves in direct contact with the coolies, and that they allow the coolies to state their grievances without the presence of the native and Chinese mandoers or European assistants. Relations between the planters and the inspectors became so bad in 1930 that the Labor Office was compelled to make concessions in the manner of inspection. It was announced that reputable plantations would receive twenty-four hours' notice, but should there be suspicion, rumor, or complaint with respect to any plantation the inspectors would come unannounced. To protect the coolies against arbitrary treatment the Government felt it necessary to enact legislation protecting the European assistants against the caprices of the planters. The assistants were without rights, they could be discharged at any time, could not marry until they had reached a certain salary level, and generally stood in complete subordination to the planters.

The planters were strongly organized and resisted the Government as a solid economic unit. The East Indian Government was in a difficult position, since on the one hand it was so dependent upon the increased public revenues which flowed from the European industries, and on the other hand public opinion was overwhelming in its demand that the sanction be abolished within the course of the next decade. The European industries are naturally loath to support the Government in policies which increase both their production costs and their taxes. This fundamental conflict of interest ran through the whole problem of the penal sanction. The planters admit that the penal sanction could be justified only as an exceptional regulation made necessary by exceptional conditions. Now, an exceptional regulation cannot be maintained or justified as a long-term policy. The European cultures had been on Sumatra's East Coast since 1870, and yet during all this time the European industries did little or nothing to remove the exceptional condition of an inadequate supply of native laborers. In 1931 only about 25 per cent of the imported laborers were free or noncontract laborers. Early colonization of Javanese would certainly have done much to solve the problem.

But there are reasons for believing that the planters were not wholly sincere in desiring an adequate supply of free native laborers. In the first place, Javanese colonists with their own little farms to till might not be very regular workers. Secondly, the long labor contract with penal sanction afforded the planters a cheap source of labor. It is true that the costs of contract labor on Sumatra's East Coast are about 70 per cent higher than that of free labor on Java, but because of the overpopulation of Java wages are very low there, while they are very high in Sumatra because of the labor shortage. The coolie recruited in Java is unaware of the high wages in Sumatra and contracts for a wage which is high only as compared to conditions in Java. The system creates a closed labor market to the advantage of the employer. And lastly, the European planters had reason to oppose bringing an adequate supply of free laborers to Sumatra in the form of colonists because it would ultimately destroy their own industries. One of the fundamental policies of the Netherlands Indian Government is the prohibition of the alienation of the land to non-natives, and the preservation of the use of the land for the natives. The planters of Sumatra hold their land in long-time leases from the Government, but the Government grants such leases only on wild lands not yet needed for native agriculture. Colonization sufficient to produce a cheap labor supply would also automatically produce a situation under which the Government could not release the land to the planters. Some of the earlier leases will soon expire and already the natives are clamoring for the lands.

The labor contract with penal sanction was long a burning issue in Dutch politics. In 1902 a Dutch lawyer in the East Coast of Sumatra published a series of shocking revelations of conditions prevailing upon the plantations employing contract coolies.[28] Several improvements were at once made, including a special inspection of labor service. Mr. Idenburg, the Minister of Colonies at the time, wished to see the penal clauses gradually suppressed. The controversy was really never ended, but a sort of truce was signed in 1924 when the Dutch Parliament declared that the contract with sanction "cannot be done away with in the interest of the State, as long as local circumstances do not make superfluous a sanction stronger than a merely civil one." While the system was accepted as necessary for some further time it was understood that it must go as soon as possible. A periodical revision of the ordinances would be made every five years, beginning with 1930.

In the meanwhile two events occurred outside of the Netherlands and the East Indies which brought the whole issue again to a head. One was the action of the International Labor Office in placing the labor contract with penal sanction on the agenda of the Conference. The other was the Blaine amendment to the United States Tariff Law of 1930, prohibiting the entrance of the products of convict, forced, or indentured labor under penal sanctions unless such products could not be produced in the United States in quantities sufficient to meet American needs.[29] Tobacco is apparently the only East Indian product affected by the amendment. To make sure that Sumatran tobacco would not be denied entrance into the United States under this clause, the tobacco plantations in 1931 gave up their right under the penal sanction clause of the contracts, and henceforth will employ none but free laborers. This action was made possible without injurious consequences, for the reason that the economic depression had turned the East Coast of Sumatra from a region with a labor deficit to a region with a great surplus of laborers. Thousands of coolies were sent back to Java. This surplus of laborers changed the whole face of the problem. The free coolies and those whose contracts expired were permitted to return to Java.

The ordinance passed in 1931 replaced the various coolie ordinances which had been promulgated separately from time to time in fifteen different districts in the Outer Islands between 1880 and 1930. A few important changes were made in the ordinance which previously obtained for the East Coast of Sumatra; and these were extended to all the Outer Islands. On plantations and in industries which had begun the use of contract coolies before 1922 the number of free coolies employed had to be 50 per cent by 1935, and other plantations were required to reach this percentage soon after. The maximum term for immigration contracts remained three years, but reengagement contracts could run for only one year, a term which could be extended to fifteen months in the tobacco industry. Violation of contract was punishable only for coolies with a first contract, though desertions remained punishable for all contract coolies. A new minimum wage prescription was inserted, to the effect that a decent wage must comprise an amount for the daily necessities plus 15 per cent for special needs. Another ordinance promulgated in 1936 provides for the complete disappearance of the penal system by 1946. Already the number of laborers under contract with penal sanction has been reduced to a small number. Of the contract laborers only about 5 per cent are employed under penal contract, the remainder being employed under free contract. The use of the penal contract was abandoned by the Government in the tin mines of Banka and Billiton on January 1, 1940. It is now pretty well demonstrated that the labor contract with penal sanction is no longer necessary.

The Dutch East Indian Government also permits recruiting of Javanese for labor in foreign countries. Javanese contract coolies have gone to Surinam, Malaya, British North Borneo, Indo-China, and New Caledonia. The East Indian Government reserves the right to send its own inspectors to these countries to observe the conditions under which its coolies work.

FOOTNOTES

[1]Meyer Ranneft, "The Economic Structure of Java," The Effect of Western Influence on Native Civilizations in the Malay Archipelago, edited by B. Schrieke, p. 78.

[2]Though part of this flows out again in the form of pensions, furlough allowances, and so on.

[3]The writer must state in all fairness that Western capitalists in the East Indies have complained bitterly of the high taxes.

[4]Van Gelderen, Voodezingen over tropisch-koloniale staathuisbondkunde, pp. 94-124.

[5]The sugar production in 1920 had a value of 820,000,000 florins, which according to Mr. Treub of the Entrepreneurs' Council, was divided as follows: East Indian taxes, 165,000,000 florins; to the natives in land rent, wages, etc., 109,000,000 florins; European personnel in the East Indies, 97,000,000 florins; liquidations, renewals, etc., 112,000,000 florins; of the remaining 339,000,000 florins at least two-thirds remained in the East Indies in the form of reinvestments. Nederland in de Oost, p. 336.

[6]Verslag van den economischen toestand der inlandsche bevolking, 1924, p. 348.

[7]The inquiry into the welfare of the indigenous population instituted in 1924 indicated that there had been a slight decline in welfare over the last two decades. The final conclusion is that the purely agricultural population now consumes more food on the average, but of poorer quality than before the war, and can import somewhat fewer goods in exchange for the surplus of its production. Verslag van den economischen taestand der inlandsche bevolking, 1924, p. 109.

[8]Gonggrijp, Het arbeids vraagstuk in Nederlandsch-Indië.

[9]Ibid., p. 21.

[10]Boeke, "Auto-activiteit naast autonomie," Indisch Genootschap, May, 1922; idem, "Het zakelijke en het persoonlijke element in de koloniale welvaartspolitiek," Koloniale Studiën, XI, Pt. I, pp. 157 ff.

[11]See Krafft, Co-operatie in Indië—een socieal paedagogisch vraagstuk.

[12]See chap, ii, "Social and Economic Structure."

[13]The plague, for instance, is more prevalent in the more densely populated districts of Java than elsewhere.

[14]The unique educational program developed during the last eight years is largely the work of Dr. John Lee Hydrick, an American who was sent to the Dutch East Indies by the Rockefeller Foundation. His work was begun in close cooperation with the Public Health Service and has since been entirely taken over by it. This section is very largely based upon a pamphlet by Dr. Hydrick, The Division of Public Health Education of the Public Health Service of the Netherlands East Indies.

[15]Ibid., pp. 2-3.

[16]Flieringa, De zorg voor de voikshuisvesting in de stadsgemeenten in Nederlandscb Oost-Indië in bet bijzonder in Semarang.

[17]Handbook of the Netherlands East Indies, 1930. This compares very favorably with a death rate of 30 per 1000 in India; 23 in the Philippines; and 32 for the Straits Settlements.

[18]Dr. A. de Mol van Otterloo, "Het opiumschuiven als vraagstuk in Nederlandsch-Indië," Indisch Genootschap, 1931, pp. 145 ff.

[19]There were originally nine European registered smokers, of whom there are still five.

[20]De Mol van Otterloo, op. cit., p. 157.

[21]Survey of Opium Smoking Conditions in the Far East, p. 12, published by the Foreign Policy Association.

[22]With respect to the Philippines, May states the following: "It is not difficult after an unofficial investigation of opium and smuggling in the Philippine Islands to understand why the United States is somewhat under suspicion internationally for failing to produce Philippine opium statistics. Illegal opium is coming into the Islands in such quantities as to make smoking opium procurable freely at very low prices, but lack of reliable figures on the number of Chinese in the Islands makes any estimate of the extent of opium smoking difficult." Op. cit., p. 15.

[23]Also other countries like Persia and Turkey.

[24]It should not be overlooked that the prohibition of alienation of land except to natives is itself a great protection to native labor.

[25]See de Kat Angelino, op. cit., II, 492 ff.

[26]For a detailed history and discussion of labor laws see Boeijinga, Arbeidswetgeving in Nederlandsch-Indië.

[27]For a fair treatment of the system see van Blankenstein, De poenale sanctie in de practijk. The number of convictions for breach of contracts is less than 5 per cent of the total number of workers under the contract with penal sanction.

[28]Van den Brand, De millioenen uit Deli.

[29]The clause as first formulated would have excluded all goods produced by such labor, but when it became clear how many essentially necessary goods would be kept out this phraseology was changed.

From Agrarian Unrest in Southeast Asia by Erich H. Jocoby. Published by Columbia University Press. Used by Permission.

CHAPTER 2

British Burma

The people who dominate modern Burma originally came from the area of Tibet and Western China. They came to Burma as migrant tribesmen during the eighth and ninth centuries and gradually made their home in the central regions of present-day Burma. From the time of their arrival down to the present, the Burmans have been the dominant peoples in shaping Burmese culture and life. Racially the Burmans are members of the mongoloid race and are physically similar to the western Chinese. Despite this racial kinship with the Chinese, the Burmans kept few cultural traits reflecting their Chinese origin and have resisted the adoption of Chinese culture down to the present. In place of their original culture, they began to adopt a form of Indian civilization from neighboring India. The impact of Indian culture tended to be relatively second-hand and never reflected a complete adoption of high Indian civilization. Several factors account for the limited absorption of Indian life in Burma. The difficult lines of communication between the two areas and the very definite lack of affinity between the Burmans and the Indian account for part of the limited impact of India on Burma. Perhaps the most important reasons for the lack of Indianization of their culture was the growth of Buddhism among the Burmans. Buddhism came from Ceylon to Burma. This Ceylonese aspect of their culture gradually became the most important cultural force in the development of Burma. Almost every aspect of Burmese life came under the influence of the religious teachings of Buddah and the Buddhist monastic orders. (Most every Burman male spent a portion of his early life as a Buddhist monk.) As the acceptance of Buddhism spread throughout Burma, the influence of Indian culture gradually gave way to the pressures of the new cultural-religious life of the Buddhist oriented Burman. Though the Burmans borrowed much from the surrounding peoples, as time progressed they gradually developed their own unique culture, blending early Indian civilization with the religious influences of Ceylonese Buddhism and by the beginning of the nineteenth century one can safely speak of Burmese culture as a distinct cultural entity.

35

Over the centuries Burmese culture and government slowly developed and gradually came to dominate central or heartland Burma. By the eleventh century, a culturally creative and dynamic society had developed with a unified government which complemented her cultural achievements. In general, the eleventh century represented the high point in Burmese achievement. Beginning in the twelfth century, the accomplishments of the past began to gradually disappear. The culture of the Burmans lacked the strong drive of the previous generations and the quality of governmental leadership slowly declined. This deterioration of Burmese life was encouraged by numerous wars between the Burman and the neighboring tribesmen which served the dual purpose of furthering the fall of central Burma and increased her isolation from the outside world. In later periods these small Burmese wars frequently went against the Burman, thus encouraging further decline and isolation. Despite the wasting of resources and power on meaningless wars and occasional military defeat, Burma, prior to the nineteenth century, maintained her independence.

Surrounding central Burma are a series of semi-primative peoples who have remained, in varying degrees, culturally and racially separate from Burmese life. Relations between the outlaying peoples and the Burmans have been cool throughout most of Burmese history and on many occasions, there have been long periods of open hostility. In general, these peoples have served as a barrier between central Burma and the surrounding centers of culture in Southeast Asia. The combination of the hostile tribes encircling central Burma and the difficult terrain made communications with Siam, India and China exceedingly difficult, and in many cases impossible. Consequently, prior to the age of rapid communications, Burman culture developed as an isolated community; a small world which had little knowledge or use for the outside. Burmans, over the centuries, became one of the most exclusive peoples in Southeast Asia.

Prior to the beginning of the nineteenth century, the Burmese could afford the luxury of isolation with little fear of foreign conquest. However, important changes occurred in the Orient which made it impossible for the Burmans to continue to avoid foreign involvement. One of the most dramatic changes to occur in the East came with the growing power of the British in India. From the early years of the seventeenth century, England had gradually constructed a vast sphere of influence in neighboring India. The Burmans were well aware of the presence of the English, but they failed to appreciate the importance of the growth of Western power in this region and chose to ignore the growth of English rule in India. By 1820, England had emerged as the most powerful Western nation in the Orient and had made India the most important part of her empire. Each decade that passed brought greater British involvement in India, and with the ever-increasing role that Great Britain played in India, the British Imperial Army and the East Indian Company reacted to any possible threat to her security in this area. By the beginning of the nineteenth century any form of threat, direct or implied, to her supremacy in India usually brought immediate military and colonial action against the suspected agressor. Furthermore, as part of her protective policy, Britain chose to absorb surrounding territories which would further isolate India from rival colonial powers and outside influence. This policy, combined with several specific events during this period, gradually drew Britain's attention toward Burma. During the wars of the French Revolution and the age of Napoleon, the French indicated an interest in reviving their involvement in India. Burma offered an ideal area for initial French advance toward India. Though French policy remained theoretical, Britain took official notice that Burma presented a potential base for a future attack against India. Secondly, British-Burmese relations became strained over the problem of refugees from Burma who sought and received British protection in the Bengal. Britain's willingness to protect these refugees led to small burmese attacks against the Bengal. These attacks would require some form of British response. Finally British merchants in Lower Burma sought to exploit the rich teak forests in that area. Though the Burmese only partially controlled Lower Burma, the presence of foreigners in this area displeased the central government. The presence of traders and an assorted variety of missionaries combined with Anglo-Burman hostility in the Bengal and the expressed interest in Burma by the French, brought Burma into direct conflict with the outside world, more precisely, the British.

Burma at this time neared a state of chaos, particularly in the South or the area known as Lower Burma. Local government, traditionally one of the strengths of the Burmese political system, and the monastic orders had lost most of their influence. Economically, the region had partially reverted to jungle, and the Mons, a local tribe, had come to dominate most of the area. In 1823-24, the first armed clash between the Burmans and the British East India Company occurred. The direct cause came from a series of disputes between the teak traders and the Burman government over foreign trade in this area. The British-Indian army defeated the Burmans and Britain chose to occupy a small portion of Lower Burma to protect future trading activities in this region and to prevent the area from falling under French influence in the future. Between 1824 and 1852, the Burmese government continued to decline while the territory under British control showed definite signs of recovery and prosperity. Rice land replaced jungle, the teak industry flourished and, on a moderate scale, law and order prevailed. In 1852, after a series of small incidents, Britain again defeated a Burman army. After the second defeat of the Burmese, Britain occupied all of Lower Burma. Soon after British occupation of this area the region revived economically while Upper Burma continued to falter. Owing to the declining environment in Upper Burma, large numbers of Burmese began to migrate into Lower or British Burma. The result of this migration created additional problems for the newly organized government of British Burma. The combined problems of establishing order after conquest and providing for the needs of the increasing number of Burman immigrants taxed the British governmental resources to the extreme limit.

In the post-1850 era, Lower Burma gradually began to experience the impact of mid-nineteenth century colonial rule. Railroad and steam navigation replaced the traditional means of communications, liberal capitalism challenged the economic teachings of Buddah, and Western values began to compete with the ethical systems of Oriental Burma. While change descended on Lower Burma, Upper Burma remained unchanged. The corrupt native government failed to respond to the advances of the British and to further complicate the plight of the native government, tribesmen from the surrounding area began to move against the old government, seeking revenge for past difficulties between the Burmans and the native tribes. In an attempt to gain support against the natives tribesmen and the British, the monarchy abandoned its isolation and began to negotiate with the French for military aid and protection. From the British point of view, French influence or occupation in Upper Burma could not be tolerated. In the mid-1880's, Britain occupied Upper Burma and abolished the royal government, resulting in overwhelming hostility toward the British. Though the monarchy had failed to respond to the needs of the Burmans, it had represented a long tradition in Burman life and had served as a symbol of Burmese culture. This rapid break with tradition resulted in an armed insurrection against British authority under the leadership of the monastic orders, the defenders of tradition and Burman culture. The Burman insurrection lacked both coordination and leadership. As a result, the British easily broke the uprising and established complete colonial rule. The rebellion of the 1880's produced two lasting results in the future development of British Burma. First, a deep and lasting hostility arose between the Buddhist monastic orders and the British government. The monks believed that the British would destroy their power and influence over the Burmans, while the British viewed the monastic orders as antagonistic to British rule and must therefore, be stripped of their sources of power, namely education of the young. Secondly, all important aspects of traditional Burmese government disappeared. The monarchy, monastic authority, and local government were abolished and in the area of government, they were replaced by new organs of authority. This abrupt break with the past intensified the problem of restoring order and establishing profitable and creative colonial rule in Burma.

After the 1880's, England had to begin the process of rebuilding Burman life. Outside of the Anglo-Indian army there was almost nothing left in Burma to assist in the reestablishment of order. Probably the only vestige of the old order which could have pulled burma together was the Buddhist monastic order, and this element had been ruined in the post-1880 era. Thus, Britain not only had to restore order in Burma but had to construct a government capable of commanding the respect of the Burmese people, a task which she never fully accomplished.

The initial conquest of Burma began under the direction of the East India Company. Each section of Burmese territory added to British control up to 1855 fell under the direction of the Company. This initiated a policy in which Burma became a part of British India, a decision bitterly resented by the Burmans. Burma had always maintained her independence and now, with British rule, Burma lost not only her traditional form of government but her independence was lost to India. Britain introduced Indian law, permitted unlimited Indian migration to Burma, and oriented the Burmese government toward India. To the Burman, foreign rule was bad, but to be placed under strong Indian influence was even worse. The decision to treat Burma as a part of India proved to be a lasting error associated with British rule in this area. Policies affecting Burma came from India or the colonial office in London without consultation and consideration of the people concerned, and most of these government orders proved to be both unacceptable and highly offensive to the Burmans. Finally, the interests of British India and the London government took precedence over Burmese interests, or at least this appeared to be the impression given the Burmese by the colonial officials and later by native nationalist leaders. As a result of early British policy, Burmese nationalism rapidly developed. The nationalists used Buddhist cultural and religious traditions as a basis of furthering their cause and added to this a strong hatred of both British rule and Indian influence in Burmese life.

During the last years of the nineteenth century and continuing into the post World War I era, colonial philosophy concerning empire changed. Britain, like most colonial powers, began to shift political authority from the home government to a shared system of political power. Colonies received greater responsibility for domestic affairs, and where possible, elements of democracy were introduced into these new governments. The British planned to develop a semi-democratic government in Burma. They introduced a system of government in which the Burmese received a voice in the decision making process, but final authority remained with the London colonial office. This system began in the 1920's and was called the Dyarchy. The Dyarchy did not satisfy the Burman because the association with India remained and the Burmese voice in the decision making process was not as important as the nationalists had anticipated. As for the democratic aspect of the new government, the Burmese found this system foreign since the limited British educational system had not sufficiently educated them in the value of democracy and the role of elected officials.

In 1935, Parliament attempted to remodel the Burmese government to satisfy the growing nationalist movement. Under the new system, Burma was separated from India, gained greater autonomy in the national assembly, and almost complete independence in purely local affairs. Final authority in major Burmese matters still rested with the London government. Thus, Burma, after almost sixty years of foreign rule, now was in a position to dominate a considerable portion of her domestic future. Unfortunately, the Burmese were not ready for such a high degree of democratic responsibility. The educational system had failed to provide an adequate base for the understanding and comprehension of the Western idea of democratic government and the responsibilities of both the governed and the governing. Since the old colonial governments had not provided Burma with an example of a democratic government in action, the immediate result of the new Burmese oriented government was a decline in the efficiency and authority of the government over the population. To judge the new colonial scheme in Burma is almost impossible. Soon after Burma gained her autonomy, World War II began and shortly after, the Japanese occupied the country. British rule abruptly terminated, and the 1935 experiment ended. After World War II, there was little chance to restore the 1935 system. The Burmans demanded complete independence; this they received in 1948. Though independence was achieved with relative ease, the legacy of British rule survived both to assist and to haunt modern independent Burma.

The most dramatic impact which Britain had on Burmese life came with the rapid introduction of Western civilization into traditional Burman culture. This region, even as late as the nineteenth century, had had almost no contact with the outside world and viewed with disdain foreign ideas and values. With the introduction of nineteenth century Western civilization into Burma, a cultural conflict quickly developed which created a vast variety of problems on all levels of Burmese society.

One of the first aspects of British rule to produce a cultural conflict and a disruption of society came in the general area of economics. Under British rule, Burma prospered. The area offered rich potential in agriculture and with the discovery of petroleum and mineral deposits, additional wealth was added to the colony. The teak forests also contributed to the economy of the colony. Teakwood brought a high price on the European market, and the Burmese forests produced some of the finest woods in the world. Soon after British occupation of Lower Burma, the forests fell under rigid state control to prevent destruction by overly eager lumbermen. Laws governing the cutting of the wood and regulations in marketing prevented excessive exploitation. In this instance, colonial rule meant a reasonably just balance between the preservation of natural resources and economic stimulation. Under British supervision, a thriving industry developed involving the cutting and milling of teak and a ship building industry. Rice also offered the potential for increasing Burmese wealth. In the past, Lower Burma had been an important producer of rice, but in the immediate pre-British era, large portions of the former rice producing lands had been allowed to revert to jungle. The British encouraged the reclamation of these former rice producing areas. Rice production increased and Burmese rice found a ready market in Southeast Asia. In later periods, the British developed a mining industry in Upper Burma and began the exploitation of the petroleum resources. Of particular importance was the growth of Burmese oil interests, for the by-products from Burmese oil proved to be exceptionally valuable. With the growth of the agricultural and mineral industry came considerable prosperity and colonial Burma participated in world trade with a favorable balance between exports and imports.

The exploitation of Burmese teak, rice, minerals and petroleum gave to colonial Burma a strong financial orientation. Unfortunately, despite this prosperity, the Burmese failed to profit from the increased economic activity. Investment in the new industries came from the British, Chinese, and Indian communities. The Burmese neither understood Western and Oriental business techniques nor attempted to participate in these activities. Burmans with wealth chose to remain isolated from the new economic growth in their homeland. The Burman lower classes also failed to profit from the new flurry of activity. In industry, foreign managers found the Burmese worker highly unsatisfactory and preferred either Indian or Chinese workers. The Burmese preferred agricultural work rather than urban or mining labor, and where they did drift into the urban labor force they neither understood the requirements of the job nor appeared to be reliable as steady employees. The Indian and the Chinese proved to be just the opposite. These foreign workers had the laboring skills sought by employers, agreed to work for rock bottom wages, and could be counted on for continued and reliable employment. Under British rule, Indians could migrate to Burma without restriction. Since Burma offered superior working conditions than commonly found in India they came by the thousands to urban Burma. By 1940, these Indian workers dominated the cities and most of the skilled and unskilled labor community. Burmese cities became Indian cities where Indians worked and controlled almost every trade and small business. The British government failed to protect the Indians who demanded little except a humble living wage, fearing that a well paid Indian labor force in Burma would lead to similar results in India. A second group to compete with the Burmese labor force were the Chinese. However, the Chinese did not come to Burma in as great a number as did the Indians, and therefore did not present as serious a problem for the Burman society. In the early days of British rule, the Burmans showed no interest in the role played by foreign labor, but near the end of the colonial era, many Burmans had been forced to leave the land and seek employment in the cities. When economic necessity drove the Burman to the city, he found that the market had been filled to capacity with Indian and Chinese labor and no place remained for the Burman. In rural Burma, the Burman ultimately failed to profit from the increased rice lands made available under British rule. When rice lands were opened up, the Burmans did move on to the new lands, but their need for cash to develop these lands drove them into the hands of the Indian money lender called the Chettyar. Under British law, all land could be mortgaged, whether foreign or native owned. The Indian Chettyar belonged to a money lending caste in India who found the Burman a good and ready customer. This group lent millions of pounds to the Burmans at exceedingly high interest rates. Eventually, through foreclosure, the Chettyar gained control of the riches of the Burmese rice lands. To remain in rural areas the Burmans had to become tenant farmers subject to the will of an absentee landlord, usually an agent of the Chettyar. The heavy investment by the Indian money lender was one of the reasons the British had to be cautious in separating Burma from India, since any change in the status of the Chettyar in Burma might destroy part of the economy in India. A second negative aspect associated with the role of the Chettyar came with the growth of nationalism in Burma. The nationalist used the Chettyar as one of their best examples of foreign exploitation under British rule. In this situation, the nationalists appeared to be correct in charging that Burma had become a land of prosperity but the reward for this prosperity went to the British, the Chinese and Indian worker, and the Chettyar rather than the Burman. In terms of a cultural conflict, the Burman found that the old values and ways no longer proved satisfactory. Foreign money lenders seized his land and the urban employer preferred foreign labor to the Burman. As a result most Burmans had no choice but to drift to the bottom of colonial Burman economic and social society.

Not only in the realm of economics did Burmese life change; it also changed with the growth of social service projects imposed on the Burmese by the British. Britain, like all colonial powers, attempted to introduce a variety of social service programs into

Southeast Asia. These colonial social service programs usually included public and western education, communication improvements, public welfare, public health and sanitation, and rural development schemes. Programs of this nature are extremely expensive, and in the age of colonialism, foreign aid programs were not accepted as customary. Therefore, colonial budgets had to stand the expense of any major social development programs. European humanitarians and civil servants could provide technical knowledge, but they did not provide the money to finance the various proposed projects. This meant that the cost of these programs had to be carried by the native and the business community. Generally the natives hated to pay taxes and the business community was reluctant to see its profits disappear into social welfare taxes unless they could be persuaded that the social service programs would assist them in expanding their potential for further development and exploitation. A second complicating factor associated with social service projects was that most social programs conflicted with native tradition and religious beliefs. As a result, all colonial governments had to struggle with the dual problem of reluctant tax payers and conflicting values between the colonial power and the native.

In the area of communications and travel, the British expanded the use of the river system and developed a fairly extensive road and railroad system. Pre-colonial Burma had relied on the river system for travel and trade, and for the most part, the rivers did provide good north-south transportation opportunities. Traditionally, a large number of Burmans operated an extensive riverboat system. The British introduced the steam boat which not only expanded river travel, but produced a revolution in the labor force involved in river travel. The steam boat quickly replaced the native boatman who could not compete with mechanical transportation resulting in severe unemployment among the native community. Furthermore, since the Burmans refused to work on the steam boats, the navigation companies had to turn to the Indian community for workers. Once again, the Burman found himself the victim of Western life and the Indian labor force. Using the rivers as a base of operation, modern road building and later railroad construction expanded communication within Burma. With the completion of a road and rail system, vast new areas of rural Burma could be tapped for economic development. Improved communication facilities usually produced severe cultural conflicts between the old isolated life and the rapid Westernization of the area. Western businessmen and investors frequently seized the prime lands for large scale farming or began the exploitation of the natural resources of the region. With the increased activity in a newly developed area, Chinese merchants and Indian laborers arrived to compete with the native Burman community. Generally, the outsider prevailed over the native. By the end of the British era, Burma had adequate transportation facilities for the exploitation and development of the land. But the price paid for the expansion of communications within Burma was the ever-present struggle between the old life and the new values of the West.

The introduction of a Western educational system into Burma produced a rather unique colonial problem. Owing to the accomplishments of the Buddhist monastic schools, old Burma had had an exceedingly high literacy rate for an Asian nation. In theory, every Burman boy had to be educated by the monks. By the beginning of the nineteenth century, the monastic school system had begun to decay. However, with the abolition of the royal government and official British hostility toward the monastic orders, the native school system was almost totally destroyed. Finally, as British penetration of Burma increased, traditional education had little value in the more Western oriented aspects of Burmese life. The educational void left by the disappearance of the pagoda schools was replaced, in part, by the introduction of British and missionary schools at all levels. The British, like all Western colonials, hoped to develop extensive educational facilities but, owing to a shortage of qualified persons to teach the required subjects, the quality of education and the number of schools established remained far below expectations. In Burma, the educational changes introduced by the British resulted in a decline in literacy for the lower classes. As for higher education, Burmans, like most Southeast Asians, preferred a literary rather than a vocational education. As a result, the Burman student, believing that an educated man should not do vocational work, chose to become lawyers rather than engineers or skilled workers. In an area where there remained a tremendous demand for technical and skilled workers, there remained a terrible shortage of trained Burmans, while at the same time there existed an abundance of lawyers who had no hope of employment. Many of the literary educated Burmans turned to politics as a solution to their problem of unemployment. They assisted in organizing protests against the government and civil service, believing that if they drove the foreigner out, there would be adequate positions available for the educated native. In theory, the demands of the unemployed intellectual might be correct, but in actual practice, to drive the foreigner out of the country would only solve part of the problem for only a very short period of time. The real problem lay with the choice of education the Burman preferred; literary rather than vocational.

The British health record proved adequate but not outstanding. The major epidemic diseases of the tropics such as cholera, smallpox, plague and dysentery were reasonably controlled. This in itself can be used as a partial justification for European occupation of tropical Southeast Asia. However, lasting solutions to the prob-

44

lems of health in the tropics involved far more than mere control of dreaded diseases. In order for Western medicine and medical technology to produce lasting results, native ignorance and superstition had to be destroyed. This, like so much of Western colonialism, produced the traditional conflict between the old and the new. Natives generally refused to co-operate with the local health officer and the regulations he sought to impose on native life. Where science could have succeeded, ignorance and tradition often prevailed. In 1948, Burmans still deposited night soil near local water supplies as they had done in the past, thus keeping the village water supply continually infected. A second barrier toward better health in Burma came with the Buddhist taboo against killing, even rats and mosquitoes. To control malaria and plague, the rat and mosquito had to be destroyed. Yet, to accomplish this task, the Buddhist religion had to be attacked. Any attack against the Buddhist religion produced a major reaction to foreign rule. Urban Burma faired better in the battle against disease. Hospitals and dispensaries distributed medicine to those in need and conducted research in control of tropical disease. Hospitals normally also served as training centers for native medical personnel. Unfortunately, Burmans generally refused to work in hospitals and indicated no interest in a medical education. As a result, hospital staffs fell under the domination of the Indian rather than the Burman, which meant that Burmans lacked the training to continue the job of controlling tropical diseases after the British departed.

After World War II, the Burman nationalists demanded that the British get out. In 1948, partially in conformity with British policy to disengage herself from the empire, Burma received complete independence. With independence, the new state cut all ties with the British empire and the commonwealth. Though Burma achieved its independence, the legacy of British rule remained. The following two articles suggest the most dramatic aspects of British rule in Burma. Erich Jacoby's analysis of the agrarian problem in colonial Burma and John Cady's analysis of Burmese lawlessness provide the reader with a vivid account of the conflicts faced by modern independent Burma. It has been suggested that the British were basically well intentioned in Burma, but that the road to hell is paved with good intentions.

BURMA *

Introduction. The economic development of Burma had been different in many respects from that of Java. While the Dutch administration in Java protected the natives' property rights to the soil, the British in Burma observed a policy of laissez-faire that finally resulted in an unparalleled land concentration. Increasing population pressure has marked Java's development, but Burma is still a country with vast areas of agricultural waste land. Political and economic dependence has created in Burma the typical colonial conflict, with its social and racial aspects. Conditions became further complicated by tension between the native population and immigrants from India who were urged by the British Administration to participate in the development of the fertile plains of Lower Burma.

A century ago, the British administration took over the lower part of Burma (partly in 1824, partly in 1852). In contrast to densely populated Upper Burma, with its highly complex, though not rigid, social organization, the greater part of Lower Burma then consisted of large areas of sparsely settled waste land. As a result of a series of devastating wars in the middle of the eighteenth century, only limited groups found it possible to cultivate cotton in the jungle, and this only as shifting cultivators, in small, scattered clearings. [1]

The revolutionizing factor in the development of Burma was not British rule as such, but rather the opening of the Suez Canal in 1869, which made it possible to sell tropical surpluses on the Western market. British rule established the needed political and economic conditions for the exploitation of this new trading opportunity, and thus the basis for Burma's adjustment to the expanding world economy. In the years following the opening of the Suez Canal, large-scale rice production was developed in the delta region of Lower Burma, also called the Delta land. Long before the British finally took over Upper Burma (1886), a stream of individual immigrants had gone from there to settle in the Delta land. Later there followed well-organized Indian immigration on a large scale.

Contact with Western economy strongly influenced the social organization in the Delta land, disintegrating the traditional economic and social life of the people much faster and more intensely than was the case in Java, where Western penetration had been more restricted. Whereas the old economic life of Burma had been mainly feudal and based on the tradition of the village economy, the new economic setup in the Delta land became individualistic, exalting freedom of contract and freedom of enterprise. [2] The Brit-

*Erich H. Jacoby, Agrarian Unrest in Southeast Asia, lst. ed. (New York, Columbia University Press, 1949) pp. 70—88. (By permission of the author)

ish school of economic liberalism applied its principles to this remote part of the world. Individual property displaced family property, and imports of superior manufactured commodities displaced the original local handicrafts. Land became a commodity[3] and credit arrangements conquered first the people and later the soil. J. Russell Andrus points out that the new immigrant villages in Lower Burma were composed of individuals and no longer of clans and groups, and that the head man of each village had jurisdiction over all its residents. Thus, the principle of geographically based administration displaced the ancient tribal administration, a fact which has contributed in large measure to social rootlessness and confusion, during a period in which a new and stable social system could not be developed.

It cannot be denied that British rule was highly successful in opening Burma to world trade. Burma (until 1937 an integrated part of India) has become the world's main exporter of rice (with an annual average of 3 million tons) and an important exporter of timber (teak), petroleum, and valuable metals. An efficient flood control was established in the Delta land, and in three generations vast jungle areas were cleared, thereby increasing the rice acreage of Lower Burma from 1 to 10 million acres and developing it into one of the most productive rice areas in the world. Seen from a purely technical point of view, this colonial penetration and development of Burma's economic resources was a first-rate performance. However, it lacked the somewhat more liberal-minded social considerations characteristic of the Dutch administration in the Netherlands East Indies. [4]

Foreign investments (partly in agriculture and partly in oil, mining, and lumber) decided the colonial development of Burma. [5] Before the war they were estimated at approximately 50 million English pounds, roughly three times as much as in 1914. Dividends averaged 20 per cent or more on stocks outstanding, and the remittances of commercial profits were as high as 10 to 12 million pounds annually. Ninety per cent of the total investments were British controlled. However, the estimate of the foreign investments does not include the large investments by the Chettyars[6] and other Indian moneylenders, who have financed the expansion of the rice economy in the Delta land and who have been considered "foreigners" in Burma since the separation from British India in 1937. Their investments are of particular interest to this study. According to an estimate of the Provincial Banking Inquiry Committee in 1930, the loans of the Chettyars on security of agricultural land alone amounted to Rs. 500 million, or $190 million. [7]

Colonial development is concentrated in the Delta lands, where agriculture has become largely commercialized and has taken on the typical industrial characteristics of large-scale production and minute division of labor. [8] An almost unlimited supply of land, security of rainfall, and the practice of concentrating on a single crop have permitted a division of labor by alloting each process to a different man. Large-scale production has been made possible by an abundant supply of cheap labor flowing into the area from Upper Burma and crowded South India. It has been financially supported by easily borrowed capital. Consequently, Lower Burma's land ownership is represented by stocks and shares. [9]

Today the agricultural wealth of rice-producing Burma is concentrated in the lands around the deltas of the Irrawaddy, Sittang, and lower Salween rivers. These areas, together with the Arakan region, comprise Lower Burma. It differs greatly from Upper Burma, where a stable population continues cultivation under more traditional conditions, and which is characterized by less dependable rainfall, less fertile soil, and frequent crop failures. The Chettyar moneylenders, who have provided most of the capital for developing the Delta lands, fear the risks of farming in Upper Burma and perfer the fertile plains in the south, where the rice crop is more regular. Upper Burma owes to its relatively unfavorable natural conditions its more stable social development, free from the disturbances of an unbalanced commercial economy. It is today a country of small independent holdings yielding a variety of crops (rice, red millets, sesamum, cotton, beans, ground nut) that insures the farmer in a problematical climate against a total crop failure. In fact, only one-seventh of the land in Upper Burma is controlled by nonagriculturists, in contrast with one-half in Lower Burma. Since this study, however, is primarily concerned with areas having a typically colonial economy, it will deal mainly with the economic and social conditions in the Delta lands.

In Burma, as in other dependent areas, there is almost no manufacturing, and only some processing and extracting. Large imports of cheap consumer goods cripple native handicrafts and practically eliminate the possibilities for development of any native industry. The dependence on the Indian market for rice exports (one million tons) prevents the imposition of protective tariffs against cheap Indian-made consumer goods, a fact which Burma's nationalistic leaders deeply resent. [10]

For the last decades Burma has been one of the most problematic of Western possessions in Southeast Asia. The war not only damaged its economy severely but at the same time shattered its entire political and social system. However, the great economic problems with which Burma is confronted today have a new basis for solution in the political agreement signed in London between Great Britain and Burma on January 27, 1947. Displaying superior British statesmanship in acknowledging political facts, the agreement contains the procedures enabling Burma to achieve, in the near future, self-government with the option of remaining in the Commonwealth. [11] Burma decided, however, to leave the British Commonwealth, and on January 3, 1948, proclaimed its independence. The Republic of Burma is the first state to separate from the British Empire since the American colonies did so in the year 1776. Independent Burma will now have to find the right solution for the numerous difficulties that accumulated during a period of unparalleled economic expansion terminated by a war of disintegrating effect upon the economy of the country.

Population and Land Utilization. The Census of 1931[12] reported a population of 14,700,000, of which more than 50 per cent lived in the Delta land, 30 per cent in Upper Burma and the remainder in the Shan States in the east, or in other tribal territories on the western, northwestern, and northeastern frontiers. [13] The 1941 Census, which had not been analyzed before the Japanese invasion, reports a population of about 16.8 million; today the population may have passed the 18 million mark, thereby reaching that of the Philippines.

Indebtedness and Land Concentration—Tenancy. All over Southeast Asia we encounter a very urgent credit and indebtedness problem, intimately related to the structure of colonial agriculture. It is the natural result of Western economic penetration, of the elimination or crippling of native handicraft, and the lack of diversification. But in the case of Burma it developed far beyond the general economic and social limits. The mechanism of colonial expansion operated here more or less undisturbed by governmental interference. The consequence was that the people were forced either to part from their land or become heavily indebted to a foreign moneylender group.

The Delta land was not developed by the traditional imposition of a colonial economy upon an existing native economic system, but was, rather, the actual organization de novo of a pioneer colonial economy. Taking this into consideration, certain features in the picture may be more easily understood. The British colonial administration had to deal mainly with immigrants, and not with a stable population. Its task was to achieve "the blending, harmonious or otherwise, of three distinct economic systems, the original Burmese economy, the economy of the Chettyar moneylenders, and the increasingly important capitalist economy of Western nations."[14] The immigrants from Upper Burma and south India lacked the needed capital to develop the Delta area in a manner commensurate with the opportunities presented by an expanding world trade. This brought about the unique combination of British administration and Indian moneylenders, mainly represented by the Chettyars. British law guaranteed the Chettyars that the loan secured by mortgage (an instrument unknown to native custom)

would be honored and protected by the British courts. Now the
Chettyars could come to the rescue of the immigrant peasant,
gradually expanding their credit system over the entire Delta land,
following, and even ahead of, the expanding cultivation. Confident
in the law and order of British rule, and anticipating the economic
prospects of Lower Burma, within two generations the Chettyars
loaned out an estimated Rs. 750 million (equal to $U.S. 270 mil-
lion), two-thirds of it on the security of agricultural land. [15] The
result was that by 1936 the Chettyars owned two and a half of
Lower Burma's ten million acres of rice land, and had heavy mortgages on an additional 10 and 20 per cent. [16]

As the Chettyars are professional moneylenders and not
agriculturalists, they have taken full advantage of the unprepared
and easy-going native population. Their rates of interest have
been between 15 and 36 per cent annually, averaging 25 per cent;
this was often lower than that of indigenous moneylenders, but it
was extremely high considering the first-class security covering
the loan and the normal profit rate of the native cultivator.

In spite of the tremendous amounts involved, the Chettyar
credit system was far from being economically efficient.
Furnivall[17] gives excellent reasons for the inability of the Chettyars
to solve satisfactorily the problem of agricultural finance in Burma.
While subagents in all large villages combined access to large
credit capital with local knowledge, the custom of changing personnel every three years—probably necessary on account of technical banking considerations—was prejudicial to agricultural efficiency. Longterm loans were rarely granted, and loans which
should have been extended over periods of from ten to twenty years
(considering the backward economic development of the area) were
granted for a term of only three years. The inexperienced native
farmer almost inevitably was forced to default on his debt and to
lose his property.

As the Chettyar agents could not possibly acquire a satisfactory knowledge of their clients within only three years, they
covered the risks involved by charging a higher rate of interest.
Furnivall[18] estimates the consequent additional cost to Lower
Burma, in 1931, at Rs. 7.5 millions (1 per cent of the capital).
The Chettyar thus makes his calculations exclusively with regard
to the amount of security at hand and not with regard to the increase
of agricultural productivity. Consequently, the cultivator frequently finds his credit exhausted just when the land is about to repay the initial expenditures made for developing it.

Too much lending, rather than too little, is generally the
greatest drawback to the Chettyar credit system. The temporary
agent is seldom interested in a stable, prospering clientele which

he hopes to develop economically, as does a Western banker. He, as a mere moneylender, is concerned only with securities and interest. He seldom cares about the economic use of the money; frequently he encourages his clients to continue to borrow as long as they can give additional security. It is estimated that less than 10 per cent of the money lent on Burmese rice lands was actually used to improve the land or to purchase additional holdings[19]— an estimate, which, however, seems to be exaggerated.

This system has been detrimental for a new country like the Delta, cultivated by people unaccustomed to dealing with large sums of money and inexperienced in the use of credit. Consequently, the most recently cultivated lands were usually the first ones to pass out of the control of the original owners.[20] Some students emphasize that the strict religion of the people does not encourage the accumulation of wealth and that this is no less responsible than the Chettyars for the losses of the cultivators. No doubt, the fact that religious Burmese Buddhists are prohibited from making legally valid wills has brought about a minute division of family property, which naturally has not favored the accumulation of wealth. The elaborate spending of money for pagodas in order to accumulate credit for the next transmigration neither favors the establishment of a capitalist class nor does it foster sound economic thinking. Thus, the Burmese were completely unprepared for the new problems of a money economy.

The boom times at the beginning of the century, when the price of rice increased by 50 per cent within only eight years, made the population still more adaptable to the credit system of the Chettyars.[21] The mere fact, however, that this system was able to operate unrestricted and uncontrolled in an area like the Delta land must be considered the main reason for the present situation. Other factors may have prepared or emphasized the development, but these are too remote to be causal. It is true that the Chettyars are not actually land grabbers, but prefer straight, profitable accounts to the trouble of taking over the land. Andrus[22] asserts that they are often more lenient that native creditors, in order to avoid foreclosures. However, the logic inherent in such a credit system ultimately leads to the most unfavorable consequences.

Although the British administration emphasized that it favored peasant proprietorship rather than large estates, the trend toward the elimination of native ownership was already apparent at the beginning of the century. Some legislative acts, such as the Land Improvement Loans Act of 1883, the Agricultural Loans Act of 1884,[23] and the Debt Conciliation Act of 1905, stressed the graveness of the situation, but brought little actual financial relief. After serious rebellions, the government proposed in a press communique, May 19, 1931, "to re-examine the very difficult question of agrarian legislation, but that it will be come time before they can come to any conclusions on this controversial matter."[24] Not until shortly before the Japanese invasion in 1941 was legislation passed on land alienation, tenancy and land purchase. It came too late, however, since the process of land concentration in the hands of nonagriculturists was so far advanced that a mere legal measure was of little consequence.[25]

Statistically, the history of the colonization of Lower Burma shows an almost uninterrupted loss of land by native farmers. The periods of high rice prices at the beginning of the century, and during and after World War I, did not stop this trend. Land concentration has been almost exclusively in favor of foreigners, mostly Chettyars and Chinese. From 1915 to 1930, native owners lost 1, 300, 000 acres in the Delta land because of indebtedness.[26] By the end of June, 1931, one-third of the occupied area was in the hands of nonagriculturists.[27] This detrimental development increased during the depression. The collapse of the rice price caught the Burmese farmers completely unprepared, and a wave of foreclosurers swept over the country, leaving the foreign moneylenders in control of the best part of the land. The thirteen principal rice-growing districts of Lower Burma—that is, the area from Arakan to the region of Moulmein, focusing around the Irrawaddy delta—were the center of this serious development.

Classification of Occupiers of Agricultural Land In
Thirteen Principal Rice-Growing Districts of Lower Burma
(In Thousands of Acres)

Year	Total Agricultural Area	Occupied by Non-Agriculturists	Percent	Occupied by Chettyars	Percent
1930	9, 249	2, 943	19	570	6
1932	9, 246	3, 770	36	1, 367	15
1934	9, 335	4, 460	47	2, 100	22
1936	9, 499	4, 873	49	2, 393	25
1937	9, 650	4, 924	50	2, 446	25

Source: This table was computed by the Land and Agriculture Committee.

The share of the Chettyar in these districts increased within seven years from 6 to 25 percent. However, it was still higher in certain key areas of rice production. According to the Report of the Land and Agriculture Committee, the titles to 275, 000 acres alone in the Myaungmya district have passed to the Chettyars. According to the Pegu Settlement Report of 1932—34, the share of the Chettyars was 36 per cent; according to the Insein Report, 31 per cent. In 1938—39, nonagriculturists occupied 47.7 per cent of the agricultural area in Lower Burma (as against 14.2 per cent in Upper Burma), of which 38.6 per cent was held by absentee landlords.

Andrus[28] asserts that these figures may still be too optimistic, as many "statistical" agriculturists are, in reality, nonagriculturists, and that it is likely that more than 50 per cent of the agricultural area of the Delta land has passed to absentee landlords. This assumption gives the only valid interpretation of the fact that 59 per cent of the land in Lower Burma in 1939 was let to tenants at fixed rents.[29]

These conditions did not change during the more prosperous years following the slump. The best and most fertile rice lands remained in the hands of nonagriculturists, who, according to Andrus, owned 70 per cent of the agricultural land in the Hanthawaddy district, 68 per cent in Insein, 67 per cent in Pegu, and 71 per cent in Pyapon in June, 1939. In this connection, Andrus quotes the estimate of an official who had "excellent opportunities" to study this problem, and according to whom the Lower Burma lands in the hands of nonagriculturists was worth between Rs. 540 and 672.5 million, while the total value would have been between Rs. 655 and 787.5 million. In the five years ending June 30, 1941,[30] 51 per cent of the occupied area in the 13 main rice growing districts was reported to have been in the hands of nonagriculturists. Decrease of the Chettyar share in one particular locality was compensated by large increases in other districts. Of about 5 million acres held by nonagriculturists in this area, the Chettyars controlled about one-half.[31]

The wholesale liquidation of the stable Burma farming class was an integral part of the process of land concentration. Statistics taken from the Census of India, 1931[32] show that within the period 1921 to 1931 the group of male tenant cultivators increased only 512,000 to 578,000, a 13 per cent increase, while the group of agricultural laborers increased from 622,000 to over 1 million, a 60 per cent increase. The group of male owners decreased at the same time from 1,160,000 to 927,000, a 20 per cent decrease, and female owners from 903,000 to 321,000, a 64 per cent decrease. This very unfavorable development took place in a period of relative prosperity. However, no statistics are available for the years of the slump, the period of most rapid land concentration. Furthermore, the census figures for 1931 do not indicate how many of the owners economically were little better than tenants in the sense that they had to pay high rates of interest on loans which were covered by security on their property.

Landlordism, in general unfavorable for agricultural and social development, had particularly negative effects in the case of Burma. In Lower Burma, landlordism is in fact absentee landlordism, established by moneylending transactions. In some agricultural centers, as in Hanthawaddy, in Pegu and Pyapon, 80 to 90 per cent of the landlords are nonagriculturists, mostly moneylenders without any agricultural interests, with little knowledge of the land, but with greediness for high rents. [33] In addition, the unfavorable effects of such a tenure system were multiplied by the competitive pressure of the Indian immigrants, whose lower living levels enabled them to rent land at higher prices than the Burmese farmers. The pressure of Indian immigration is frequently mentioned in official documents. As early as 1910, an increase of Indian tenants is quoted. [34] In 1914, it is mentioned that "in or near Rangoon the steady pressure of the Indian immigration is slowly but surely ousting the Berman."[35] It is added that even Burmese landlords prefer Indian tenants because they pay higher rentals and are more obedient. However, seen as a whole, this was of less consequence than the effect of Indian competition on the scale of rents. [36]

Ever since the Labor Act of 1876, the British government and British and Indian employer groups have favored immigration from India, as cheap labor was urgently needed for the development of the Delta land and the immigration from Upper Burma was not rapid enough. But even when immigration no longer was supported by government subventions, the number of immigrants remained consistently high.

Indian competition, strong on account of the considerably lower level of living, steadily increased contract rents. In the years before the war, parts of the Delta land were so heavily rented that the economic rent level was reached or often exceeded. [37] No doubt such conditions must be prejudicial to efficient cultivation. The tenants frequently leave their holdings immediately when their contract period of one year has expired, pressed by the burden of debt, or they are evicted after two or three years. According to the statistical tables of the Report of the Land and Agricultural Committee, [38] about 50 per cent of the tenants in Pegu and Insein, the key districts of rice production, left their holdings contracted for in 1932—34 or 1933—35, after only one year's occupancy. In almost all other important districts, far more than 50 per cent of the tenants who had contracted their holdings partly in the years 1930—33 and partly in 1933—37 had left after only two years. [39] Therefore, a migrating tenant class without the protective background of a home is one of the most characteristic features in the Delta land and has influenced greatly the standard of land utilization. The migrating tenant will refrain from investing additional labor or care, expenditures for fertilizer, implements, and animals; even if he had the means to do so, he would hardly want to enrich the landlord to that extent and thus enable him to demand a higher rent from the next tenant. [40]

In very few countries is the relationship between land tenure and social and moral standards as evident as in Burma. At the beginning of the war in the Pacific "the typical rural Burman was a landless laborer, often drifting from village to village and contributing to a crime record that gave Burma proportionately the highest rate of murders of any country for which accurate statistics are available."[41] Criminal statistics for 1935—36[42] record 7,699 serious offenses against persons (6,839 in 1925) and a heavy increase of minor offenses against property. Within that year, major crimes numbered about 1,500, a very high figure especially in comparison with India. The Tharrawaddy region is noted as a center of crime, whereas the noncommercialized Shan states and frontier areas are little troubled by it. [43] Since 1936, the number of major crimes has again shown a clear tendency to increase. Taking only the first six months of the year, the number of murders increased from 539 in 1936 to 743 in 1940. The latent racial tension, which since 1930 has resulted in a series of race riots, was an additional cause of the high rate.

The colonizing of Lower Burma gradually dissolved the village community, with its fixed moral standards, and replaced it by a migrating tenant class. The tenant in Lower Burma—in contrast, for instance, with the tenants in Upper Burma and the Philippines— is no longer in contact with his native community and is thus deprived of its controlling influence on his social behavior. Isolated from the social order, he has lost the normal restraints which mark life in a decent community. [44]

Land concentration has not resulted in large scale agriculture. The landlords have preferred to let out the land in parcels of 15 to 30 acres[45] to tenants whom they themselves have financed by loans at 1.75 to 2.50 per cent interest per month. [46] Money lending "has, thus, in the Delta, become a corollary to land owning," and is frequently the main source of income for the landlord. He controls the tenant's disposal of the crop by almost invariably insisting that rice to the value of the debt is sold to him or through him. However, if the landlord has come to the limit of his lending capacity or readiness to lend, the tenant must resort to outsiders, and his last possibility is the ill-famed "Saba-pe" transaction. Of course, the services of outside agencies, such as traders and village shopkeepers are even more expensive and restrictive. Their rates are between 7 and 15 per cent monthly.

The average cultivator, whether small owner or tenant, is forced to part with the bulk of his crop immediately after harvest and to meet his commitments directly from the thrashing floor. Consequently, the market is flooded with sellers, ready to sell at any price, for two or three months after the harvest. . . . If the cultivator is a tenant, he will have to pay rent amounting to from one-quarter to one-half of his produce; subsequently he must repay loans for cultivation expenses and borrowings for the support of his family, for the feeding and payment of laborers, food for cattle, and seed for sowing. In general, the tenant-cultivator is indebted to the landlord, while the owner-cultivator has borrowed from Chettyars or traders. In addition, capital and land taxes are due soon after harvesting time. Consequently, the cultivator is forced into a typical buyer's market and has to face an elaborate purchase organization of shrewd brokers and speculators, with no possibility of bargaining or resistance. Such an economic system hardly ever makes it possible for a tenant, however thrifty, to work his way up the social scale by saving enough capital either to acquire or lease land without being heavily indebted. This fact has largely contributed to the general agrarian dissatisfaction in Burma.

FOOTNOTES

[1]J. S. Furnivall, An Introduction to the Political Economy of Burma (Rangoon, 1931), p. 40.

[2]J. Russell Andrus, Burmese Economic Life (Stanford, Calif., 1947), p. 15.

[3]Furnivall, An Introduction, p. 58, quotes a saying "that land in Lower Burma changes hands almost as frequently as securities in a stock exchange."

[4]Helmut G. Callis, Foreign Capital in Southeast Asia, pp. 80 ff. See also Helmut G. Callis, "Capital Investment in Southeast Asia and the Philippines," pp. 22 ff. However, Callis's estimate of the foreign investments in Burma is not complete. J. R. Andrus, "Burma, an Experiment in Self-Government," Foreign Policy Reports (Dec. 15, 1945), pp. 264 ff., estimates them to be including Chettyar investments and government debts, £150, 000, 000.

[5]See note 4.

[6]The Chettyars are a caste of hereditary moneylenders in South India (Madras). They are famous for their alertness, shrewdness and charity. They are intimately acquainted with the English banking system and cooperate with British banks in India.

Their strong organization and almost unlimited credit, thanks to their long-standing connections with British banks and their firsthand knowledge of local conditions, completely exclude any native competition. They work through an organization of sub-agents in the large villages, thus monopolizing the banking business. See Furnivall, An Introduction, pp. 119 ff., and L. C. Jain's Indigenous Banking in India (London, 1929), p. 30.

[7]The normal exchange value of the rupee was 15. 6d., or 36. 5 American cents. The range was 24—37 cents during the decade 1930—40. As of October, 1940, the rupee was valued at 29. 85 cents.

[8]Furnivall, An Introduction, pp. 44 ff. Andrus op. cit., p. 16, recognizes that the rapidity of the development and the degree of division of labor are uncommon features in agricultural communities, but indicates that conditions are still far different from those in a large factory.

[9]Furnivall, op. cit., p. 45.

[10]Kate L. Mitchell, Industrialization of the Western Pacific, pp. 194—95.

[11]Clarence Hendershot, "Burma Compromise," Far Eastern Survey, Vol. XVI, No. 12 (June 18, 1947).

[12]Here and elsewhere in this chapter is referred to the Census of India, 1931, Vol XI, Part I, Report on Burma. All figures mentioned in this chapter are based on official material.

[13]Institute of Pacific Relations, "Problems of the Post-War Settlement in the Far East" (United Kingdom Paper, Eighth Conference, Quebec, 1942), p. 2.

[14]J. Russell Andrus, "Three Economic Systems Clashed in Burma," Review of Economic Studies (London, February 1936), pp. 140 ff.

[15]Burma Provincial Banking Inquiry Committee, Report (Rangoon, 1930); Christian, op cit., p. 120, points out that land foreclosures since 1930 have reduced the Chettyar loans on Burma land to about Rs. 100 million.

[16]Andrus, p. 68.

[17]Furnivall, op. cit., pp. 121 ff.

[18]Ibid., p. 123.

[19]Christian, op cit., p. 118.

[20]Ibid., p. 119

[21]O. H. Spate, pp. 74 ff.

[22]Andrus, p. 67.

[23]The Acts of 1883 and 1884 made possible small loans at low rates of interest, but the administration was hampered by much red tape, which, in turn, caused many inconveniences for the cultivators. In the years 1919 to 1929, the total amount loaned by the government under the Acts averaged less than Rs. 2,000,000 per year, while the average agricultural borrowing from the Chettyars was Rs. 500,000,000 per year. According to the Land Revenue Report of 1938—1939, the over-all picture showed for loan and interest a figure of only Rs 1.5 million. See also Furnivall, op. cit., p. 126.

[24]Published in the CMD Papers, 3900, XII, 1 (London, 1931), 16.

[25]This legislation was based on the Report of Land and Agriculture Committee, Part I, Tenancy; Part II, Land Alienation; Part III, Agricultural Finance, Colonization, Land Purchase, Burma, Dept. of Land Records and Agriculture (Rangoon, 1938), The Land Alienation Act (1941) was designed to prevent land from coming into the hands of nonagriculturists. The creditor can only retain it for 15 years, after which it has to be returned to the original owner without further payment. But, in fact, ever since the slump, the Chettyars had ceased to loan to any but their own tenants. Furthermore, mortgages already existing at the time the law was passed were accepted and should be respected. The Act was without much actual importance, as, by 1941 (according to an estimate of Andrus, p. 81) the land of Lower Burma owned by genuine agriculturists and not mortgaged amounted to only 15 per cent of the total.

The Tenancy Act (1939), designed to solve the rent problem, proved unworkable because the individual judgment of local officials decided what constituted a fair rent. It was replaced by a government communiqué which transferred outstanding cases for judicial settlement.

Only the Land Purchase Act (1941) might have been favorable for future agricultural reconstruction. This law deals with the purchase of Chettyar and other lands by the government, which has the alternative to sell it on long-term contracts with provision for very low rates of interest, or to lease it to tenants.

After the war, the Moneylenders Act of 1945, the Land Disputes Act of 1946, and the Agriculturists Debt Relief Act of 1947 were passed. They gave, however, only transient relief and did not affect the real problem.

[26]Burma Provincial Banking Inquiry Committee, Report (Rangoon, 1930), I, 24.

[27]Census of India, 1931, Vol. XI, Part I: Report on Burma, p. 130.

[28]Andrus, p. 70.

[29]The last published Report on the Administration of Burma (1935–36), p. 24, mentions that the area let to tenants in Burma amounted to more than 9 million acres, of which far more than 7 million were located in Lower Burma. The Census of India, 1931, p. 130, mentions a figure of 5, 260, 000 acres as leased to the tenants. The figure of 59 per cent is quoted from Andrus, p. 70.

[30]Season and Crop Report, 1941, p. 8.

[31]The 1941 figure exceeds the 1937 figure by more than 100, 000 acres.

[32]Pp. 128 ff.

[33]Report on the Administration of Burma, 1935–36, p. 23. The report quotes the proportion of land occupied by nonagriculturalists at 38. 76 per cent of the total. It can be assumed that these figures have increased within the last decade.

[34]Season and Crop Report of 1910, p. 7.

[35]Season and Crop Report of 1914, p. 8.

[36]J. S. Furnivall, op. cit., pp. 68 ff., 73.

[37]Ibid., pp. 68 ff., 73.

[38]Part I, Tenancy.

[39]In Insein, 68 per cent; in Pegu, 65 per cent, Andrus, op. cit., pp. 71–72, asserts that approximately half of the tenants change holdings every year, and "that an economy of this kind is not a satisfactory basis upon which to build a sound society."

[40]Furnivall, op. cit., p. 66, gives an excellent picture of the tenant situation in Lower Burma.

[41]J. Russell Andrus, "Burma; an Experiment in Self-Government," p. 258.

[42]Report on the Administration of Burma (1935–36) p. 31; Christian, Burma and the Japanese Invaders, pp. 158 ff.

[43]Christian, op cit., p. 158.

[44]Furnivall, op. cit., pp. 66–67.

[45]Andrus, Burmese Economic Life, p. 71, mentions this size as typical. Also, the Markets Section Survey No. 9, "Rice," p. 32,

cities a holding of 25 acres as a typical average unit. However, Furnivall, op. cit., p. 58, indicates that the normal size of the agricultural holding has risen from the small patch of a few acres, such as is needed for subsistence cultivation, to larger holdings of 30 to 60 acres, or more, the size which will give the maximum yield in production to the costs.

[46]Markets Section Survey, No. 9, "Rice," pp. 31 ff. The Chettyar rents are 1 1/4 and 1 3/4 respectively, monthly. Frequently the landlord has borrowed from the Chettyar part of the money he gives to the tenant and increases the Chettyar rate by one-half per cent monthly.

ECONOMIC AND SOCIAL DEVELOPMENTS *

Cultural and Religious Decline

The decline of indigenous Burmese culture under British rule became increasingly apparent in the decades prior to World War I. One factor was the disappearance of the royal court, which had functioned as the inspirational center for literature and learning, religion, music, and all forms of art expression. Exquisite craftsmanship and artistic performance lost much of their motivation when superiority was no longer appreciated and rewarded. The best work was often not as salable as the inferior, and the older tradition declined accordingly. Skilled craftsmen were reduced to the cultivator level when manufactured imports displaced their products in the markets.

With the disappearance of trained secretarial posts at the king's court and at the headquarters of the many grades of Wuns, high literary competence in the Burmese language also became an unremunerative luxury not widely esteemed. English became in time the language of the law courts, of the best secular schools, and of the legislative council, while use of Hindsutani vied with Burmese in the hospitals and the urban bazaars. Burmese speech reduced to its rudiments and shorn of its refinements, continued to be used mainly in rural areas and in domestic circles. Local communities in many areas ceased to be social units sponsoring entertainments, sports contests, and gala occasions. Restless spirits accordingly found their excitement in gambling, dacoity, or other antisocial activities. [1] The whole picture of cultural decline was a somber one.

The sad state of social and religious indiscipline was particularly apparent among the Burman Buddhists of Lower Burma. The participation of monks in the rebellion of 1886—1887, in violation of all the rules of the sacred order to eschew mundane affairs, was itself an overt demonstration of religious decay. For a time in Upper Burma, Sir Charles Bernard was able to enlist the aid of the Mandalay thathanabaing and other prominent pongyis in restraining belligerently inclined monks and in promoting the restoration of law and order. This was accomplished largely as a result of British promises not to interfere with religion and to continue the primate in office, even though the government refused support for his decisions. Sir Charles even persuaded the incumbent thathanabaing to visit Rangoon, where the government built a special resthouse for his accommodation on the slope of the Shwe Dagon eminence. Bernard discovered to his disappointment, however, that the Mandalay dignitary exercised little authority in faction-ridden Lower Burma, which remained reprobate religiously. [2] After

*Reprinted from John F. Cady: A History of Modern Burma. @1958 by Cornell University. Used by permission of Cornell University Press.

Crosthwaite took over in 1887, he rebuffed the proffered assistance of the hierarchy by refusing its request for official recognition of its status and authority. [3]

Since the British authorities were not willing to take over the traditional responsibilities of the royal court in sponsoring the disciplining of the Sangha through its own agencies and since the monastic order without royal support was incapable of controlling disorderly members, an inevitable decision was reached. Government ruled that all wearers of the yellow robe must be treated as subject to the control of the secular courts and the police, just as were other citizens. [4] Thereafter even in cases where disputant or disorderly monks consented to the primate's or a gaingyok's handling of their problems, the decision rendered carried no legal sanction. Ecclesiastical authority was virtually destroyed after 1891, when a secular judge overruled a disciplinary decision of the Sangha. This was a fateful step. When the last royally appointed thathanabaing died in 1895 and a division developed over the selection of a new one, the post was simply left vacant. The surviving regional gaingyoks and the Sayadaws at leading pagoda shrines continued to settle minor ecclesiastical squabbles in their respective districts, to hold examinations for probationers, and to try monks accused of misconduct. But the inevitable trend was in the direction of increasing laxity and decline, with Burman opinion becoming increasingly sensitive to any criticism leveled at religion or the monks. [5] At the turn of the century a sympathetic British observer reported that, although every rule of Buddhism was violated daily even by the Sangha, the religion still tended to make the Burman humane, tolerant, kindhearted, and charitable. Some saintly monks did good work preaching, but errant and wandering rahans tended toward sedition. When any monk started to practice magical incantations or to tattoo followers, it was time for the policy to jail him. [6]

Apart from continuing to pay high popular deference to the monks, Burma's traditional structure of society disintegrated. The destructive process at the local level was much more rapid in the south than in Upper Burma, where traditional patterns of economy and landholding remained intact. [7] After 1900 the educational function of the monks declined rapidly, mainly because well-to-do Burmans began sending their children to the government and mission schools where English subjects were taught. The traditional pongyi kyaung education lost out primarily because it came to lead nowhere vocationally or professionally. On the other hand, students who were subjected to instruction in English and an alien curriculum struggled with a frustrating handicap, while at the same time they developed an attitude of contemptuous superiority toward their elders. [8] The academically competent could aspire to a post in the governmental bureaucracy, but few could hope to rise beyond the level of township myook, which was far inferior to the civil service stratosphere. Government service contributed envied social status to incumbents because of the authority and the high salaries attaching to it, but the prestige of the bureaucrat was destined to evaporate in the politically charged atmosphere of post-World War I.

In the economic field, few Burmans were a match in experience, resources, or general aptitude for competing British, Indian, and Chinese businessmen. In any case the effort to attain social prestige by amassing wealth violated all established Burmese traditions. The Burman landlord and moneylender were often more grasping than the Chettyar and enjoyed correspondingly little respect socially. The village thugyis enjoyed some prestige as perhaps the largest landowners of a given tract area and as the local representatives of governmental authority, but they were obliged to perform unpopular tasks, and their prestige was in no way comparable to that of the old hereditary myothugyi. [9]

One difficulty associated with the solitary pre-eminence enjoyed by the pongyis in the changing social order was that their personal prestige held up better than did their religious influence. In view of the increasing indiscipline and declining educational function of the Sangha, the overnumerous monks were making, in fact, a diminishing contribution to the national life. [10] The social loss incurred from the weakening religious influence was universally deplored, for Buddhism was potentially the humanizing, tempering, and integrating social factor, intangible but very important. [11] The situation was at its worst, of course, in Lower Burma's newly developed agricultural areas, where disorderly migrant communities were engaged in the demoralizing speculative scramble for economic advantage and usually included no pongyi kyaungs at all.

The displacement of monastic education by that of the government schools, especially after 1910, not only reduced the amount of religious and moral instruction imparted to the youth but also discredited in the eyes of the educated elite the prescientific lore of the pongyis. Even where Buddhist families paid token deference to tradition by enrolling youth in monastic schools for short periods of time and by continuing the shin pyu ritual, religious instruction inevitably suffered in substantive content and in disciplinary effect. The artificial and often difficult requirements imposed by lay schools for obtaining passing marks, [12] as a condition for qualification for government jobs or clerkships, had no relevance to social ethics. Nor did the new schools help much in the clarification of Burma's emerging world orientation. Monastic morale itself suffered from the loss of educational responsibility and influence. In the course of time the yellow robe ceased to be a friendly, integrative social influence and became too often a cloak for antiforeign traditionalism and for ulterior political designs, which properly were not the concern of the Sangha at all. Buddhism's tradition of withdrawal from mundane affairs and its defensive posture intellectually disqualified it in large measure from making any positive contribution to the fashioning of the new social order. Nevertheless undisciplined, half-indoctrinated monks, as shall presently be apparent, did not refrain from exploiting their social influence in the political arena. [13]

An intimate picture of the transitional process through which Burmese society was passing is presented by Mi Mi Khaing, [14] the European-educated daughter of a Talaing government official. Her father was trained as a youth in a pongyi kyaung school and had fled from the school under threat of corporal punishment for disobedience. Journeying to Moulmein, he learned English and other knowledge which eventually qualified him to be a township myook. He sent his children to the English schools despite misgivings concerning the excessive length of the foreign educational program and the absence of religious-moral training. He gave food to the monks on their morning rounds. After he retired as an official, in 1935, he looked after the family plantations, contributed generously to pagodas and zayat (resthouse) construction in order to accumulate kutho (merit) and possibly to rationalize his acquisitiveness. While in retirement he gradually reimmersed himself in the nostalgic atmosphere of his Buddhist-oriented youth. He eventually gave up his Western shoes and socks, shifted from tables and chairs to mats and polished floors, and even dabbled in alchemy. But he still played tennis, drank lime juice, and used the knife and fork in preference to eating with his fingers.

Such a person's children could not possibly follow his pattern of life completely, for they lacked his early experience as a monastery koyin. Attendance at pagoda feasts gave place to the Rangoon cinema. There were also foreign-made goods to buy, a daily newspaper and English language books to read. Marriages were still arranged through the traditional go-between; the astrologers still did a profitable business; but there were few nostalgic religious memories for those born of myook-status parents after 1900. [15]

The Problem of Growing Lawlessness

The evaporation of community vitality and the accompanying inability of custom or government to control the antisocial forces unleashed by the expanding economy of Lower Burma spelled out in an alarming increase of crime, especially during the decade prior to World War I. [16] Much of the crime was apparently the work of youthful wanderers, lacking access to land and periodically unemployed. Village elders had the habit of putting such idlers to work on unpaid village services. Their departure from home might be good riddance locally, but it created difficulties elsewhere. They usually took to theft and then to dacoity, partly to find excitement and sometimes to obtain funds by which to hire persons to go their surety as "bad livelihood" suspects who otherwise could be jailed by the police for as long as six months' time. They also quickly learned that successful thievery could pay the cost of keeping on good terms with the local police. [17]

Some evidence of increasing criminality had appeared during the late 1870's among the carelessly selected immigrant laborers from India who virtually monopolized labor opportunities in the transportation, manufacturing, and public works fields. The coolie traffic at the outset was not far removed from slave trade. [18] From 1875 to 1877, the Indian jail population was proportionately nearly five times as numerous as that of the Burman Buddhists. By 1880 the virus of lawlessness had spread to the uprooted migrant Burman population which had been caught in the confused economic toils of commercialized rice production. Official observers in 1880 were concerned over what they called the reckless passionate character of the Burman, his fascination for riotous excitement, and the "indisposition of the people to . . . resist criminals."[19] Criminal statistics covering the five years 1880—1884, when compared with those of the preceding half decade, revealed that the number of murders had increased by 34 per cent and that of dacoities by 77 per cent. The gathering disorder eventually merged with the rebellion of 1886—1889.

Conditions in Upper Burma improved markedly in terms of order as soon as the fury of the rebellion had subsided. Social controls were re-established, and for the next decade and a half crime was held effectively under control. The exceptions were caused by Kachin depredations in the northern districts and by periodic lapses in localities suffering famine conditions. [20] Under normal conditions of stable government, neighborly relations, and resident land ownership on a permanent family basis and in the absence of commercialized agriculture and speculation in land, epidemic crime had never been a serious social problem in Burma. [21] The people of Upper Burma disliked many aspects of British rule, such as prevailing water and forestry regulations and the general leveling of society gradations, but such political resentment did not prior to World War I contribute to lawlessness. On the other hand, the large number of emigrants from the same area who sought to improve their fortunes by migrating southward contributed more than their full share to the growing disorder. [22]

In Lower Burma, the situation deteriorated steadily after 1890. Chronic debt and conditions of semianarchy on the agricultural frontier as well as transiency and seasonal unemployment contributed to disorderly conditions. During the two long breaks in the agricultural season, one at the end of the rains after the rice was transplanted and the other during the latter half of the dry season following the harvest, foot-loose paddy farmers normally found excitement and some profit in lawless escapades. In the absence of agencies for mediation and settlement, petty disputes were magnified into passionate conflicts to be settled by antagonists with their dahs (long knives). Criminality, it should be noted furthermore, was confined almost entirely to the male population. Sometimes criminal elements got control of entire village tracts.[23] Concealment was usually easy. The police authorities encountered increasing difficulty collecting dependable evidence against offenders. During the pacification period and as late as 1896, youthful offenders had confessed offenses quite freely, and the voluntary surrender of criminals to the authorities was common. By 1902, as already noted, an increase in cases of perjury and false witness was widely reported.[24]

Police and courts faced a losing battle. Jailing, whipping, collective fines on villages, and the disciplining of errant headmen had little effect. Nor did the passage of the Habitual Offenders' Restriction Act and the Criminal Tribes Act do any good. The more vigilant the police were, the more criminal offenses were brought to light. Obviously much petty crime went undetected. From 1904 to 1912, cognizable offenses increased 17 per cent and noncognizable crime 40 per cent. In 1912, violent crime was twice the level of 1904. More than half of the serious crimes in Burma in 1913—1914 were committed in the Pegu and Irrawaddy divisions. From 1906 the annual police reports for Lower Burma repeated a dismal refrain concerning the inferior quality of the police recruits, the almost total failure of headmen to act against gambling and excise violations (liquor and drugs), and the alarming village apathy with respect to the defense of villages from armed attack. Convictions were made more difficult by perjury, concealment, and the faking of evidence, sometimes on the part of headmen themselves.[25] In 1913—1914, some 637 headmen were fined for being derelict in their duty, while 221 village tracts were fined collectively.[26]

Sir Herbert Thirkell White, who was governor of Burma from 1905 to 1910, was more baffled by the growth of crime than by any other aspect of the country's problems. He explained that he could understand crimes of passion and impulse, but not the increasing prevalence of theft and embezzlement. His statement follows:

> Children are treated with indulgence, not always according to discretion. . . . No orphan is left desolate. No stranger asks in vain for food and shelter. Yet these good people . . . produce dacoits who perpetrate unspeakable barbarities on old men and women. Sudden and quick in quarrel . . . with a strong if uncultured sense of humour, they can be cruel and re-

vengeful. . . . The courts reveal a mass of criminality
as shocking as it is surprising. Murders, dacoities,
robberies, violent assaults are far too numerous. [27]

An Explanation of Burman Lawlessness

It has been noted that whereas girls in old Burma early found
an assured and useful status in the home, the boys were usually
pampered in childhood and were subjected to their first arbitrary
discipline in the monastic school. As youth, they tended to drift
away from family ties to find fellowship among persons of their
own age. When confronted by disagreeable inhibitions, a Burman
youth could either bully his way through or could by-pass the frustration by joining up with a dacoit band in order to experience the
desired thrill of uninhibited power. Violence and cruelty, whether
perpetrated in dacoity or in heated resentment of alleged personal
indignity, were therefore not necessarily the expression of sadistic
tendencies; often they were only an expression of fierce hostility
toward frustration crossing one's path. Burmese youth could also
attain the valued experience of individual autonomy in the free
gaiety of association as equals (the "Ko" of formal address), none
of whom enjoyed superior status or exerted power over their
fellows. [28]

Under British rule the public service and the police afforded
legitimate, and sometimes illegitimate, outlets for the exercise of
power. The first was accessible to the student, the second to
those lacking high educational qualifications. Even a petty official
like a post-office clerk might like to show his authority by keeping
the stamp purchaser waiting. The police could employ threats,
blackmail, and personal abuse on occasion. But all of these were
poor substitutes for what had been destroyed. Within the system
of jealously guarded social gradations of old Burma, each person
had carried about in his own head a set of criteria which determined appropriate behavior toward royalty, government officials,
military leaders and captains, pongyis, myothugyis (whether
ahmudan or athi), local gaungs and village elders. The Buddhist
Sangha itself provided a complete hierarchy of status permitting
escape from outside competition. It afforded an avenue for eventual social recognition of one's superiority in wisdom, holiness,
religious learning, and magical lore. At the same time, exit from
the Sangha was always easy and carried no stigma. Under British
rule, by contrast, the upper rungs of the social ladder including
the high government offices, the wealthy merchant status, and
positions as large landowners and business executives were pretty
largely closed to Burmans. With the exception of the favored
("heaven-born") few who achieved posts in the civil service and a
larger number who got minor government jobs, social mobility
tended to be downward, descending from the small landowner or

67

trader to the artisan, the landless cultivator, and finally to the unskilled laborer. It was the sense of suffering social degradation quite as much the economic hardship entailed in being classified as a coolie along with Kalas from India that made the Burman unhappy and resentful under the new order. The creation of the post of village headman compensated very meagerly for the social loss sustained in the general leveling of Burmese society. [29]

Although traditional deference for officials, pongyis, elders, and teachers carried over for a time, the degrees of respect to be accorded tended to blur as status disintegrated. In village situations, where bachelor youth had to provide labor gratis at the behest of the newly elevated headman, the boys became adept at circumventing what was distasteful. Since reverence for law in the abstract had never been part of the Burman tradition, the growing dissipation of respect for personal authority meant the elimination of customary restraint. Infliction of personal insult usually brought quick retaliation. Personal prestige was frequently sought in feats of strength or daring, perhaps in violence or personal intrigue, or in sheer Robin Hood adventure divorced from all established loyalties. Until later challenged by nationalist-motivated rebellion, police duty was attractive to many Burmans as affording opportunity for bravado in face-to-face encounter, for harsh handling of captured criminals, and, incidentally, for the collection of gratuities from bullied clients in order to supplement low salaries.

Those persons who lacked a spirit of daring could, of course, cultivate rice or possibly retire on a pension, but they were not admired for their peaceful moderation. Little premium, as a rule, was placed on deferred values or the calculated long look ahead; act action usually took place not as sustained effort but in narrow time span. Thus were both anxiety and sense of guilt minimized and delightful moments cherished as they occurred. Careless of system, evasive of responsibility, oblivious to consequences, the Burman male enjoyed those "exalted seconds" when through spoken utterance or physical violence he could gratify his yearning for freedom from threat and frustration. [30]

Such generalized considerations could not, of course, be regarded as applicable to every instance of lawless violence, but they probably go far to explain the eventual coalescence between crime and political disaffection. This situation was to become far more serious after the war when the rise of nationalist sentiment tended to dissolve all reverence for status, especially that of headman and police, as set up under the new categories of British rule.

FOOTNOTES

[1]Furnivall, Political Economy of Burma, pp. 227—234.

[2]Nisbet, II, 126—127.

[3]The Cambridge History of India, VI, 411.

[4]O. H. Mootham, Burmese Buddhist Law (Oxford, 1939), pp. 123-127. The thathanabaing was denied jurisdiction over civil cases in Upper Burma by Article 8 of the Civil Justice Regulations in 1886. The individual monk remained under the personal disciplinary authority of his pongyi superior only to a very limited and strictly religious sense.

[5]Nisbet, II, 126—127; White, A Civil Servant in Burma, pp. 191-192. The Government did give moral recognition to one of the candidates for thathanabaing in the form of a sanad setting forth the terms of recognition, but this recognition carried no substantive authority.

[6]White, A Civil Servant in Burma, pp. 192, 196—199, 264.

[7]White (ibid., p. 183), writing in 1912, referred to the pongyis as "the most influential and respected class of the community . . . wielding indefinite but real power."

[8]The most undisciplined youth often came from Burman families in good circumstances. They ridiculed their elders, sometimes carried deadly weapons, got drunk, and fought each other at pwés (dramatic performances). See Nisbet, II, 233—243.

[9]Ibid.

[10]Fielding-Hall, A People at School, p. 244; Nisbet, II, 120—122.

[11]Fielding-Hall (A People at School, p. 247) called loss of religious vitality "the greatest possible calamity" for Burma.

[12]RAB for 1913—1914, pp. 56—59, for 1914, p. 99. The results of the Anglovernacular high school final examinations (tenth standard) for the two years 1913—1915 were 56.8 per cent and 46 per cent passed respectively. About 250 candidates per year qualified for matriculation in the University of Calcutta out of 360 to 440 taking the test. Almost half of the candidates for the B.A. degree failed to pass.

[13]Furnivall, Colonial Policy, pp. 199—200; Shway Yoe, p. 36. The lowered standards and discipline within the Sangha were reflected in the deflated value attributed to traditional modes of address. Thus the term Sayadaw (royal teacher, or thathanabaing) came to be applied to any monastery head; the venerable term pongyi ("great glory") came in time to be used for almost any wearer of the yellow robe. In post-World War II, even bus drivers were called Sayas. Nga, the traditional address used for athi commoners, was degraded after 1900 to apply only to criminals. Similarly the term thugyi was applied to the traditional ywagauny. See Mya Sein, p. 74.

[14]The Burmese Family (Bombay, 1946).

[15]Ibid, pp. 42—44, 66—73, 120.

[16]Donnison, pp. 35—36.

[17]G. E. R. G. Brown, Burma as I Saw It, pp. 85—86.

[18]J. T. Wheeler, Journal of Voyageing up the Irrawaddy (Rangoon, 1871), p. 26. Shipmasters active in the coolie traffic in 1870 sold the services of their passengers to Rangoon employers to recoup transportation costs and to realize a profit.

[19]British Burma Gazetteer, I, 509, 513—514. In 1884, cognizable crime was 50 per cent higher than in 1879.

[20]RPA for 1880—1884, 1889—1894, 1897. Violent crimes in Upper Burma numbered 3, 409 in 1889 and only 296 in 1894.

[21]F. B. Leach, The Future of Burma (Rangoon, 1936), p. 121.

[22]The Cambridge History of India, VI, 440.

[23]J. S. Furnivall, Political Economy of Burma, pp. 26—27, and "Reconstruction in Burma" (MS., 1943), pp. 16—24; RPA for 1905, p. 13.

[24]Fielding-Hall, The Soul of a People, p. 101.

[25]RPA for 1905, 1906, 1909, 1911, 1913; RAB for 1914—1915, pp. iv, 29.

[26]RAB for 1913—1914, pp. 13—15. Headmen convicted and fined were, of course, a small proportion of the total subjected to criticism. There were more than 17, 000 headmen all told.

[27]White, A Civil Servant in Burma, p. 66.

[28]For a full statement of this interpretation, see L. M. Hanks, Jr., "The Quest for Individual Autonomy in Burmese Personality," Psychiatry, XII (1949), 285—286.

[29]Ibid., p. 287.

[30]Ibid., pp., 288—300.

MALAY STATES

International Boundary

Malay State Boundary

Unfederated Malay States

Federated Malay States

Straits Settlements

SIAM

SOUTH

CHINA

SEA

PERLIS

KEDAH

Penang I.

Georgetown

WELLESLEY

KELANTAN

TRENGGANU

PERAK

PAHANG

SELANGOR

Kuala Lumpur

NEGRI
SEMBILAN

MALACCA

JOHORE

Strait
of
Malacca

SUMATRA

Singapore

Miles

Philip   80   0   50   100

From Agrarian Unrest in Southeast Asia by Erich H. Jocoby. Published by Columbia
University Press. Used by Permission.

CHAPTER 3

British Malaya

The term Malaya is used to describe the British colonial arrangement over the various regions known collectively as the Malay States. The States are divided into three parts: the Straits Settlements which include Penang, Malacca, and Singapore; the Federated Malay States; and the Unfederated States. Early in its history, this region assumed an important role in Southeast Asian affairs. The Malay Peninsula extends Southward from Siam or Thailand, and with Indonesia forms a barrier between the South China Sea and the Indian Ocean. This barrier dominates trade lines between the Indian world to the West and the Chinese world to the East. For the European traveler, trader, and seaman the Straits of Malacca between Malaya and the island of Sumatra in Indonesia are critical for communications between Europe and the Far East, and the nation or nations which control the Straits of Malacca controls the China-Western trade. With the advent of Western colonialism in this region, domination of both Malaya and Sumatra quickly emerged as vital to the interests of the colonial world. Thus, as a matter of geographical determinism, Malaya became an important trade depot and communications center for the entire world.

The Malayans or the Malayo-Polynesians, share with the Indonesians a common ancestry, in that the peoples of both areas reached this area several thousand years before the coming of the European. The Malayans settled on the land and established an agricultural based economy. In later years they developed a command of the sea which brought them into contact with the surrounding areas of Southeast Asia, China and India. This interest in the sea gave to the native inhabitants an opportunity to trade and communicate with the more advanced cultures in the surrounding areas. In particular, the Malayans began to visit India as far back as the time of the Roman Empire. In terms of cultural orientation, the peoples of both Malaya and Indonesia looked to India for cultural, intellectual and religious leadership rather than to provincial mainland China. Because of this Indian orientation, Hinduism and Mahayana Buddhism found their way into Malaya and Indonesia. With

73

the adoption of Indian religious attitudes much of Malaya fell under the economic and cultural dominance of India, thus ensuring the continuation of the Indian orientation to the life patterns of Malaya. However, by the end of the twelfth century, Indian influence in both Malaya and Indonesia gradually declined. In the years immediately preceding the coming of the Westerners, a revival of communications between Malaya and India occurred, and a new source of religious influence came to both Malaya and Indonesia from India; Indian Islam. With Islamic penetration of India, Indian life quickened, and with this, Indian trade revived. Soon Islamic traders and missionaries from India reached Malaya and Indonesia, bringing with them the new religion. When the Portuguese arrived in the East, they found that the Islamic faith had been firmly established in both Malaya and Indonesia.

With the exception of travelers such as Marco Polo, the first important group of Europeans to reach Malaya were the Portuguese. They, like the succeeding waves of European colonials to reach the East, realized the economic and strategic importance of the Malay Peninsula and they quickly seized the Malayan port city of Malacca, a region which offered the best potential for trade and defense of the more valuable spice islands of Indonesia. The Portuguese dominated Malacca for a little over a century, and by controlling this area and the coast line of Sumatra, trade between the South China Sea and the Indian Ocean became a Portuguese monopoly. Though the Portuguese provided the initial contact between the Malayans and the Westerner, the impact of the Portuguese remained exceedingly limited, primarily because the zealous religious activities of the Christian Portuguese offended the Islamic community. A second factor to limit the Portuguese influence in Malaya came with the pattern of Portuguese settlement in all of Southeast Asia. The Portuguese did not come in great numbers, but rather as individual businessmen and missionaries. They tended to dominate the port cities of this area and never truly attempted to control the interior of any portion of Southeast Asia. Furthermore, the contact between the trading cities of the coast and the interior remained exceedingly limited, thus preventing the penetration of early Western influence into rural Southeast Asia. By the beginning of the seventeenth century, the Portuguese gradually began to lose their hold over Malaya and the rest of Southeast Asia. Part of the reason for the decline of the Portuguese power was the arrival of the Dutch as a new colonial force in the East. Basically, the Dutch found it relatively easy to secure native assistance in driving out the Portuguese. The native willingly supported the Dutch because of the almost universal hostility between the Portuguese and the native community, and with this support the Dutch destroyed most of the Portuguese Eastern empire.

The cooperation between the natives and the Dutch eventually enabled the Dutch to seize the port city of Malacca and with this, a voice in Malayan politics. During this same period, the Dutch also managed to exclude their rivals, the British, from gaining a foothold in the Malay area. The British defeat at Amboina, in Indonesia, coupled with a growing interest by the British in India, gave to the Dutch almost an exclusive control over Malaya, Indonesia, the entire South China Sea area, and Japan. In the seventeenth and early eighteenth centuries, the Dutch concentrated their efforts on the island of Java, but through military and naval power they could dominate the more important areas of both Malaya and Indonesia. Dutch influence in Malaya remained primarily economic. The Hollanders showed little interest in establishing Christianity or in colonizing the peninsula. From a Malayan point of view, the lack of Dutch missionary zeal made the Dutch acceptable neighbors. Though the Dutch remained the dominant European power in Malaya during the eighteenth century, by the 1780's, both the British and the French began to show interest in Malaya; despite French and British activity, the Dutch managed to maintain their monopoly over the Malay peninsula until the nineteenth century.

British involvement in Malaya began in the 1780's primarily through the interest shown in this area by the colonial government in India and by the London economic community. Indian officials sought to trade in Malaya and hoped to acquire naval and military establishments which would be useful to prevent any possible French military and naval success in the Bay of Bengal and the Indian Ocean. Indian officials believed that the growth of French power in this area would ultimately weaken British control in India and interfere with British trade in Southeast Asia. Also, the London and Calcutta economic community hoped to expand their activities in the spice trade and to increase the Anglo-China trade. To accomplish this, the Dutch control of the Straits of Malacca had to be broken and a trading and naval station had to be established in Malaya. The first specific British move in acquiring territory in Malaya came with the acquisition of the Island of Penang located off the northern coast of Malaya. The British secured an agreement with the sultan who controlled the island, and in return for permission to establish a trading and naval station on the island, the British agreed to pay an annual rent to the ruling sultan. This rental arrangement continued until the 1950's. As a trade center, Penang proved to be an economic failure, in that the island was located too far from the spice producing areas and the mainland territory offered little opportunity for trade. The island did serve one important purpose in that it became a base for military operations against the Dutch.

The next major event to encourage British intervention in Malaya came during the age of the French Revolution and Napoleon.

During this period the French began to consider the possibilities of developing an empire in Southeast Asia. British concern that the French might attempt to initiate a colonial program for Southeast Asia was encouraged by the French occupation of Holland. In theory, France now had the opportunity to assume control over the Dutch East Indian interests. In an effort to prevent any possible growth of French power in that area, the British occupied the Dutch island of Java as a precautionary measure, and with the occupation of Java, Dutch involvement in Malaya virtually ended. The British administrator of Java, Sir Stamford Raffels, was an avowed imperialist who believed that the survival of Britain as a world power depended on the extension of her empire. Raffels hoped to integrate Java into the British empire thus giving Britain indirect control over the Straits of Malacca and a dominant voice in the spice and China trade. Raffels' scheme failed to materialize, in that after the conclusion of the French wars, Britain chose to return the islands to the Dutch government. As for Raffels, he received a relatively minor position with the British East Indian Company. However, his dreams for an expanded empire continued. He appealed to the Governor General in India to act against the Dutch in such a fashion that their control of the South China Sea trade would be permanently broken. He eventually received permission to develop a British trade center in Malaya. Raffels immediately sailed for the island of Singapore, located at the southern tip of the Malay Peninsula. At the time of Raffels' arrival, the island belonged to the Sultan of Jahore. In the past, the island had been used as a major pirate stronghold by the Malays and little or no Dutch influence existed in this area. Raffels offered the Sultan a large sum of money for the purchase of the island. The Sultan agreed, the pirates moved to another nearby island, and Raffels now possessed the island. Under his careful eye, modern Singapore was founded. He encouraged Chinese to settle on this new outpost of British power. With the assistance of the Chinese, Raffels developed a major British trade center in Malaya. British occupation of the island created considerable difficulties between the Dutch and the British East India Company. The Dutch resented the rapid growth of British power into their sphere of traditional influence and they quite rightly realized that Raffels' settlement of Singapore would eventually challenge the economic leadership of Batavia and Java in Southeast Asia. As for the British East India Company, they decided that Raffels had exceeded his authority, but they appreciated the economic and naval potential of the island and therefore, did not disavow Raffels' activities in Singapore. Owing to the difficulties created by Raffels' activities, the Company never forgave him for his actions in founding the colony. After his retirement from the Company, the colonial government accused him of mismanagement of funds and attempted to collect an exceedingly large sum of money from Raffels.

The shock of the accusation and the enormity of the fines laid against him killed him. Though Raffels died under the shadow of official scorn, his accomplishment, the founding of Singapore, ranks as one of the most colorful and exciting events in the story of the building of the British Empire.

The founding of Singapore laid the foundation for the growth of British influence, not only in Malaya, but in the entire South China Sea area and it permanently broke the Dutch monopoly of trade in Southeast Asia. The location of the island made it a perfect trade and control center for communications between the Orient and Europe, and with its fine natural harbour, this former pirates den became one of the most active trade depots in the entire world. Another reason for the rapid growth of Singapore came with the economic philosophy put forward by Raffels. Raffels believed in free trade. He hated the traditional Dutch policy of high tariffs and restrictive trade regulations. He believed that if Singapore became a free trade area, the island would quickly prosper and that the Dutch would be economically destroyed. His free trade policy worked perfectly and within a very short time Singapore became the major trading depot between the East and West, while Batavia slowly declined as the Queen City of Southeast Asia. Finally, in order to even further the economic trading aspects of Singapore, the British established the tradition that all paperwork associated with trade in Singapore be kept at an absolute minimum. This not only encouraged business firms to establish trading associations in Singapore, but assured traders that official red tape would be kept to an absolute minimum, thus making it even more attractive to use Singapore as a base of operations in Southeast Asia. London business interests quickly made use of the facilities of the new British colony and willingly invested in the development of the island. Furthermore, as the British proved their ability to maintain an environment favorable to trade, Chinese merchants began to migrate to Singapore. Generally the Chinese and the British found it quite easy to cooperate with one another. The British used the Chinese as middlemen in matters of trade and domestic development of the island. In return, the Chinese appreciated the British ability to maintain law and order and an environment favorable to economic growth. Thus by the mid-nineteenth century, both the British and the Chinese used their talents to assure the success of Singapore.

As a means of regularizing their position in Singapore, the British found it necessary to conclude an agreement with the Dutch. By 1830, the Dutch acknowledged the British occupation of Singapore and Penang. In exchange for Malacca, the British abandoned all interest in the Island of Sumatra in the Dutch East Indies. With this agreement, Britain now had acquired a free hand to dominate Malaya. After the agreement with the Dutch had been reached, the

British government eventually organized Singapore, Malacca, and Penang into the Straits Settlement. As for the rest of the Malay Peninsula, the British did not directly interfere with the internal developments in this area. This hands-off attitude by the British government toward the peninsula lasted for about fifty years. However, by the beginning of the 1870's, this policy no longer proved to be expedient. Several factors account for the change in British policy. During the mid nineteenth century, Malayan government broke down. Lawlessness and disruption of civil authority became the order of the day. One reason for the decay in Malayan political life was the old-fashioned form of native government. In each of the Malay States, a sultan attempted to rule as an absolute monarch. The typical Malay sultan appeared to be a feudal lord, occupying a position similar to the feudal lords of the European past. Up to the nineteenth century the sultans had managed to hold their positions of power, but during the nineteenth century, the feudal structure of the Malay states began to fall apart. Inept sultans, an overly aggressive nobility, piracy, civil wars, lawlessness, and pressure from Siam on Northern Malaya created a chaotic atmosphere within each of the various independent states. This internal chaos did not in itself invite British interference in Malayan affairs, but by 1870, the breakdown of authority in Malaya did interfere with trade in the Singapore area, a matter which would require British attention. A second factor which drew British interest into internal Malayan affairs came with the growing importance of the Malayan tin mines. By 1870, Malayan tin had become an important part of the economic activity in both Malaya and Singapore. Generally, the Malays did not concern themselves with the mines, preferring agriculture as their basic economic activity. However, the Chinese migrated by the thousands to the mining districts and dominated most aspects of the entire tin producing industry. Around 1870, the Chinese began to fight among themselves over labor and mining rights. The local sultans did not have sufficient authority to prevent the spread of the Chinese civil disturbance. Since Britain generally acted as the protector of the Chinese, they had to acknowledge the dual problems of the weakness of the native government and the internal difficulties within the Chinese community. Thirdly, British self-interest began to emerge as a factor in encouraging direct involvement in Malayan affairs. With the opening of the Suez Canal and a general upswing in interest in foreign trade and investment, British businessmen began to cast an eye toward Malaya as a good place for profitable investment. Furthermore, they received support from Singapore in that an economically prosperous Malaya would mean greater economic potential for Singapore. Finally, 1870 marked the beginning of a renewed interest in colonial expansion among all European powers, and Britain found that if she did not act in Malaya, possibly her traditional rival, France, might take advantage of the troubled situation in Malaya. The combination of the above suggests that Britain had no choice but to expand her influence in this region. Basically, empire begets empire, and in the case of Malaya, this concept holds a particularly high degree of truth. The expansion of British interest in Malaya, like her expansion into Burma, became an expediency of empire building.

The organization of British colonial Malaya began with the creation of the Straits Settlement which included Singapore, Malacca, and Penang. This territory fell under complete British sovereignty and all persons born or naturalized citizens of the Straits Settlement automatically became British subjects. The Governor General of Singapore (a position which automatically made him the supreme authority over Malacca and Penang) eventually became the general supervisor over the entire territory of British Malaya, and from this position he provided general direction to the development of all British activities in the Malay Peninsula. The beginnings of British government over the Peninsula began in 1874 and gradually expanded with the passage of each decade. To regularize the British position in Malaya, colonial officials negotiated treaties of semi-submission with each independent sultan. These treaties called for the establishment of a British resident who advised the sultan on most all domestic matters except for questions involving religion and Malay customs. In foreign relations, Britain acquired a free hand to handle all matters of diplomacy. With this grant of power, the British hoped to bring peace and order to Malaya, to protect the region from outsiders such as the French or the Siamese, to maintain a healthy relationship between the Malays and the non-Malays, and to provide a safe area for Chinese and British investment. Two decades later, in 1896, those areas in central and southern Malaya which had signed agreements with Britain were organized into the Federated Malay States. In those areas affected by the organization of the Federation, the sultans continued to exercise independence in matters of religion and native custom and each state maintained its financial independence. In matters affecting all states, the sultans had to agree to abide by a British supervised Federal Council and the advice of the Governor General. The capitol of the Federated Malay States was established at Kuala Lumpur, in the center of the Federated region of the Peninsula. In 1909, five additional Malay states were organized into the Unfederated Malay States. Four of the five states had previously fallen under the protection of Siam, but in 1909 Britain concluded an arrangement with the Siamese government whereby Siam relinquished its control over Northern Malaya in exchange for various pledges by Britain to abandon certain British controls over Siamese domestic affairs. The four Northern states refused to accept a federated status, but did agree to permit British resident advisors to remain in their individual capitols where they could offer advice and explain British policy in Malaya. In most cases the sultans in Northern

Malaya accepted British advice except in matters of religion and native custom. The fifth state to join the Unfederated States was the Sultinate of Jahore, located at the extreme southern end of the Peninsula. Jahore had traditionally remained independent from British influence. However, since the territory of Jahore surrounded much of Singapore, both the British government and the Sultan of Jahore deemed it necessary to come to some working arrangement. Owing to this situation, Jahore joined the Unfederated Malay States.

The explanation as to why Britain permitted the high degree of variation of control within the Malay area can best be explained in terms of economic necessity. Areas which emerged as important regions for investment and trade received the greatest degree of colonial control, while areas of limited economic value remained more independent. In the Straits area, the British and the Chinese dominated the entire economy, and with this came almost complete domination of the colonial government. In south and central Malaya, investment in tin and rubber by the Chinese and the British required moderately firm European control, while in northern Malaya, the economy remained relatively traditional and little or no domination of the government was required.

British rule in Malaya generally served the interests of all peoples involved in Malayan life. Under British indirect rule, the native Malay found that he could still identify with the traditional form of government, that his customs did not change, and that the Islamic faith remained under the protection of the sultan. For the highly conservative Malayan, life changed very little because of British domination of his government. As British occupation and administration of Malaya continued, the home government sought to provide an atmosphere whereby the Malayan could eventually assume greater responsibility for their own political affairs. The English believed that through self government, the Malays would be protected against foreign domination and exploitation. In adopting this policy, the British attempted to train the Malays in the arts of modern government and civil service. Some of the native community did avail themselves of this opportunity, but the program did not accomplish as much as anticipated because of the general native resistance to participate in the European aspects of Malay life. Another change to occur in Malayan life was the restoration of law and order. This had been one of the reasons for British occupation of the Peninsula and once Britain assumed authority in Malaya, lawlessness declined and eventually law and order came to characterize colonial rule in this area. In an effort to maintain law and order, the British modernized the judicial system and the administration of law which helped preserve civil order and benefitted all persons living in Malaya. Another positive aspect of British rule in Malaya came with the use of tax revenue from the tin and rubber interests. Throughout the entire British era in Malaya, the government enjoyed a considerable income from these two areas of investment. Rather than send this money to London, the government used this revenue to introduce a sizable social service program and to establish an education system for the Malayans. One problem associated with British rule in Malaya came from the Malayan reluctance to participate in the rubber and tin development of the area. To develop these resources, the British had to find a new source of labor. This problem was solved by the introduction of thousands of Chinese and Indian laborers, but in so doing, they increased the Chinese role in Malayan life and introduced the Indian as a new element in Malayan society. From the Malayan point of view, they responded favorably to British rule, a factor which served to keep friction between the British and the Malayan to a minimum. The Chinese community also remained contented with British rule. In Singapore, they were free to conduct their own business activities in almost any manner they chose, providing they did not interfere with basic British concepts of colonial rule. The Chinese living in the Straits Settlements took advantage of British citizenship which offered considerable political and economic rights in Malaya and within the British empire. In the Federated and Unfederated areas, the Chinese merchants did exploit the Malays, which, on occasion, did create difficulties, but the British attempted to settle these difficulties in a fashion which appeared fair to both the Chinese and the Malays. Generally, the British believed that they were responsible for both the Chinese and the Malayan and therefore tried to protect both elements. The British also assumed responsibility for the rise of an Indian community in Malaya. Because of this, the British tried to protect the Indian resident in Malaya against exploitation by either the Chinese or the English business community.

The colonial social service record in Malaya, as compared to most other colonial social service programs, achieved considerable success. This success came not only because the English tried harder than other colonial governments, but because Malaya tended to have a greater source of revenue than most other colonies in Southeast Asia. Malaya had a consistently good source of revenue from both tin and rubber. In both the tin and rubber producing areas, the British could tax the owners and operators of these businesses, they could tax the mining and farming equipment brought into Malaya, and they could tax the export of these products from Malaya. These taxes provided considerable revenue for the social service program. This is particularly important since European governments did not give money to colonial areas for social service programs. For Malaya, she had the advantage of a large domestic revenue and a responsible colonial government willing to use the money wisely. This combination of adequate funds and the wise use of money made it possible to establish a relatively successful social service program.

The colonial administration in Malaya, in the realm of social service, acquired the reputation of being a twentieth century form of benevolent despotism. Prior to British arrival in Malaya, this region traditionally had a reputation as being particularly unhealthy. Tropical diseases abounded and little or no effort had been made to improve this aspect of Malayan life. Once the British assumed control over Malaya, they immediately began to consider the problems of tropical health. Part of this interest in health programs came with the acceptance of the concept of the "White man's burden," and part with the realization that a healthy environment in Malaya would ultimately make it more profitable to invest in Malayan resources. The British approach to the problem of tropical health was to attack the problem through research into tropical diseases and by the application of the best medical services available during the last years of the nineteenth century. Of particular importance was the discovery of the cause of malaria which plagued the entire Malayan region. The discovery that the mosquito carried the dread disease resulted in an all-out assault against the mosquito. The British attacked the bothersome insect in all possible ways. Swamps were sprayed and where possible, drained. Education programs were introduced into native areas to train the Malays to use preventive methods to prevent the breeding of the insect near inhabited areas and the local population was taught the best methods available to control the disease and treat those stricken with malaria. To further the battle against all tropical diseases, medical institutes in both London and Malaya studied the general methods of tropical disease prevention and control. To ensure that the advanced medical practices introduced by the British were continued after the British left Malaya, Asians of all races were given special training in Europe and Malaya to continue the fight against diseases common to the tropics. By the end of the British period, Malaya emerged as a medical showplace in Southeast Asia. Towns, for the most part, proved particularly safe for both Asians and European habitation, and in rural areas, traditionally a difficult place to combat disease, considerable progress was made. Without question, British efforts in medicine contributed to the improved health situation in Malaya. Critics have indicated that the motivation behind this advanced medical program came from a desire to expand rubber and tin production. This in part may be true, but as a comparison, Indo-China and Indonesia were also rubber producing areas, and the colonial governments in these areas did not come close to achieving the success of the British program. It is reasonable to assume that the British record suggests more than merely economic motivation but a combination of both economic and humanitarian reasons for the achievements of the British medical-social service record.

A second area of success came with the British record in education. Generally speaking, provision for educational facilities for all races became the goal for the colonial government. The Chinese maintained their own school system in which their culture, language, and social values remained dominant. These schools taught the children that they were Chinese first and that some day, they would eventually return to China. To ensure that the Chinese student received the proper kind of education; books, teachers, and most related reading material used by these schools came directly from China. The Chinese preference for their own cultural schools ran counter to the British attitude concerning education. For the most part, the major British complaint concerning the Chinese schools stemmed from the fact that they did not train the young to identify with Malaya and learn a working command of the English language. To avoid any official disagreement between the Chinese and English communities over education, when a colonial school inspector visited a Chinese school, the class immediately switched to English to satisfy the inspector. The British government accepted this situation, though they would have preferred greater Chinese cooperation. In the post-colonial era, the Chinese sought to continue their private Chinese oriented schools. However, this situation had created considerable trouble with Malayan nationalists who preferred Malayan schools over alien culture oriented schools. A second group of residents in Malaya to present an educational problem were the Indian laboring communities. During the colonial era, most Indians came to Malaya to work on the rubber plantations. Eventually a substantial number of Indian migrant workers settled in rural Malaya. The Malayans disliked the Indians because the Indian eventually began to compete with the Malayan in rural areas for agricultural employment. Furthermore, in many ways the Indian proved to be far more offensive to the Malays than the Chinese in that both the Indian and the Malayan lived in the same environment. The British attempted to educate the Indian by establishing plantation schools. Since the government's intention was to encourage the Indian to eventually return to India, the Indian young received an Indian oriented education. Both the Indian and the Chinese culture schools tended to maintain the non-Malayan orientation of these two different groups of settlers in Malaya. Government schools provided education for the Malays. Elementary schools, with government support, attempted to educate all Malay children between ages five and twelve. These schools encouraged the preservation of Malay culture and religion and attempted to acquaint the student with the values of the European. These schools proved to be successful in preserving local culture and religious values and maintaining an adequate level of learning among the Malays. For the bright Malay student, an English education could be acquired at the secondary level. This kind of education gave to the student an opportunity to advance either in government work or business. Generally speaking, the British educational system provided for the basic needs of the entire community. Perhaps the greatest weakness of the system came with the establishment of Chinese, and, to a lesser degree, Indian schools which served to maintain separate cultural communities within the Malay area.

The termination of British rule in Malaya began with the outbreak of World War II. Japanese occupation of the entire Peninsula not only destroyed the power of the colonial government, but ruined the prestige which generally surrounded the European colonial community in all of Southeast Asia. In addition, Japanese occupation offered the native nationalist an opportunity to assert a more aggressive form of nationalism than had been characteristic of the pre-World War II era. All of this worked against the continuation of British rule in Malaya. After the war, Britain did re-occupy Malaya, but the old form of colonial government had to be reorganized. One of the more important aspects of this re-organization of the government was the separation of Singapore from the rest of Malaya. Singapore now became an independent British colony. For the rest of Malaya, new treaties with each sultan resulted in the creation of a federal state, replacing the Federated and Unfederated governments of the pre-war era. For almost a decade, Britain maintained her colonial status in Malaya. During this final decade of British rule, the government had to face the very serious problem of rising native nationalism, disagreements between the Chinese and Malayan communities, and the growth of communism. With the exception of the non-communist Chinese; Malayans, nationalists, and communists all favored the termination of British rule in Malaya. Recognizing that her colonial status in Malaya would soon end, England attempted to settle the differences between the Chinese and Malayan and to prepare the Chinese-Malayan population for independence and self rule. In 1957, Malaya became independent.

The following article by Virginia Thompson examines the question of nationalism in Malaya prior to the Second World War. This material provides not only an understanding of the background to the present problem of nationalism in Malaya, but also suggests some of the basic problems created by the existence of foreign elements in all parts of Southeast Asia.

BRITISH MALAYA *

The Malay states, along with Cambodia and Laos in Indo-China, have the distinction of being the only dependencies in Southeast Asia which sought the protection of European powers against the encroachments of foreign Asiatics. This has affected not only the type of indirect rule subsequently applied to them but, more important, has created a loyalty or rather an absence of resentment toward the sovereign power.

The English East India Company concentrated its energies on consolidating its position in India after vain attempts to break the Dutch monopoly in the Indian Archipelago during the 17th and most of the 18th Century. The French Revolutionary Wars brought with them a realization of the need for greater protection for the eastern coast of India, and Napoleon's occupation of Holland gave the British a second chance to gain a foothold in the Archipelago and to share in the rich trade between that region and Europe and the Farther East. With the gaining of Penang in 1786, the capture of Malacca from the Dutch in 1791, and the acquisition of Singapore by Raffles in 1819, the English Company followed its traditional policy of establishing, albeit hesitatingly, a string of strategic trading posts along a world commercial sea lane. Its sole purpose at the time was to wrest the rich Straits entrepôt trade from the Dutch by the revolutionary means of free-trade ports, but in so doing to avoid the complications that would result from penetration of the hinterland.

The settlement of the centuries-old Anglo-Dutch rivalry in this region[1] by the treaty of 1824, followed by the substitution of state for company control after the Indian Mutiny in 1857, and the transformation of the three ports (Singapore, Penang, Malacca) into the Crown Colony of the Straits Settlements in 1867, set the stage at last for effective intervention in the increasingly chaotic affairs of the Malay states.[2] Here was repeated the old story of rival factions within each of the sultanates calling on an alien power for aid against internal enemies, even at the price of losing all but nominal sovereignty.

On the British side the impetus within the Straits Settlements was strong enough by then to overcome the aversion of the home government to territorial expansion with the cogent argument that the peninsula's rich resources might otherwise be lost to Siam in her current southward drive. Individual agreements made with the sultans of Selangor, Perak, Pahang and Negri Sembilan, stipulating that they would ask and accept the advice of British Residents on all questions not pertaining to Malay custom and religion, were followed by the Treaty of Pangkor which molded these states in 1874

*R. Emmerson, Mills, and Thompson, <u>Government and; Nationalism in Southeast Asia</u> (New York, Institute of Pacific Relations, 1924) pp. 160-181. By permission of the author, Virginia Thompson.

into an increasingly centralized federation. Johore's proximity to Singapore led its sultan to follow the same path independently, though he did not accept an adviser until 1914. The remaining unfederated states, Kedah, Perlis, Kelantan and Trengganu, came under British protection subsequent to a treaty made in 1909 with their suzerain, Siam. Thus in the small area (50, 976 square miles) that comprises British Malaya are nine states with a corresponding number of customs barriers and three types of British administration.

The explanation of this state of affairs lies in the geographical and cultural, as well as the historical, background of the region. Pre-British Malaya was colonized along the seacoasts and river valleys by successive groups of Malays who had been migrating thither from the nearby Archipelago for centuries. [3] The jungle-covered hinterland of the peninsula remained the uneasy preserve of scattered and nomadic tribes of indigenous Sakais, Semangs and Negritoes. The Malays were the controlling power in the peninsula for only about a century, [4] their decline dated from the Portuguese capture of Malacca in 1511. Thereafter states like Perak and Trengganu achieved a certain degree of independence only spasmodically, while refugees from Malacca maintained a pseudo-sovereignty over Johore. The northern countries became the quasi-vassals of Siam in the degree to which geography and the means at Bangkok's disposal permitted the enforcement of suzerain powers. The southern peninsular states were periodically overrun by Malays from Celebes and Sumatra, and later by Chinese immigrants who came to work the tin mines, principally in Perak. The golden age of Malacca was subsequently never equaled by any of these states which passed through centuries of subjection, degeneration and internal dissension. Three centuries prior to Britich sovereignty the older Indian rajahship of the peninsular Malays became influenced by the Islamic concept of the ruler not merely as a monarch, but as God's shadow on earth, and this idea with the loyalty it inspired remained the most fundamental force in Malaya's history until modern times, imbuing Malayan Islam with a national rather than a purely religious force.

The religious intolerance of the Portuguese aroused such hostility on the part of the few Malays who came into contact with them that they made common cause with the Dutch. [5] When the latter became masters of Malacca in 1641, they treated native rulers with as much deference as seemed necessary to secure their co-operation. In 1874 the Malay chiefs acquiesced in British supervision, albeit without enthusiasm, while the masses remained indifferent. The sole Malay revolt against British rule, discounting the Nanning War of 1832, was the assassination of Resident Birch of Perak, [6] whose well-intentioned but overenergetic interference in the ancient Malay institution of debt-slavery was considered by a small group of the local ruling class to be an infringement on their treaty-established control over Malay customs and religion. After the quelling of this revolt and the simultaneous suppression of piracy in the Straits, the pax Britannica was established in the peninsula, to the relief of the Malay peasantry and to the ultimate contentment of the sultans who came to enjoy greater prestige, security and wealth under Britain's suzerainty and through the rapid development of the peninsula under both British and Chinese auspices.

Despite the strongly adverse impression created in England by Birch's assassination, the government sanctioned continuance of the system of Residents and the institution of State Councils, with a few Malay representatives, in the protected states. Although the British made use of the existing governmental machinery in the Federated States and reiterated their intention of safeguarding the prestige of Malay rulers, the three types of administration that have evolved in Malaya have simply strengthened European control, and the only difference lies, as it does in French Indo-China, in the degree of their intensity.[7] The Straits Settlements merely represents the most direct form: it has a Legislative Council dominated by an official majority with unofficial representatives chosen or nominated according to their commercial or communal interests. In spite of frequent, vociferous criticism by Malays of administrative autocracy in such matters as income tax and the Malayan union, the chief protagonists have no real desire for representative government, in which they would be numerically swamped by other racial groups. They quarrel solely among themselves and with the administration. When it comes to any issue vitally affecting the colony as a whole, British, Chinese and Indian vested interests line up as a unit.

In the Federated States the decentralization aimed at by the Guillemard[8] and Clementi reforms theoretically restored greater prestige and autonomy to the sultans and their councils in relation to the increasingly centralized and rigid bureaucracy at Kuala Lumpur, which was governing efficiently enough in the interests of the country's economic development. Actually what conflict there is has remained an inter-British struggle of the producing regions against the commercial and fiscal domination of Singapore. The remarkable economic prosperity of the Federated States has never sufficiently tempted the sultans of the Unfederated States to permit themselves to be drawn into a common economic and political framework that might jeopardize their pseudo-independence and the more purely Malay character of their states. Such obviously commonsense arrangements as a uniform administration and a single tariff for the whole of so small a country as British Malaya have been blocked by the competition of rival groups, not always drawn up along racial lines, for the retention of political or economic power, and the whole struggle has been fought out above the heads of the ignored Malay majority.

This Malay majority comprises both the apathetic peasantry and a small but growing middle class of professional men and government employees which feels that such privileges as have been left or granted to Malaya have benefitted solely the ruling class. [9] The Middle class shares the view of the "Malayans" and some British that the government policy of holstering up an anachronistic sultanate and Malay way of life is futile because it is doomed inevitably to destruction in the modern world. The sultans naturally support British rule, direct or nominally otherwise, because under it they enjoy a position far above that of their "sovereign" ancestors and have indeed become parasitic upon it. What the middle class demands is a sincere British effort to train Malays in self-government beyond the subordinate sphere since government employment still enjoys the highest prestige in Malay tradition. But their more recent desire for sharing in the economic plums as well reflects the growing materialism of the younger Malay generation. The radical fringe of this group demands further the exercise of actual sovereign powers by Malay rulers, a Malay majority in the legislative councils, and the use of Malay as the official language. [10] There is a distinct feeling on the part of the few but vocal Malay nationalists that British policy in respecting the Malay cultural pattern has deliberately retarded vital national growth and that the perpetuation of the different forms of protected and directly administered states has simply strengthened Malay regionalism.

The current British policy of Malay preference did not characterize the early administration of the Malay states. The Malays' traits of timidity and courteous conservatism—characteristics which antedated British intervention—kept them for many years spectators and not participants in the changes overwhelming their country. Muslim mentality was bewildered by the spectacle of man's domination over nature and by the separation of secular and religious powers, but it acquiesced in this eclipse of the Malay-Muslim culture because the Oriental believes that temporal prosperity is the visible sign of divine favor. New means of livelihood developed under British control were theoretically open to all alike, but the passive Malays did not seek them, while Chinese and Indians swarmed over their country as clerks, overseers, laborers, policemen and schoolmasters.

In the early 20th century the Malays sought compensation for this implied English deprecation of their natural life in a renewed allegiance to Islam. In this period Malay national ceremonies were being discarded, their venerated natural laws set aside in favor of an alien code, their inherited superstitions undermined by the march of Western science, their culture often ridiculed as a futile devotion to outmoded trivialities and combated as interfering with the spread of English institutions. [11] Even loyalty to their own sultanates was condemned as the perpetuation of arbitrary territorial distinctions in what had now become a federated whole. Malay allegiance was thereby temporarily transferred from the local sultan to Pan-Islamic ideals, emanating from Turkey and Egypt.

Pan-Islam in British Malaya, in the pre-1914 period, took on an imitative and defensive character and was followed by a quickening of religious zeal throughout the peninsula. [12] Muslim and study clubs dedicated to reading the Koran and exclusively religious schools sprang up. The Malay press was flooded with translations from Egyptian journals, materially affecting Malay literary style by the introduction of Egyptian and Arabic expressions and by the boycotting of English words. [13] The movement was defensive in its fear lest the Malay and Muslim way of life be irreparably and adversely altered by the materialism pervading the peninsula. Its importance lay in its awakening of the Malays and in the termination of their traditional role as "frogs beneath a coconut shell" knowing nothing of the world outside.

But Malay interest in Pan-Islam largely evaporated as a consequence of Turkey's disregard of tradition between 1922 and 1924. [14] The abolition of the caliphate removed the political bias from the movement, while the British policy of noninterference and even endorsement of their religion did much to win over the orthodox group. Since Pan-Islam is regarded as less dangerous to the British government than a national loyalty would be, the Malays were encouraged to remain Muslim: the British shared in the cost of mosque construction, subsidized religious schools, reorganized the curriculum of state schools to permit religious observances, and they even prohibited Malays from entering public drinking and gaming establishments. [15]

Inevitably the Muslims of Malaya have divided into modernist and orthodox camps, and their views are respectively expressed in the two Malay religious journals, Lembaja Melayu and Pengasoh, which are read all over the peninsula. As in other Muslim countries, modernism has little hold on the masses or the uneducated chiefs; its adherents are chiefly the younger, English-educated men of the towns. [16] The strongholds of orthodoxy are found in the religious seminaries of Perak and Kelantan, while those of modernism center chiefly in Singapore and the western states. Even in these areas, however, the old ideas are still powerful. In July 1925 a wildly enthusiastic gathering of 2,000 Muslims at Singapore denounced the modernists as being worse than idolaters and Christians. As modernist ideas have been making headway, so the opposition had gathered strength.

In the early postwar period the modernists were represented by Kaum Muda, a party of about 100 young Malays from the growing middle class who advocated progress along Western lines despite the blind prejudices of their elders (Kaum Tua), who wanted to return to the old ways. [17] <u>Kaum Muda</u> wanted more democracy rather than the revival of an obsolescent aristocracy, and they tried to inspire in their apathetic compatriots a desire to rise to the new economic and cultural opportunities.

A strong branch of the <u>Anjaman-i-Islam</u> exists in Singapore, and the <u>Ahmadiya</u> movement has many sympathizers. Most of the Western-educated Muslims have followed the lead of Sir Syed Amier Ali and Mira Ghulam Ahmed, whose influence, directed toward the restriction of unduly easy divorce and the promotion of higher education among Muslims, has undoubtedly increased liberalism among Malays who have hesitated to identify themselves openly with an organization so abhorrent to the orthodox. The generally broader outlook of the urban Malays was evident in 1938 in their opposition to the reimposition of the Muslim Offenses Laws in Selangor and other states, involving such questions as whether a Muslim should be fined for absence from the mosque, or a Muslim woman imprisoned for six months because she had had relations with a non-Muslim, and generally whether Muslims should be still subjected to laws inspired by the hierarchy of the <u>kathis</u>. That same year witnessed the appointment of a Malay judge to the Federated Malay States Supreme Court, the admittance of two Muslim lawyers to the Bar, the promotion of a Malay to a high engineering post, the selection of a Malay woman for the first time as supervisor of a Perak school, the appearance of the first Malay woman golf champion, and the formation of the first tin company by Malay enterprise—all small achievements in themselves but marking a great triumph for the influence of <u>Kaum Muda</u>. [18]

The Muslim struggle in Malaya has remained essentially a communal one. Both traditionalists and modernists live on good terms with the foreign Malays, who have come increasingly to the peninsula and are eventually absorbed by their fellow-Muslims, and with the Christian British, who have found it in the interests of peaceful government to encourage the Muslims to continue living in their traditional and isolated fashion. In 1926 the government set up a Mohammedan Advisory Board only three of whose fourteen members have been Malays. The nationalistic reorientation of Malayan Islam is shown by the latter's growing resentment of the domination of this Board by Indian and, above all, by Arab Muslims who for centuries were revered in Malaya as quasi-divine beings.

In the past decade a number of Malay associations and journals have appeared. The Malay Association for the Advancement of Learning, founded in 1924 by two Malay officials, has only Malays as members: its proceedings are held in Malay, but political and religious matters are barred by its constitution. This interesting effort of the Malays to educate their own people has been taken up by the more nationalistic Malay associations which have been founded recently in Perak, Pahang and Selangor. In Singapore there is the Malay Union with over a thousand members and branches all over the island. Members of these groups have come to realize that the Malays—aristocrats, peasants and fishermen alike—have been relegated to the background while wealth and power and position are enjoyed by the more vigorous and money-minded immigrant races. They see the need for organization and discussion of mutual problems, and for the protection of their common interests. Their most interesting venture is in the field of improving the Malay home by the spread of vernacular education, especially for girls whose status Islam has seriously depressed. Parallel with this growth toward organization and education along Malay lines has come a crescent Malay press. Now there are twelve Malay journals published in British Malaya, whereas during the last war there was only one. Probably 60 per cent of the village Malays, at least in the more accessible western states, read these papers, of which Majlis, printed at Kuala Lumpur, is outstanding as a nationalist organization. Malays in increasing numbers listen to Malay broadcasts from Singapore, which have grown in number with the war. A definite religious, racial and national feeling is taking shape, and while Malay public opinion is far from articulate, it is being formed. Its tempo was accelerated by the economic troubles arising from the depression, and it has been sharpened by national demarcations which have come in the wake of war.

The chief Malay grievance is economic and only secondarily political. Malays are beginning to feel that the innumerable changes that have come to their country have been for the benefit of foreigners; that the British, despite lip-service to the principle of Malay preference, are no longer protecting Malay interests against inroads by the immigrant races but are simply using it to check the political demands of the latter groups; and finally that they are not being prepared either for self-government or for participation in their country's development.

As is true everywhere in Southeast Asia, agrarian indebtedness, though less acute in Malaya, underlies the impoverishment of the farming class. When the law safeguarding their land through the creation of Malay reservations was overhauled in 1933, it was hoped that the dangers of a landless peasantry had been averted, and that henceforth it would be impossible for the gullible and easily intimidated farmers to pledge their land as security for loans. [19] But time has proved that the peasant is still handing over his title to Indian moneylenders, albeit illegally, and that often the actual occupants of the land are secret nominees of the real owners. The government cannot, for its part, outlaw the moneylender, because the peasant still needs credit. The co-operative movement, though slow, has been in many ways successful, but least so in the rural districts where the membership for both the Federated States and

Straits Settlements totals just over 2,000 peasants. The British are making an effort to train the stubbornly conservative peasantry in better agricultural methods and to relate elementary education more closely to the Malays' main life work. By attacking the fundamental problem—i.e., educating the people to exercise co-operation and thrift—British policy offers a marked contrast to the purely credit function of the more numerous and better-organized agricultural banks of the Netherlands Indies.

Another seemingly simpler form of protection that the government might offer the peasant involves protecting his land against the encroachments of tin companies and Chinese agriculturists. But the pressure of war needs has greatly complicated the government's policy of reserving the monopoly of rice cultivation to the Malays, and of holding the balance between peasant and prospector. Tin interests point to the imminent exhaustion of those peninsular mines that are now being worked to capacity. The country is dependent on foreign sources for two-thirds of its food supplies and at present it is impossible to repatriate unemployed Chinese coolies, as was done at high cost during the depression. Nevertheless war production has absorbed most of the unemployed, and Malay opinion was so unanimously against reorientation of the land policy that it has secured its indefinite postponement. Malay nationalists believe the only permanent solution of the problem lies in a government program which would allot funds to the impoverished Malay peasantry, improve the health of village Malays, and above all restrict alien immigration.

Indian immigrant laborers are placed under an All-Malayan Controller of Labor, who strictly regulates their working hours, wages and living conditions in conjunction with the Indian Agent. The latter official represents the Government of India, which takes so active an interest in the welfare of its overseas nationals that it is responsible, as in Burma, for such progressive measures as have been adopted. The Chinese laborers enjoy no such benevolent supervision. They work independently, and as they are more efficient laborers they secure higher wages than the Indians. The Protector of the Chinese is an official who, it should be noted, protects local society against the turbulence of Chinese strikers, Communists and secret societies, which in the last few years have included a gangster element functioning under the cloak of patriotism. Despite Chinese consular representation, the government effectively uses the arbitrary weapon of banishment against Chinese whom it considers undesirable. By virtue of their right to acquire real property, the Straits-born Chinese have become a far more influential group than Chinese in other neighboring countries, and they differ from the China-born in respect to occupation, in patriotism toward the mother country, and above all in having predominantly local interests. The far less wealthy and influential permanent

Indian communities are almost untouched by the Congress movement in India, while the Tamil laborers, who form the great bulk of the Indian element in Malaya, are mostly illiterate transients. In either case, intellectual contacts between these alien groups and the Malays are so slight that Malay nationalism owes little to them.

Numerically the Malays consider themselves an island which is being fast submerged by the flood of aliens that have been encouraged to enter their country contrary to their best interests. Though native Malays still predominate in the Unfederated States, in the Straits Settlements they are the most numerous race only in Malacca, and in the Federated States only in Pahang—in all accounting for only 37.5 per cent of the total population, according to the 1931 census. The basis of their existence everywhere is agriculture, and their standard of living is low. In the Straits Settlements, where the proportion of Malays engaged in commerce is highest, only one in twenty-five is so employed, and in the remainder of the country only about one in seventy. Nationalists claim that it is impossible for Malays to get either commercial training or employment because all business firms are run by non-Malays. The administration is absorbing them in increasing numbers, but the total is still very small, and only in the Unfederated States do they outnumber the non-Malay civil servants. Malays have virtually no share in the tin industry, and only a limited one in rubber cultivation, accounting for only 24 per cent of total production as contrasted with half in the Netherlands Indies.

There are no statistics published on the income of Malay farmers, but it is obvious that argicultural profits are not sufficient to induce them to cultivate food crops beyond their personal needs, despite increasing governmental pressure to make the country more self-sufficient. The total revenues of the Federated States, in particular, show phenomenal increases, but in their development in the Malay plays neither a creative nor a service role. He goes his accustomed way, in which religious and agricultural duties regulate most of his waking hours and which bears no real relation to the country's economic or political life. In the village the Malay respects his hereditary chief, but is spectator to the chief's struggles with the religious element; the latter, which offers the humble their only path to power, includes all that is energetic and capable in the village. [20] The shortsighted greed of both ruling forces, united only in their oppression of the peasant, made it pointless in the past for the farmer to earn anything beyond his subsistence. Religion enjoined the simple life and the sultan and chiefs made any other life impossible for the peasant, who was forced to shift for himself with but little concern for his neighbors, and was never allowed to develop any luxurious tastes for whose gratification he would be willing to work hard.

Since Islam was brought to the Malays not by the sword but by merchants who were conscious of their position as a minority in the country, it never developed fanaticism or hatred of foreigners, but only a religio-racial feeling of apartness. The Malay is vaguely aware of the existence of non-Muslim countries outside the Archipelago, but his ideas of China and India are derived wholly from their unwanted representatives in his country. Islam is a further barrier to social contacts as it debars marriage with Chinese or Hindus. Since 1905 there has been a growing consciousness of the might of Japan, but the concentration on Singapore Island of 4,000 out of the 5,000 Japanese in British Malaya has prevented transforming contacts. When the Chinese coolies boycotted Japanese mines, plantations and shipping, the Malays indifferently took their places, insofar as they felt inclined. Malay addiction to the easy life has reinforced their contempt for the alcohol-drinking, pork-eating and usurious aliens and their foolish striving for material gain.

Alien enterprise has been concentrated in the more accessible western states of the peninsula. Only Perlis and Kedah, in addition to the eastern states of Kelantan and Trengganu, have retained their essentially Malay structure. Chinese and Indians, when confronted with nationalistic Malay demands, reply with some justice that the shiftless and unenterprising Malays alone are responsible for their backward position, and that their unprogressive pride in race and religion has kept them a static group apart, preferring the monotony of village life to working during fixed hours as coolies on other men's plantations and mines. Only in Kelantan, where alien labor is unavailable, has local labor been tested and, under special conditions, it has been found reasonably adequate.[21] In short, according to the alien groups, the spoils belong to the laborers, whether foreign or indigenous, and in the case of Eurasians and second-generation Chinese and Indians this means access to the higher realms of government employment without distinction as to race and color.

The ban imposed on Indian emigration since May 1938, and the war in China, have posed the problem of retaining a permanent labor force in Malaya, and the price demanded for this is citizenship rights for self-styled "Malayans" in the country of their birth if not of their culture. These demands have in turn heightened Malay fears, and have made racial issues out of the apparently unrelated questions of admission to the civil service, the establishment of a Malayan university, and the opening of rice lands to agricultural colonists. It is already obvious that the main problem of the future will be the preservation of harmony among the domiciled communities, who are no longer content with a semi-alien status and are in Malaya to stay.

Years of British paternalism have been built on the barrier which Islam erected between the Malays and other races so effectively as to preclude, at least for the present, any possibility of Malayan cohesion and unity. Malay nationalists want more benevolent autocracy by the British rather than the replacement of it. Leadership as well as unity of thought and aim are lacking in the steady growth of Malay nationalism. There is no organization, or a will to organize, nor is there co-operation between the Malays of the Federated States and the Unfederated States. The aloofness of Kedah, the superciliousness of Johore and the apathy of Kelantan and Trengganu reinforce the isolationist outlook of the Federated States.

FOOTNOTES

[1]Mills, L. A., British Malaya (Singapore, 1925), pp. 1-79.

[2]Swettenham, Sir Frank, British Malaya (London, 1929), p. III et seq.

[3]Wheeler, L. R., The Modern Malay (London, 1928), p. 52; Wright, A. and Reid, T. H., The Malay Peninsula (London, 1912), p. 313.

[4]Wheeler, op. cit., p. 64.

[5]Mills, op. cit., p. 1.

[6]Swettenham, op. cit., p. 138.

[7]Emerson, Rupert, Malaysia (New York, 1937), Chapters IV, VI.

[8]Ibid., p. 330; Cuillemard, Sir Laurence, Trivial Fond Records (London, 1937), p. 91.

[9]Wheeler, op. cit., p. 234.

[10]See articles and correspondence in the Straits Times, October 24, 1938.

[11]Wilkinson, R. J., Malay Beliefs (London, 1906), p. 80.

[12]Wheeler, op. cit., p. 176.

[13]Wilkinson, R. J., Papers on Malay Subjects (Kuala Lumpur, 1907), p. 62.

[14]Wheeler, op cit., p. 132.

[15]The Malays in Malaya (Singapore, 1928), p. 93, et seq.

[16]Wheeler, op. cit., p. 237.

[17]Sidney, R. J. H., Malay Land (London, 1926), p. 49.

[18]Straits Times, November 21, 1938.

[19] Ibid., August 3, 1938.

[20] Wilkinson, R. J., Papers on Malay Subjects (Kuala Lumpur, 1907), Vol, III, p. 10.

[21] See Straits Times, August 6, 1938.

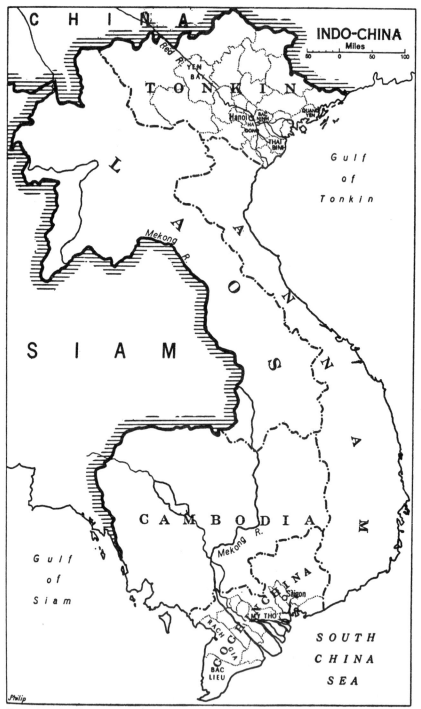

From <u>Agrarian Unrest in Southeast Asia</u> by Erich H. Jocoby. Published by Columbia University Press. Used by Permission.

CHAPTER 4

French Indo-China

The geographic area known as Indo-China has become identified with five regions in Southeast Asia. They are Cochin China, Annam, Tonkin or Tongking, Cambodia and Laos. The three states of Cochin China, Annam and Tongking are located on the eastern side of Indo-China and are known as Vietnam. Traditionally, this area had maintained strong cultural ties with southern China. On occasions, the governments in Vietnam have fallen under the control of China, but normally, the Vietnamese have sought to be free of Chinese domination. Regardless of the degree of Chinese control, owing to the nearness of China and the relatively easy lines of communications between the two areas, political expediency always required a degree of caution in Vietnam concerning matters that might offend her powerful neighbor to the north. Racially, the Vietnamese have a strong Chinese heritage. Whereas Vietnam has traditionally looked to the north for its culture and political guidance, Cambodia and Laos have traditionally looked to the Western nations of Siam and India for their cultural orientation. Both Cambodia and Laos have been forced to maintain a careful foreign policy to prevent Siamese intervention into their domestic political activities. The people of Laos are Tai or Siamese, while the Cambodians are a combination of Indian and Mongolian. From a nationalistic point of view, it is almost impossible to speak of an Indo-Chinese culture, race or nation. Culture, national traditions and racial background differ from area to area with each region having its own cultural and racial identification. Vietnamese and Cambodian culture differs in the same fashion that Burman and Malayan culture are quite separate and unique.

Cochin China, located in the southeast portion of Indo-China, shares with Cambodia and Laos the important Mekong River, a river system that has made irrigation possible for extensive rice cultivation, particularly along the Cambodian sector of the river. Saigon, the principal city in Cochin China, served as both a commercial and political center of this area. North of Cochin China lies the kingdom of Annam with its capitol, the city of Hue, known as the cultural capitol of the entire Vietnam area. Fishing and agriculture dominate the Annam economy. At the beginning of the modern colonial era, Annam dominated the whole of Vietnam. North of Annam lay the region of Tongking with its capitol city, Hanoi. The French found Tongking rich in minerals which included; coal, tin, iron ore, zinc, copper, and lead. In addition to the various mineral deposits, the Red River provides a good area for rice cultivation and communications with southern China. The area surrounding the Red River has traditionally been heavily populated and suffers from intensive cultivation. This region has been the source of migrations to the less populated southern regions of Annam and Cochin China. Laos, located in the mountainous north-west portion of Indo-China, is the least developed part of Indo-China. Laos, both before and during the French period, tended to be removed from most Indo-Chinese activities. In the southwest portion of Indo-China lies the kingdom of Cambodia. Cambodia has been a buffer zone between the ambitions of both the Siamese and the Vietnamese governments. With great difficulty, Cambodia has generally been able to maintain its own cultural and political inde-pendence. Cambodia is rich in rice lands and has been an exporter of rice to the surrounding areas. The cultural and political center of Cambodia is the city of Phnom Penh.

The first contact between the Vietnamese and the European came in the sixteenth century when the Portuguese attempted to establish regular trading connections in Annam and Tongking. The Portuguese did not establish any factories (trading forts) in this area, but they did engage in the Vietnamese silk trade by way of the island of Macao off the China coast. Aside from the Portuguese activities in Vietnam, the only other major foreign peoples to fre-quent the ports of this area were the Japanese and the Chinese who had established a long tradition of trade with this region. Though the Portuguese did not establish factories in Vietnam, they did en-courage missionaries to do so, and attempt the conversion of the natives. The early European missionaries found that the Vietnam-ese deeply resented their activities, but, owing to the persistence of the mission societies, particularly the Jesuits, they eventually gained a foothold in Vietnam. The mission work of Alexander of Rhodes was particularly important in Vietnam in that he invented a Romanized version of the Vietnamese written language and he encouraged French missionary activity in Indo-China. Because of Rhodes' work in Vietnam, the French became the principal Euro-pean power to show interest in Indochina. Neither the British nor the Dutch attempted any major settlement or trading association with this area. By the end of the seventeenth century, foreign in-fluence in Indo-China centered around the religious activities of the Jesuits, French mission societies, and the traditional Japanese-Chinese trade in Vietnam. European trade in Vietnam remained a secondary matter throughout this period of general Western pene-tration of Southeast Asia. During the most part of the eighteenth century, some European traders did visit the port cities of this region, but in terms of actual settlements or bases of operation for regular trading facilities, no major attempts occurred to expand Western commercial influence in this area. Several reasons account for this limited activity in Indo-China. The Portuguese had been excluded from most of Southeast Asia by the Dutch. After this, the Portuguese made no further attempts to revive their lost trading empire. As for the Dutch, they remained too preoccupied with the Malaya-Indonesia area to attempt any further expansion of their sphere of influence. Finally the English and the French concentrated their trading activities on India. Furthermore, neither England nor France had sufficient strength in Asia to extend their rivalry from the great Indian struggle to Indo-China. By the end of the eighteenth century European interest in Vietnam began to increase. Both France and England had begun to acknowledge the economic and strategic importance of Indochina, and both nations suddenly began to fear that the other power might attempt to expand into this portion of Southeast Asia. Of the two powers interested in Vietnam, France took the more aggressive action. French missionary activity increased and communications between the Paris government and the various rulers in this region began to develop, but owing to the problems facing pre-revolutionary France and the uneasy political situation in Indo-China, this increased French activity did not develop into any lasting growth of foreign involvement in Indo-China.

From 1789 to 1815, France underwent the upheaval of the great Revolution and the age of Napoleonic expansion. During the revolutionary period, the French remained preoccupied with internal conditions rather than imperial expansion. However, during the Napoleonic era, some consideration did occur concerning expansion of the French empire, but no overt action occurred. Moreover, since England controlled the seas, Napoleon had no real opportunity to develop an Indo-China empire. While France remained involved with the problems of revolution and European expansion, events of great importance occurred in Indo-China which would later affect French interest in this area. Prior to the French revolutionary era, Vietnam had been divided into two rival kingdoms. During the French revolutionary era, the emperor at Hue managed to unite the two states into the single kingdom of Vietnam, which then attempted control of Cambodia. The new kingdom of Vietnam adopted a highly anti-Christian policy and began to persecute the missionaries and Christians resident in this area. These attacks against the Christian community would, at a later time, provide the French with an excuse to pressure the Hue government into protecting the Christian community, extending French trading rights in Vietnam, and ultimately to accept French governmental advisors in Hue.

After the Napoleonic era, France had to recover from the

costly wars of the past and for several decades thereafter, the French made no major attempt to develop an empire. Despite this lack of interest in colonial expansion, two factors continued to involve France in Indo-China. First, the European-Oriental trade continued to grow and France, like the English and Dutch, had to protect her Asian markets. This trade with the East forced the French to take necessary action to safeguard their commercial interests in both China and Indo-China. Secondly, the Catholic community in Indo-China gradually drew France into more direct involvement in Vietnamese affairs. Traditionally, the Christian converts in Vietnam looked to France for protection and leadership. Beginning in the nineteenth century, persecutions against the Christian community began to increase. Two reasons account for the Hue's dislike of the Christian element in Vietnam. First, the European missionaries had worked against the expansion of the Hue government into Southern Indo-China. Secondly, the Hue government adopted a highly antagonistic attitude toward Western culture and European involvement. Part of the reason for this antagonism toward the West and their general isolationistic policy came from the highly Confucian orientation of the Hue government and the deep respect paid Chinese culture by the Hue monarchy. As a result of the above, the government sought to discourage foreign trade, to exclude further missionary activity, and to persecute members of the foreign religious sect. When these persecutions occurred, European naval squadrons stationed in the China Sea and in Southeast Asia usually came to the rescue of the Christian community. Since the French had traditionally protected the Indo-Chinese Catholic community, they, rather than the Dutch and British, took the necessary military and naval action against the Hue government. The combination of the desire to trade in the East and the periodic military actions against the Vietnamese kept the French, more than any other European state, involved in Indo-Chinese affairs.

In the mid-nineteenth century, French interest in empire revived. During this period, Louis Napoleon III came to power and established the Second Empire. Compared to the previous governments in France, Napoleon III adopted a far more aggressive foreign and imperial policy than had been typical of French governments prior to the Second Empire. Louis Napoleon dreamed of an expanded French empire and sought to increase French influence throughout the world. In addition, during this period, England and France agreed to cooperate in an attempt to expand their trading concessions in China. The success of the Anglo-French activities in China, combined with the agressive policies of Louis Napoleon, resulted in renewed French activities in Indo-China. In addition to Napoleon's expansionist policies, he also sought to cultivate the image that he defended the interests of the Catholic Church. The Hue government, with its anti-Catholic policy, provided an excellent opportunity for Napoleon to realize his ambitions for empire and his desire to defend the Church. Meanwhile, in the Orient, a major reaction occurred against European involvement in the East. The Chinese having been pressed into granting trade concessions and protection to foreigners resident in that area, developed a strong anti-Western attitude toward all Europeans. This attitude quickly spread to Vietnam. To protect her influence in Vietnam, the French, in the 1860's, began to exert strong pressure on the Hue government to stop their anti-Catholic persecutions and to permit the extension of French commercial interests in Vietnam. This resulted in a brief war in which the French defeated Annam. After this war, the Hue government gave to France several provinces in Cochin China or southern Vietnam, they agreed to accept continued missionary activity in all of Vietnam, and they agreed to permit the extension of French trade in Indo-China. Shortly after France acquired southern Vietnam, they occupied all of Cochin China and Saigon became the capitol of French Cochin China.

Having absorbed the area of Cochin China, France soon became involved in Cambodian affairs. In the early years of the 1860's, the Cambodian situation had become exceedingly awkward. The government in Phnom Penh had been caught between the two powerful states of Siam and Vietnam. Technically, the ruler in Cambodia owed allegiance to Hue, but as a matter of practical politics, the Cambodians feared that once again the Siamese might attempt to expand into Cambodia. In addition, Siam, though independent, accepted a degree of British advice in the conduct of their international affairs. This basically placed Siam in the British sphere of influence. The French, fearing that the Anglo-Siamese government might attempt to expand into Cambodia, argued that since Cambodia had technically been part of Cochin China, they had a right to dominate Cambodian affairs as the new rulers of Cochin China. Though the logic of the French desire to influence Cambodia might have been exceedingly weak, the aggressive activities of the French in Cochin China forced the Cambodian government to seek an alliance with French Cochin China. By treaty, the Cambodian government agreed to accept French protection and advice in exchange for a guarantee that Cambodia would not be absorbed by Siam. With this agreement, France became the protector of Cambodia.

In 1871, France suffered a resounding defeat in the Franco-Prussian War. The new government, the Third Republic, endorsed most of the colonial ambitions of the previous administration, but lacked the power to continue the agressive policies of Napoleon III. However, within a decade, French military and economic power had revived, and with this recovery she once again committed her national resources to the development and expansion of her empire. The motivation behind the renewed French imperial drive consisted of almost every justification identified with the age of the new imperialism. Imperialists sought to increase national strength and glory, to carry on the "White man's burden" by passing on French civilization to the native world, to expand their growing industrialized economy, and to prevent England from gaining too many advantages in the race for empire. With the acceptance of the spirit of the new imperialism, France once again began to expand her control over Indo-China.

The area of Tongking became the next section of Indo-China to receive French attention. From a commercial point of view, the Red River offered the potential for expanded trade with southern China, and hopefully, with increased trade in this area, the French might be able to replace British influence in this part of China. From a naval point of view, if Tongking fell under French control, they would also be able to dominate communication in the important Gulf of Tongking area. In the 1860's, the French had made a half-hearted attempt to seize this region, but owing to the internal confusion of France and a momentary decline in public interest in empire, the French had failed to take the area. Beginning in 1880, the French once again began to seek control of Tongking. In this area, conditions appeared favorable for renewed French action. During the past decade, the Hue government had gradually lost control over the area. Rebellion against both the influence of Hue and against foreigners led to frequent attacks against French commercial interests and the Catholic community. Owing to these attacks against French trading interests and the Christian community, France began the conquest of Tongking and Hanoi. By the mid 1880's, Tongking became a French protectorate. After the seizure of Tongking, the French turned to Annam and by the mid 1890's, Annam, or Hue, became a French protectorate.

Throughout most of the nineteenth century, the region of Laos remained a land of mystery to the Europeans. In the past, Laos had been an independent state, but by the beginning of the eighteenth century, the region divided into two rival nations. Owing to frequent war with Siam and Cambodia and almost constant warfare between the two rival states of Laos, the Siamese gained control over both states in Laos. Once the French had seized Cambodia and Vietnam, they turned their attention to Laos. Beginning in the late 1880's, the French encouraged the natives to rebel against Siamese authority. In the 1890's, the French government forced Siam to withdraw from Laos. During the first decade of the twentieth century, France and Siam reached an agreement which recognized French control over Laos. With the conclusion of the Franco-Siamese Treaty, France now dominated all of Indo-China. To regularize their role in Indo-China, the French organized the Union of Indo-China. Cochin China became a french colony and Cambodia, Annam, Tongking, and later, Laos, became protectorates in which the local monarchy reigned but did not rule. With the creation of the Union of Indo-China, France assumed complete responsibility for all major activities in this region.

French domination of Indo-China combined two theories of colonial government, direct and indirect rule. In some areas, the French organized direct rule and assumed complete responsibility for all political activities, but for most of Indo-China, the French, established an indirect form of government whereby colonial advisors dictated to native princes what government policy would be. What France attempted to accomplish was to influence all levels of authority, but to publicly appear to be responsible for only limited government action. Indirect rule meant government by influence. French advisors offered opinions to native rulers who then attempted to enforce French policy. Over the years the French resident advisors assumed more and more authority in determining Indo-Chinese affairs, forcing the government of the native princes to become merely a form of window dressing for disguised French rule. The advantage of indirect rule lay in the use of the traditional power and influence of the native princes as a support for the new colonial administration. Most colonial governments, particularly in areas where there had been an established form of authority, found that total direct government by the colonial power antagonized and confused the native population. The break with the past seemed too great for the native to readily accept. Where an indirect form of government was used, the native population frequently obeyed the native prince without question, particularly in the early years of colonial rule. The disadvantage of indirect rule came with the gradual loss of respect by the people toward traditional authority. To even the most casual observer, the native princes had become the tools of the European, and with this, the prestige and authority of the native rulers rapidly declined. When reaction against European colonialism in Southeast Asia emerged, the same elements that opposed colonialism sought to destroy the monarchys that had assisted the European rulers in the past. As a result, in many areas where the indirect system of government had been used, in the present era the native population not only rejected their European colonial masters, they also destroyed all aspects of traditional government.

In Indo-China, ultimate authority, whether applied to the direct or indirect forms of government, rested with the Paris government. Both the French National Assembly and the President of France had the final authority in all colonial matters. Below the President and the National Assembly, two colonial offices controlled all aspects of French policy in Indo-China, and conducted searching investigations into the activities of all resident officials in the colonies. The reports submitted by the colonial office investigators reached Paris in secret. In Paris these reports received great consideration and any suggestion that an official or supervisor attempted to innovate policy generally resulted in that official's immediate dismissal or transfer to a lessor important position within the empire. By the consistent use of the above procedure, the Paris government ensured that all officials followed the dictates of the metropolitan administration. The second aspect of the colonial office's interest in Indo-China dealt with furthering French economic interests in the colonies. Generally, this activity represented the voice of special groups or interests that hoped to profit either directly or indirectly from the French empire. This aspect of metropolitan involvement in Indo-Chinese affairs never considered the interests of the native population, but preferred to profit from the empire even at the expense of the colonial population. The entire structure of the Paris colonial government tended to be highly bureaucratic, overly concerned with special interests, confused, highly specialized, and too involved in the regulation of even the most ordinary governmental activities. As a result, French rule in Indo-China lacked local both initiative and creativity.

Below the Paris government, the Governor General of Indo-China occupied the next level of colonial authority. From his capitol city, Hanoi, he not only administered the entire federation, but had the right to issue laws and decrees, appoint lessor officials, supervise financial matters, and maintain the internal and external security of the entire area. The Governor General held his appointment for a two year period. He received his appointment on the basis of politics rather than on the merits of his colonial knowledge and experience. Owing to his short term appointment and frequently because of his limited knowledge of the area, the quality of his administration rested on the ability of his advisors and the willingness of the Governor General to follow the advice of those who knew the Indo-Chinese situation. Unfortunately, the Hanoi advisors seldom offered creative suggestions to the Governor General, preferring to remain safe by following the traditional policies of the Paris colonial office. In addition to his staff of colonial advisors, the Governor General met periodically with the Colonial Council and the Grand Council of Economic and Financial Interests. In theory, these councils represented a cross-section of Indo-Chinese interests. In practice, the councils represented only a small portion of the entire colony. The scope of the councils typified the French concept of colonial rule. In financial matters, the council could consider the colonial budget, but lacked the power to reject financial reforms and tax measures submitted to the body for discussion by the Governor General. In other matters, such as legislation, the councils had little power since most important laws originated in Paris rather than Hanoi. The composition of the councils also suggest the typical French point of view in colonial matters. Half the membership came from high government officials resident in Hanoi and from the other political units in Indo-China. These members had made a career of supporting French colonial policy and reflected the orientation of the Paris colonial offices. The second half of the council's membership represented the native population. These members received their appointment from important colonial and native officials who maintained their positions of authority by supporting French policy. As a result of the above, the composition of the advisory council reflected only the "correct" French attitude. Indo-Chinese opposition never had an opportunity to speak in the high councils of government. Finally, the Governor had the assistance of the colonial civil service. The civil service seldom used native Indo-Chinese, preferring to employ Frenchmen who understood the attitude of the metropolitan government in Paris. The entire system of government in Hanoi ensured the preservation of Paris colonial policy and the supremacy of the powerful economic interests that hoped to profit from French rule in Indo-China. This system of government always isolated the Governor General from the Indo-Chinese people. However, few Governor Generals ever showed any interest in securing native opinion in matters of Indo-Chinese policy.

The government of Cochin China was a French colony rather than a protectorate. This placed the colony under the direct control of the Paris government. As a colony, the French maintained authority in matters of government, economics, justice, and security. The French citizens in Cochin China held the unique right to elect one deputy to the French National Assembly in Paris. The Governor of this colony served a five year term of office and his powers paralleled those of his immediate superior in Hanoi. A colonial council assisted the Governor, but like the councils that advised the Governor General, the Saigon councils could neither compel him to take any specific action nor could they reject any financial matter submitted to the body by the government. Basically, all acts affecting Cochin China reflected the policies of the Governor and the higher administrations in Hanoi and Paris. Finally, the Governor remained isolated from native opinion, in that his entire staff of advisors and assistances came from either the French community or the assimulated Indo-Chinese. Native opinion seldom reached the higher levels of government.

French rule in Cambodia illustrates the concepts of indirect colonial rule. In the 1860's, the King of Cambodia agreed to permit the French to advise his government on all matters of taxation, customs duties and public works requiring technical skill. In return for this grant of authority, the French agreed to protect Cambodia and maintain the royal government. Though the native government had the right to administer French policy, in practice the French stripped the king of all authority and used royal officials as puppets to administer French policy. In theory a dual government existed, but in practice the French dominated all important decisions making posts in Cambodia. The Resident Superior represented French influence. He was directly responsible to the Governor General in Hanoi. The Resident Superior had unquestioned authority in all matters concerned with Cambodian and Indo-Chinese policy. He supervised all French and native administrators and advised the royal government on all local and domestic matters. The King, with the Resident Superior's advice, governed by means of administrative ordinances which his subjects had to obey. Though these ordinances dealt with purely Cambodian matters, the Resident Superior had to sign all royal ordinances and commands. Various councils assisted both the Resident Superior and the King. Like the other councils in Indo-China, they remained centers of French or Westernized Cambodian influence. Native judges handled legal matters between Cambodians under traditional law modified by French Roman Law. In legal matters involving Europeans, justice was administered either in Hanoi or Saigon by European judges using French law. In effect, under the indirect system of rule, power rested with the French rather than the pseudo-government of the Cambodian king. However, the governmental solution used in Cambodia appeared to be traditional as far as the native population was concerned, and therefore remained acceptable to the population. Partly because of this, the French remained reasonably popular in this part of Indo-China.

The governments in Laos and Annam were quite similar to the form of government established in Cambodia. In Laos, the native prince had the assistance of an Administrator who held a position similar to the Resident Superior in Cambodia except in some local matters where the native prince did hold some independent action free of French control. In matters affecting all of Laos and its relationship with the Hanoi government, the French permitted no opposition. In Annam and Tongking, the administration of the Emperor of Annam continued to exist. The Emperor had the assistance of a Resident Superior who ruled in the same fashion that the Resident Superior ruled Cambodia. In purely local matters, native Mandarins exercised limited power, and they, like all native officials, had to accept the role of a French advisor. Of the three areas which fell under indirect rule, Annam and Tongking had less independence than either Cambodia or Laos, primarily because of its location between Cochin China in the South and the Hanoi government in the north.

The French offered little opportunity for the Indo-Chinese to develop the arts of self-government. Preparing a colony for self-government involved the delegation of authority to the native peoples, something the French never attempted to do. Native officials had to do the bidding of their French advisors, and in cases where a native official showed signs of independence, he either lost his position in government or received a severe reminder that he owed total allegiance to the French rather than to his native land or the titular head of state. Examples of the lack of self-government abound. Local councils fell under complete French influence since only French appointees or westernized natives sat on this advisory board. Furthermore, these councils only had the power to advise, never to legislate. The only acceptable advice a council could offer was an endorsement of Paris policy. Finally, all positions of real power or influence, relating to political and economic authority, remained under the control of either Frenchmen or assimilated natives. In general, France governed Indo-China in a highly authoritarian manner with power coming from the Paris government via the Governor General in Hanoi and ultimately reaching the lowest level of civil service. Native political responsibility or independence did not exist.

French economic philosophy, as applied to Indo-China, simulated that of the mercantilist philosophy of the old British empire. According to French economic thought, Indo-China existed for the sole benefit of the mother country, and therefore, it would be highly illogical to permit foreigners to compete on an equal basis with France in her colonies. Under this system trade outside the French economic world never had a chance to compete with goods manufactured in France since import duties remained so high that foreign goods always cost the native far more than similar French items. Furthermore, the French never permitted an Indo-Chinese industry to develop which might either compete with France or consume raw materials that could be processed in France. In terms of investment in Indo-China, the French preferred to see either their own nationals dominate the areas of agriculture, banking, commerce, internal trade, and the exploitation of raw materials. For example, rubber became Indo-China's most important agricultural export product. The French held well over ninety per cent of the rubber lands, leaving less than ten per cent to native and Chinese ownership. Only through labor on the rubber plantations did the natives profit from the introduction of the rubber plant. Furthermore, the French shipped most of the raw rubber to Europe where the processing of the raw material provided additional jobs and profit for metropolitan France.

Indo-China had the economic potential for the rise of a strong and varied economy. In terms of natural resources, this area has a variety of minerals which could have led to a thriving metal industry, she has good land for rice cultivation, and her potential for rubber development rivaled the best areas in Malaya and Indonesia. During the years of French occupation of Indo-China, most of these areas saw some economic development, but the full potential of Indo-Chinese resources never occurred. For years, the French government considered the possibility of industrializing the colony, but the programs never passed the discussion level since most businessmen and industrialists fought to prevent any form of Indo-Chinese competition from developing or a reduction of the French monopoly over manufactured goods. The power of the industrial class remained sufficient to prevent either the Paris or Hanoi government from developing industry in Indo-China. France never broke with the old philosophy that colonies existed for the benefit of the mother country and that colonies must remain the suppliers of raw materials and the consumers of manufactured goods. As a result of her occupation of Indo-China, France grew rich at the expense of the Indo-Chinese. This exploitation policy emerged as the most negative aspect of French rule in Indo-China and formed the basis for considerable native hostility toward their European masters.

Prolonged contact between the Indo-Chinese and the Westerner produced one possible advantage for the native population; the growth of nationalism. This proved to be particularly true in the area of Vietnam. The French had not intended to do this, but owing to her colonial policies, nationalism became one of the few positive results of foreign rule in Indo-China. Prior to French occupation of Indo-China, nationalism had had little opportunity to develop. In the past, there had emerged a degree of localism among the natives and in the area of Vietnam, some feelings of cultural identity had developed. Though a cultural identity had begun to emerge, no one truly unified movement among the peoples of Indo-China had occurred. By the mid-twentieth century, a rather well-developed nationalist movement had become a reality. The causes for this are many, some beyond the bounds of French rule, but in general the existence of the Westerner in Indo-China and the policies of his domination of the area formed the major cause of the growth and acceptance of nationalism in Indo-China.

One of the more interesting aspects of French rule which produced the rise and growth of nationalism came with the cultural conflict between the Chinese-Annamite civilization of Vietnam and the "cultural mission" of the French. The Vietnamese population in the late nineteenth century, held the traditional negative Oriental attitude toward the Westerner. With the arrival of the French and the determination of the French to force their culture on the Vietnamese, the Vietnamese found it necessary to re-examine their institutions and values in order to defend their traditional life against the foreign ways of the French. Through this examination and defense of their culture, a new awareness of the past and its traditions rapidly emerged. A second reason for the rapid growth of cultural awareness came with the French policy of assimilation. According to the French, through proper education and guidance, Oriental Frenchmen could be created out of the native population. In theory, the assimilated Asian would be as much at home in Paris as he would be a metropolitan Frenchman, and that Siagon and Hanoi could easily become French centers of culture and civilization. In terms of race relations and tensions that can exist between peoples of different race and culture, the French theory of assimilation can be defended. However, from both a colonial and native point of view, this policy can produce highly negative results both for the colonial masters and the native society.

To realize her policy of assimilation, France began to destroy many native institutions and traditions, and in place of the abandoned native life, substitute Western ways, many of which the Indo-Chinese believed to be unacceptable. Of the many changes in the political, social and economic life of Indo-China that occurred under French rule, the educational system produced the most dramatic alterations in the Indo-Chinese life both by challenging tradition and fostering the growth of nationalism. The French educational system introduced Western culture into the local environment. At the height of the age of the assimilation policy, the goal of the educational system was to produce Asian Frenchmen out of all educated Indo-Chinese. In later periods, after the abandonment of the extreme assimilation policy, the education system was divided into two parts, vernacular schools which stressed native culture over French civilization and French language schools which gave to the students a complete French education. In general, the bright student went to the French culture school while the less promising student went to the vernacular schools. As a result of this system, the highly educated and the bright students became assimulated Asians. These highly educated and assimulated Indo-Chinese found themselves in an extremely difficult position. From an economic point of view, higher education did not involve financial reward. The business opportunities offered the educated native remained limited, in that the economy could only use a few educated persons, and these positions generally went to Frenchmen who had important contacts in the government or the business world. As for government employment, most all administrators preferred Frenchmen to assimulated natives. Social isolation also became a problem for the assimulated natives. To secure a French education, a student had to deny most of his cultural heritage. He soon found it next to impossible to communicate with his local community, and since metropolitan Frenchmen seldom treated the westernized natives as equal, they had no one to turn to except their own kind. Having failed to secure government or business employment, and having been rejected by both his native community and by the French colonial society, the educated native slowly turned to revolutionary activity. In their long years of acquiring an education, the assimulated native had been taught the values of the French Revolution and the long history of Western man's struggle for liberty and freedom. Using this education, the educated native elite added their numbers to the growing resentment toward the French and used their talent to encourage revolution and Vietnamese nationalism. The French tried almost every means possible to destroy the growing revolutionary-nationalist movement, but their efforts only added additional fuel to the flames of nationalism which increased with the passing of each decade. By the mid-twentieth century, the Indo-Chinese, particularly in the Vietnam area, had developed a deep concept of nationalism and with this, an even deeper hostility toward France and all that symbolized French rule in Indo-China.

World War II brought a momentary end to French rule in Indo-China. After the Second World War, France attempted to reassert her control over her former colony, but native opposition to French rule, combined with the awesome problems faced by metropolitan France, prevented the complete restoration of her empire. Furthermore, the French not only failed to appreciate the strength of the native nationalist movement. Also she failed to offer any reform of her theory of colonialism. As for the native opposition, they refused to return to the pre-1940 era of colonization and they refused to accept any form of restored French government in Indo-China. The nationalists quickly turned to guerilla warfare to prevent a restoration of French power. Also, many of the native leaders, in opposing the French, adopted a very hostile attitude toward many of the doctrines associated with imperialism. In so doing, the natives assumed an anti-capitalist orientation which eventually resulted as a pro-communist, anti-imperialist attitude. Indo-Chinese nationalists fought against both French imperialism and the economic system identified with colonialism. Almost a decade of guerilla warfare followed. The war proved costly in terms of men, money and morale for the French. The guerilla forces inflicted a particularly heavy toll against the poorly trained French soldiers, which in turn produced a strong anti-war attitude among the metropolitan French, who had just begun to recover from World War II. Furthermore, the cost of the war proved to be much greater than the national economy could stand, and to the average reluctant French taxpayer, he believed that this war only benefited a small class of French society, namely the business community. Finally, the political left in France opposed colonialism and tended to favor the goals of the nationalist movement in Vietnam. By 1954, the desire to continue the struggle came to an end. All that France needed was an excuse to abandon Indo-China. The chance came after the battle of Dien Bien Phu. In this battle, the French suffered a heavy defeat. Defeat in battle, combined with domestic turmoil, brought France to the conference table. In 1954, at Geneva, treaties were signed ending French rule in Indo-China and with these agreements, Cambodia, Laos, North and South Vietnam once again achieved their independence.

The following article by Virginia Thompson suggests the cultural conflicts the native and the colonial overlords. The problems presented by Virginia Thompson can be applied to most colonial situations existing in Southeast Asia.

REACTION OF COLONIALS TO THE NATIVES *

Discouragement with the country and disillusionment in the exotic charms of its people characterized almost without exception the reaction of the first French in Indo-China. Men of such varied temperaments as Bourde, Bonnetain, Dutreuil, and Lyautey found the Annamites, from top to bottom of the social scale, totally un-heroic, lacking in virility, essentially servile, incapable of spirit-ual growth. The case was hopeless: the modern Annamite was only the degenerate débris of a race formerly great but now found-ering beyond redemption. Physically he was repellent, his face bestial, hideous, and petrified with idiocy. [1] The aristocratic Louis de Carné felt an unconquerable repugnance for his Khmer companions though they were all of royal blood. [2] None of the Indo-Chinese could compare with the colourful and artistic Hindus, or had the dramatic beauty of the Arabs. [3]

Later, when the French had recovered from their initial disappointment and found an aristocratic elegance in these people, even their most ardent admirers could not help reflecting upon the extraordinary combination of refinement and dirt. They were like carved ivory buried in grime. They might wash frequently, but in muddy water; they burned incense at the ancestral altar yet reeked of decayed fish; the children were covered with sores, yet even the poorest of them wore silver necklaces; they put on exquisitely embroidered tunics, yet at even the greatest ceremonials gave unmistakable evidence of being vermin-ridden.

Unfortunately, the first unfavourable impressions were only strengthened by association with the interpreter-servant class of Annamites, and to this day for the majority of colonials they con-stitute their sole contact with that people. They are either unaware or forget that such Annamites are the dregs of native society, iso-lated from the restraining discipline of communal and family life, and so they are peculiarly subject to the disintegrating effects of European contact. The conversation of Frenchwomen in Indo-China is largely devoted to the misdeameanours of their servants—chiefly their thefts and lightning-like escapes. The shocks given to European households by their servants have often been narrated, but nowhere more amusingly than by Madame Vassal. [4] At the end of her first month's residence all her linen had disappeared or was in rags. She found that the special cloths designed for glassware had been devoted to cleaning shoes or serving as turbans. The rest had been sold or mislaid. All the food provisions disappeared with the same haste as the linen. Meals were very expensive, despite the cheapness of food in the market. Eventually Madame Vassal discovered the co-operative system between her cook and

*Virginia Thompson, French Indo-China, (New York, Octagon Books, Inc., 1968), pp. 434—475. By permission of the author.

that of a neighbour: each cooked meals for both families on alternate days. Dishes were washed cheerfully in the drinking-water well. A table that was ostensibly for dish washing and cleaning silver was used for a couch.

Annamites simplify every operation by using as few utensils as possible. They will not use a corkscrew so long as they have teeth, or a shovel where their fingers could serve. Madame Vassal's cook used his manly chest on which to roll potato croquettes. Servants, like other Orientals who dislike routine work, ask for periodic leaves of absence. They appear in a white turban with the announcement that their mother has died. When the same process is repeated a few weeks later, the uninformed European calls them liars, not realizing that a mother's demise is the Oriental equivalent for the Occidental office-boy's permission to attend his grandmother's funeral. The frequent recurrence of stories of this nature is apt to make one forget that, in general, the Annamites make excellent servants. They are very observing, assimilate rapidly, are clever with their hands, and astonish newcomers by the excellence of the meals and service. But the natural French impatience is augmented by a trying climate and linguistic misunderstandings. The colonials who have a vast retinue leave their servants with more leisure than they are accustomed to, with naturally disastrous results on a none too strong moral fibre. For the servant who steals, there are others who have become so invaluable to their masters that they are taken back to France with them.

The ignorance or indifference of colonials to native culture is largely attributable to laziness. The Annamite language, to be sure, is one of the most difficult extant, and few are willing to make the effort to overcome this first barrier. The majority of civil and military residents have a restricted cultural outlook at best, and for the most part it never occurs to them that the country is anything but a place of exile to be endured just to make a fortune. The first soldiers roamed through the towns looking suspiciously at the native food which they never dreamed of eating. Even the fruit and rice cakes were suspect. Of cautious peasant stock, these men distrusted the Yellow Race on principle and made fun of whatever was different or strange. But was throwing paper in tombs any more absurd than refusing to sit thirteen at table? They were totally unaware of the profound side of native culture. Hué was only a mass of broken-down buildings: its emperor just a backward schoolboy. There was a more aggressive turn to this non-appreciation of Annamite civilization. Many of these soldiers earned for themselves the name of colonial apaches by their cruel violence towards native coolies and shopkeepers. Their attacks were not confined to the natives and for a time they practised profitable hold-ups on Europeans as well. [5]

115

Frequency of contacts and the will to understand are the indispensable preliminaries to a study of any foreign culture. Most colonials are not brutes or Machiavellian schemers trying systematically to oppress the native population. For them the native problem does not exist, because they think of them only in terms of labour. The most liberal theorists are often the last men willing to expatriate themselves to apply their ideas. This also applies to functionaries who, though they do not accumulate fortunes so rapidly, are nevertheless attracted to the colonies by the larger salaries offered there. The perennial charm which office-holding has for the French is shown by the great number of applicants for even the most humble positions in the colony. The desire for such a form of security has been even more pronounced since the depression. The lower ranks of officialdom are notoriously more hostile to a liberal native policy than the upper—undoubtedly because of their greater fear of native competition. The bloc of anti-liberal opinion, made up of the vast majority of functionaries and colonists, is almost impossible to overcome. The majority of the French residents in Indo-China are functionaries—that is transients in the colony who, having assured positions, naturally favour a policy of domination. They must refuse to see virtues in the Annamite civilization and intelligentsia, as the price of their continued survival in the colony. Their hostile obstinacy is a greater stumbling-block than either indifference or laziness to mutual understanding.

Another group of fear-ridden conservatives are the Frenchwomen who have come to the colony. Often the congaie, "the sleeping dictionary," was an excellent medium for learning the native people and their language, and her gradual elimination has been harmful to better inter-racial understanding. The desire felt by Frenchwomen to undermine a rival influence and to find compensation for exile by creating a second France has reduced the contacts between the races. Before they came there was a more primitive social life, and the lack of diversions made the French seek out natives as a way of passing the time. But natives in a salon add nothing to the world of fashion, with their blackened teeth, bare feet, and betel-reddened mouths. Women who are unused to having servants in France abuse their new status by treating all natives as inferiors, ignoring the traditional hierarchy among them. With some notable exceptions Frenchwomen have formed themselves into a wedge between their men and the native population.

The motor-car, impersonal as it is, has become another means of reducing contacts. The administrator who used to take a week to inspect his province on horseback, conversing with the village Notables in the evening hours, was able to learn their grievances in this way and their viewpoint. Now in a car he can cover his territory in a day. And he has no longer time for idle conversa-

tion. The increase in bureaucratic red tape has tied him to his
desk and away from his people. The motor-car gives him the
means of yielding to the rising pressure of office work, and spares
him some of the fatigue engendered by an energy-draining climate.

The men who first studied Annamite culture seriously naturally approached the problem from a French viewpoint. Many students found Annamite justice arbitrary, property poorly divided,
and above all the sacrifice of the individual to the group revolted
their individualistic upbringing. It was no wonder that compatriots
of Victor Hugo, who proclaimed that he would not sacrifice a child
to save a whole people, believed that the Annamites were subject
to an incredibly oppressive régime. The assimilationists, with
generous if ignorant idealism, wanted to share with their Oriental
brothers French institutions and ideas that would with time erad-
icate the superficial differences between them, and fashion the
Annamite after the French image. Initial misunderstandings were
only natural in view of the obstacles in language and different out-
looks. And the Annamite intelligentsia were sulking in their tents
and not making any effort to enlighten the Western barbarians.
Each interpreted everything in the light of his own culture without
appreciation of the other viewpoint. The French who distributed
copies of the Rights of Man, who abolished the lays to superiors,
who refused with righteous indignation the traditional gifts tendered
by their subordinates as attempts to corrupt their republican integ-
rity, were insulting the Annamites or making themselves absurd
with the best intentions in the world. It took many years for both
sides to appreciate the necessity of ridding themselves of their
particular mental setup before understanding each other.

To the important though negative handicap of infrequent contacts may be added the most ominous of all forms of Oriental-
Occidental misunderstanding—the white man's assumption of superiority. Almost inevitably this feeling settles over the Occidental,
no matter how liberal his viewpoint may have been in his own country. Idealistic young Frenchmen have come to the colony longing
to play Cyrano to the oppressed natives, brutalized by his compatriots. He is often disillusioned upon arrival. Old colonials tell
him condescendingly that he will outgrow such notions, or he may
have an experience that confirms their worst prophecies. Try as
he would, Jules Boissière could find no profoundly learned and dis-
dainful bonze who would instruct in the secrets of the East one
benighted Occidental who burned to drink of his wisdom. In addition
to the discouragement afforded by a difficult language and a profoundly different culture, it was even more disillusioning not to
find a qualified teacher, and to feel that all one had amassed is but
arid and banal. If further study proves Annamite civilization re-
warding, almost all scholars agree that they are at first disappointed by its dull mediocrity. The totally inaccurate and romanti-

cized cult of exoticism that prevails in France is largely responsible for these early disillusionments. The amount of perseverance and discipline required to master even the technique for understanding the East has given birth to the legend of Asiatic impenetrability. This is the solution encouraged not only by laziness but by the attraction which the very mystery of the East has exercised over the Western mind. Understanding Asia would probably lessen its charm for Europe. The obstacles to penetrating Eastern thought are real enough without deliberately swathing it in thicker veils. The Orient does nothing to further Western understanding, but even opposes it by the force of inertia and ridicule.

For the few who are disappointed, there are the many more who are immediately ripe for that state of mind known as the esprit colon. This unhappy attitude is an aggressive composite of smugness, laziness, fear, and racial prejudice. Though colonial society is less class-bound than in France, it is an aristocracy in its relations to the natives, a return to the feudal regime. According to this philosophy the most miserable white man is above the best native. This attitude is further encouraged by the average native acceptance of inferiority. They understand the Europeans' presence in the colony only in terms of the latter's leadership. When the European treats the Annamite as an equal the latter responds by treating the European as an inferior. Under these circumstances, the champion of egalitarian principles feels his ardour dampened. If under the ancien régime the good side of feudal morality was reflected in noblesse oblige, there is no corresponding benevolence to mitigate colonial arrogance. A human tendency to abuse power is augmented by a difficult climate and by the fact that the aristocracy is a minority fastened by force upon a numerically superior and potentially hostile mass of different nationality. The obscure menace of revolt makes for colonial solidarity. Fear creates injustice in an unequitable leniency towards Europeans and no mercy shown to native delinquents in their conflicts with them. In racial prejudice there is an admixture of physical repugnance on both sides, and the isolation in which it results may be further strengthened by a fear of going native—essentially the instinct of self-preservation. This narrow pride emphasizes those very differences which mark racial groups, and long residence in the colony only accentuates this barrier. If the natives accept, without visible protest, domination on these terms, they are despised, for the weak are necessarily wrong. Their hostility, which the colonial feels, further alienates him. This attitude is more characteristic of the English colonies. British visitors have expressed this viewpoint, and were astonished to see French soldiers commanded by an Annamite officer, and to hear that a touch of colour in a Frenchman is thought to make him the more interesting . . .

NATIVE REACTION TO CONTACTS WITH FRENCH COLONIALS

When the Court of Annam sent ambassadors to Paris in 1893 they took with them a letter for the French President, in which the character representing Annam was placed so as to dominate that of France, thus reducing the latter to the position of a vassal state. This insult was characteristically Oriental. The fact that the French failed to grasp its significance did not prevent the Annamites from relishing their insolence. The Annamite language abounds in insults and compliments but it takes an expert to appreciate the shades of irony under the respectful exterior. The Chinese domination of Annam is responsible for this characteristic, which is based on the fear of openly expressing contempt for those who are superiors by force of arms, and disdain for the Western Barbarian as inherently inferior to the Chinese.

It was natural that the Scholar class, impregnated with Chinese culture, should add disdain of the West to their resentment of the French destruction of the mandarinate, of which they were the mainstay. They regarded as traitors any who were willing to cooperate with the conquerors—which made it impossible for the French to find good native officials. This hostility extended to the French language and even to quoc ngu. An Annamite mandarin who wanted to learn French dared not do so openly. Ignoring the ignoble present by burying oneself in the past, through study and meditation mixed with opium and tea, harmonized with the cultural ideals of this group. If the lower classes were unable to indulge themselves so agreeably, the harsh necessity for daily toil and daily rites absorbed all their energies and effected an equal insulation. Immersed in the past or absorbed by current material preoccupations, the great majority of Annamites lived for many years without real contact with their conquerors.

The hostility of the intelligentsia was matched by the superstitious fear of the masses. Even obvious differences in external appearance frightened them. The French were not like other men. The stiff way in which the soldiers marched led the nhaqués to conclude that they had no knee joints. But the awe they inspired by feats of arms did not convince the natives of their innate superiority. This was illustrated by the speech of a mandarin at the funeral of a French officer:

> You are a curious personage. You have curly hair, a nose which stands out. You ride horseback, and whistle for your dog to follow you. You place bottles on your table for ornaments, and plant grass in your courtyard. Despite your military talents, you have succeeded in getting yourself killed. How sorry I am for you. [6]

To the majority of Annamites, excepting those in the towns, all Europeans look alike, and their prestige rises and falls collectively. Yet in 1905 a curiously double reaction was produced by the Japanese victory over Russia. Western science took on new lustre because Japan had used Occidental methods, but Europeans themselves inspired less awe, because it was thought that anyone could master their machines and beat them at their own game. The Annamites shared this belief. They stormed the gates of the new Hanoi University with renewed self-confidence, yet simultaneously they resented the presence of the purveyors of these now desirable ideas. Pride of race has from the outset dominated Franco-Annamite relations, but most Westerners forget that the vanity of the Oriental at least equals if not exceeds that of the Occidental.

The Annamites have adapted themselves to Westernisms with astonishing facility. Their powers of assimilation are remarkable. Even detractors of their moral qualities admit that they can be readily trained into making splendid cooks and mechanics. They have adopted Western clothing, though not always in the best taste, and Western sports, though they formerly despised bodily exercise. Many observers claim that this Annamite transformation is purely imitative and superficial . . . .

Oriental pride is the great uneasy factor in any acceptance of Western supremacy, and it is felt most keenly by the upper classes, who are weighed down by the knowledge that they are the heirs of a great civilization. Being so sensitive to the marks of respect, they are constantly being outraged by the French who, often unconsciously and sometimes deliberately, humiliate them. They do not take into consideration a natural ignorance of native customs, a different viewpoint, or good intentions—everything is subordinate to the external results. French officials often fail to show the proper respect, tutoyer the high mandarins, are over-familiar through bonhomie as well as condescension, and wound Annamites by going straight to the point in conversation instead of respecting the traditional form of a devious approach. The necessity for using interpreters has increased the opportunities for misunderstanding, partly involuntary and partly—when profitable—intentional.

When the insult is deliberate, as is too often the case in colonies where the white man feels himself a god, the Annamites' already sizeable inferiority complex is enlarged. The French seem unable to compromise between an exaggeratedly favourable and an unjustifiably unfavourable attitude towards the natives. The Annamites are very sensitive to injustice and will not be put off with indulgence or pity—which they find equally insulting. The whole relationship is dominated by the enforced proximity of conquered with conqueror.

Brutality characterized far more the early days of colonization than the post-war period, yet it is only within the last ten years that French writers have begun to publicize the fact. During the pacification the treatment of French prisoners by both Annamites and Chinese was anything but gentle, and their cruelty engendered reciprocal brutality. A rebirth of this violence recurred with the industrialization of the colony, when the usual capital-labour struggle was aggravated by the race problem. Léon Werth is the historian of abuse on the French side, especially in the master-servant relationship, and his book makes sorry reading. He records the anger of Annamites at the presumption of the Occidental barbarians in mistreating a people more civilized than themselves. Unfortunately it is the petty official—la mentalité sous-off, of which there are legion—who casts terror wherever he goes. At word of his coming whole villages are deserted. He is regarded as a carnivorous and alcoholic brute, and his servants inspire even greater fear and hatred. He either does not thank the Notables at all for their gifts, or in such a way that it diminishes their prestige. All breathe a sigh of relief when he has passed on to make the life of another village miserable, by threats of fines and imprisonment.

But in condemning, and rightly, the brutality of the white race towards men who have no recourse against their caprice, one must not forget that the example was first given by the Annamites themselves. The most ardent native nationalist cannot but admit that the worst exploiter of the Annamite is his own countrymen. This is true throughout the whole economic scale, from the rich landowner who evicts the poor farmer to the plantation foreman who physically and morally abuses the men under him, and like the jailers even use torture to elicit money. No Westerner could equal the atrocious cruelty that characterized the Communist uprising. Those Annamites who resent so bitterly the disdain with which they are treated by the French, forget their own history. They wiped out the Chams and were in the process of cruelly exterminating the Khmers and Laotians at the time of the conquest. They despise these nations, as they do the Hindus and Africans, as inferior peoples. They have been the ruthless exploiters of primitive tribes like the Mois. This trait in the Annamite character as well as their deification of success-at-any-price, makes their denunciation of French race-pride hypocritical. The only difference—and it is an important one—is that the Annamites are not purveyors of the principles of '89, nor do they have to reconcile their former attempts at colonization with a civilizing mission. But one is forced to conclude that it is not their humanitarianism but their pride which the French have offended, and both sides have been busier pointing out the weak spots in the other's armour than in taking active measures to remedy the situation. . . .

121

NATIVE REACTION TO FRENCH CULTURE

The divergence between two racial cultures is nowhere more clearly shown than in the Annamite reaction to Western education. Chinese instruction was thoroughly utilitarian. Although the child absorbed a complete system of ethics, as part of the paraphernalia of learning, he continues to study not in order to expand his viewpoint by new knowledge, but to win honours that lead to high government positions. The European ideal of disinterested scholarship is incomprehensible to the Annamite, who regards knowledge as no dynamic growth based on study and experience, but as a vast memorizing of texts which embody the sum total of knowledge. When the Annamites demanded more educational facilities they meant more administrative openings. It is true that the earliest schools in the colony trained interpreters and that the French agregation is the equivalent of a teaching position for life, nevertheless, it was not true of the colony's educational system as a whole, and the deception felt by the frustrated Annamite students is shown by the number who have joined the revolutionary ranks. Those who have received diplomas and positions are almost equally undesirable. Their arrogance is unbearable, and they have acquired no humility from a realization of the immensity of knowledge. This attitude towards education has been an important factor in alienating liberal opinion in France. The Academician Brieux was touched by the Annamites' wish for education, but only recently has it been realized that those very Annamites who have been most generously educated lead the anti-French agitation.

Annamites who have made sacrifices to send their children to French schools find them changed: the old respect and courtesy have become impudence and conceit. The patriarchal system and the gods who supported it have been shattered. The culture of the Occident has brought the individual out in relief from his social background. Here the missionary and functionary have joined hands. The glory of God and of the Third Republic were thought to be equally served by encouraging Annamite individualism. The results have discouraged those who encouraged it most. The educated Annamites have not received the recognition or positions to which they feel themselves entitled, and they are hopelessly uprooted from their own setting without being transplanted into Western culture. Their parents have undermined their own authority and have lost their children in trying to fit them for a new world that has come too suddenly upon them. The French have alternately reproached themselves with parsimony in fulfilling their cultural obligations towards their protégés, and at the same time of having given them the desire and the means of driving out their foreign conquerors. The deception has been universal, but it is too late to turn back.

The Confucianist ideal of self-control and self-effacement has, in one generation, been swamped in the rising tide of individualism. At first the Annamites were horrified by the outbursts of feeling to which the French gave vent, and even more by the self-analysis and cult of sensibility inherent in French culture. The classic drama, for example, to the Annamites did not mean moderation and reason, but the exaltation of the emotions. As is natural with emotional adolescence, the Annamites have developed sentimentality, a love of rant and bombast, and of the sensational. In political reading they love the fiery passages of Rousseau. An investigation of sales in Tonkin bookships shows a love for French romantic writers, ranging from Dumas to Victor Marquerite, and of detective stories. The modern sentimental Chinese novel also has great success with the Annamites, and it has created for them an unreal and fantastic world. Even the poor buy books entitled On the Ocean of Love and Where, Then, Is Thy Promise? To conteract this rush of sentimentality to the heart of government has subsidized translations of the soberer Western classics.

The utilitarian aspect of the Annamites' interest in education is partly the result of being cut off from Chinese classics and partly the desire to profit by the new opportunities. When the missionaries invented and propagated quoc ngu they were trying to burn Annam's bridges with Confucianism in order to leave a virginal mind, ready to receive the imprint of Christianity. By destroying respect for the traditional authority they unloosed—much to their surprise—a critical spirit which was no more docile to Catholic than to Chinese doctrine. Quoc ngu became the symbolic bridge over which the Annamites have passed from the old to the new. It is an instrument by which the native who has perseverance and a textbook may acquire literacy and a veneer of Occidentalism within a few months, but it is not a subtle medium for thought. Some natives have not been willing to make even this small effort. When in 1906 quoc ngu schools were opened the Annamites at first cooperated eagerly, thinking that it meant the beginning to a new era of wealth. But the lack of immediate advantages—always in terms of government jobs—as well as the necessity of paying the teacher, soon chilled their enthusiasm so that few pupils were left. Those who persevered and rose in the world felt that there was nothing left for them to learn.

The old type of Annamite scholar whose life was devoted to the pleasures of learning, and who dreamed and discussed philosophy, agreeably lying on a mat in his garden, had been abolished to give place to an upstart go-getter. The old scholar was stagnant, complacent, contemptuous of manual labour, and quite out of touch with the practical world, but he made an art of living. He was bound to disappear because he was an anachronism, but his successor is far less sympathetic, for he has lost the best in the old

and acquired only the worst of the new. Western culture in Annamites hands is deformed, just as the French language is distorted
by their pronunciation. Both the language and ideas are hybrid.
Annamites learn to live like Occidentals, dress like them, and repeat what they say. But though they can be trained in analysis,
they are inept at synthesis and grasp of general ideas—even the
most brilliant among them. Just as in the economic sphere they are
extraordinarily subtle in serving their own immediate interests but
inadequate in large-scale enterprises, so in the realm of ideas they
are incoherent and clumsy when handling the abstract. Assimilation and memorizing rather than criticism and creation are, up to
the present, their forte. They have evolved marvellously in a short
period, but they have accumulated emotions more quickly than their
ability to appraise or utilize them. They are suffering from an in-
digestion of Western culture. Time alone will reveal whether they
or the superficial learning they have acquired will be the master.
In the future they may be constructive, but up to now the destructive
side has triumphed.

Altruism is conspicuously absent from Oriental psychology,
and the Annamite mentality is not propitious for the propagation of
Christianity. The family and commune are responsible for their
own, and not the individual, beyond membership in those two
groups. In fact, to some Annamites pity, charity, and benevolence
are effeminate emotions. A European does good for the comfort-
able feeling it gives him—more for the satisfaction of his vanity
than for its efficacy. From the Buddhist viewpoint the emotional
effect either on oneself or on others is incidental: one should do
good, if at all, without knowing or caring to know how it is received, or whether the recipient is undeserving or otherwise, with
the sole desire of remedying universal injustice. Charity that ends
with the family and village harmonizes with the provincialism of
old Annam. The universality of Christianity is inconceivable to
men whose religion is that of their village gods. It does not neces-
sitate public spirit—a complete void in the Annamite character.
One who occupies himself with general welfare is suspected of neg-
lecting a more imperious duty to his family. Christianity for the
Annamite has been a disruptive force cutting across the closest of
his ties. The highly localized character of Annamite life, encouraged and enforced by religion and law, has been a primary cause
of their immaturity as a people, both politically and emotion-
ally. . . .

Proselytizing to the native intelligentsia is but another proof
of European discourtesy. The assumption of superiority inherent
in the assimilationist idea is part and parcel of missionary work.
Christianity with its confusing and metaphysical preoccupations
has not the ordered clarity of Chinese philosophy, and seems in
consequence an inferior superstition. Differences in dogma are

not striking enough, nor the Catholic liturgy sufficiently aesthetic to lure the cultured classes. Annamite religion is essentially practical, whereas Catholicism is based on revelation. These considerations pale beside the important obstacle—that Catholicism runs counter to the social and political fabric of Annamite society. Catholicism, with its concern for the individual soul, subordinates society's interests to its salvation. Even more, Protestantism, by making the individual conscience the supreme arbiter, undermines the religious sanction Confucius gives to society and the state. Polygamy and the ancestral cult are but two illustrations of the irreconcilable differences between the Christian and Confucianist outlook. Hierarchy, firmly ingrained in the Annamite soul, finds satisfaction in graded religions: Confucianist doctrines for those who can appreciate its subtleties, and a profoundly modified Buddhist-Taoist practice for the masses. In short, the Annamites are satisfied with a religion which they are used to and which confirms their socio-political order. The only advantages which conversion offers in their eyes are material. Hence in studying the problem one must differentiate between abstract Christian ideals and Mission practice.

The rising materialism of the Annamites, a consequence of the French conquest, was regarded by the Mission as both an obstacle and an aid to conversions.

> With the rich it is the burning desire to become even richer; with the poor it is the sharp prick of necessity which is increasing with the ever heavier public burdens. The spirit of insubordination, of absolute liberty, of disdain for good traditions, disorganizes families and perverts individuals. Any pretext is good enough for a young man to leave home. Married couples abandon each other without a thought for their children. Even our Christians do not escape this epidemic of insubordination and vagrancy . . . [7]

Like the administration with whom it had co-operated to destroy the traditional culture the Mission found that it had simultaneously demolished moral discipline and respect for authority—Confucianist and otherwise. On the other hand the current materialism was a two-edged sword. It might work to Mission advantage. Preoccupation with the things of this world was not wholly due to preference but to necessity. The prevalent misery of the masses is a leitmotif that runs through Mission reports. It caused seasonal displacements for work and this neutralized any effect the missionaries might have by lives of self-abnegation, toil, and even martyrdom. To make any headway at all the Mission had to adapt itself and make it worth the Annamites' while to convert themselves—not a high plane of appeal but an effective one. The Mission held a privileged position as landowner, dating from the pre-conquest period. Rice-fields would tempt the land-loving Annamite as nothing else. The missionary, too, could be a good friend at court, and a powerful intermediary with the administration.

Many Annamite families pride themselves on having been converted to Christianity at the time of the conquest, and incidentally of having thus laid the basis of their fortunes. If some of them were later massacred by the mandarins as French partisans, if subsequently the survivors' hopes of being treated as a privileged group were deceived, nevertheless many had profited by their perspicacity to see at an early stage which way the wind blew. Conversion statistics reflect accurately the Mission's influence, notably after security was assured and anti-clericalism influenced the government, and show that there was a vast decline in conversions. Spring and Fall pastoral visits, exhortations to attend Mass, inquiries into absences—all show the native Christians' constant need for stimulus to piety and tendency to backslide. It is curious that the Mission has in itself and in its converts deliberately encouraged greed and materialism as a means of spiritual salvation.

Efforts to adapt Christian doctrine have been frowned upon by the Church. A Papal Bull forbade assimilating the ancestral cult to Purgatorial dogma. An experienced missionary, [8] recognizing the difference in native mentality, concocted a new Paradise to suit variegated Annamite tastes. He found that sitting on the right hand of God was too vague a formula to stimulate Annamite ambition. The tortures of Hell were far more comprehensible. To make a Paradise to match, he filled it with fruit trees, cock-fights, plenty of good food, gaming houses, and libraries. But his superiors, safely tucked away in Rome, where they were too remote to understand and too enmeshed in theory, removed this dangerous missionary to another field. This inelasticity and rigidity of the Church has cost it many a convert, and forced the Mission into a colonial career of temporal possessions.

Not only were many French colonials not attractive exemplars of Christian virtues, but the type of Annamite who forsook all to acquire rice-fields was of so low a social and moral fibre that he alienated the best of his compatriots from Christianity. Whole villages had to turn Catholic to avoid the moral and physical isolation that individual conversions would have entailed. When converts came to claim their share of the family heritage the ensuing struggles made the Mission hated and feared. The mandarinate, since the pre-conquest days, had persecuted the Mission and the feeling was later enforced by their privileged position. Since the War the Mission has made an effort to improve the quality of its converts, to attract the indifferent, and to propitiate the hostile. Secondary education, newspapers, lectures, organizations like the Feunesse Catholique and the Cercle Annamite des Etudes Catholiques have succeeded in attracting a certain number, but the influence of Communism has made many of the young Annamites incurably hostile.

Communist hatred of the Mission is not based solely on its dislike of Christianity per se, but on the economic role it plays in the colony. Natives working Mission property are depicted as serfs in the usurious stranglehold of the Mission. They point to the nefarious role played by the Mission during the conquest, when it aided the French against Annamite patriots. Similarly they claim that during the 1931 uprising the Mission betrayed secrets of the confessional and delivered over Annamite nationalists to the scaffold, and that it used this occasion to take revenge on those villages which had refused to be converted. The Mission is so much disliked that it has become the target for contradictory attacks: the Communists hate it for being the government's ally, and the government in turn fears the Mission as a state within a state because of its influence over the natives. The Communists have an additional grievance in the resistance which native Christians have shown to the siren voice of Moscow. On both sides the uprisings covered revenge for a multitude of old grudges.

Nor has nationalism spared the bosom of the Church. Even at the time of Japan's victory there were not only fewer converts but fewer candidates for clerical ordination. Now the formation of a native priesthood is the primary preoccupation of the Society of Foreign Missions: the conversion of the infidel is but secondary. This is especially important as the War and anti-clerical laws have cut down the number of French missionaries sent out from France. Though the native clergy had a most honourable record during the era of persecutions, nevertheless the Society has shown a marked reluctance to promote Annamites in the ecclesiastical hierarchy. They have accepted the idea in principle, but in practice the French missionaries cling to the top positions. Right after the War the Annamite clergy showed a marked spirit of insubordination, paralleling the general nationalist movement. In 1922 a scandal broke out over the treatment of native priests supposed to be implicated in the theft of a French missionary's possessions. The following year a native priest a Chaudon murdered a French missionary, and the Bishop of Pnom-Penh was accused of muzzling all complaints and the evidence of discontent. During the Emperor Khai Dinh's trip to Paris, an Annamite priest succeeded in presenting to the Vatican the native clergy's demands for equality of status with the French missionaries. In January 1926 an encyclical letter, Rerum Ecclesia, tactfully rendered homage to missionary devotion in Indo-China, but recalled to them the duty of Christian charity in making native priests their collaborators. A Papal Legate was sent to Hanoi as evidence of Rome's watchful care. Further steps taken by the Annamite clergy led to the nomination of a remarkable native bishop, Père Six, who was given the diocese of Phat Diem. In 1925 a second native bishop was named. Père Six had had a splendid record during the heroic period[9] and after the French conquest he was made cure at Phat Diem, a parish formed by alluvial deposits in the Red River. His remarkable organizing ability was shown not only among his parishioners but by the building of dykes and a cathedral in the Annamite style, with only the resources of his followers. Men like Joffre and Lyautey visited him and many came to ask his advice. The court of Hue, his erstwhile prosecutor, now made him honorary Minister of Rites. He was named Baron of Phat Diem, he was made Officer of the Legion of Honour, and, as crowning glory, 40, 000 people attended his funeral. His life is an illustration of the Mission thesis that Christianity is the best bridge which can span the abyss between Oriental and Occidental cultures.

It is not coincidence that the religious movement, both within and without the Church, took on a nationalist tincture. The self-assertion of the Annamite clergy synchronized with the birth of a new politico-religious sect in Cochin-China called Caodaism in 1926. On the religious side it has an eclectic character—a reform version of Buddhism which includes Taoist and Catholic dogmas. It is a compromise between the old and the new, a reconciliation of Eastern and Western concepts. Its guiding deity is a spirit named Cao-Dai, whose Pope was an extremely able Annamite named Le-Van Trung. The headquarters is at Tayninh, where a pagoda has been constructed, manned by a priesthood, nourished by a domain of rice-fields and flanked by a village, school, printing press, and weavers' looms. There is a Ghandiesque flavour about creating a community which is economically self-sufficient. At first the government, true to its policy of protecting native religions, encouraged the movement, but its enormous growth, its close-knit organization, its clandestine meetings, and the presence of dubious characters, in government eyes, among its disciples soon made the state nervous. It might be Communism masquerading as religion, and there was an undeniable similarity between the two organizations. It has also created a hitherto unknown fanaticism in the colony: the spirit of Cao-Dai can save the Indo-Chinese who have lost their independence as punishment for their sins. Nationalists and Caodaists use to good effect the plea for liberty of conscience, and claim that the state's persecution—the mild Pasquier was particularly virulent—of this religion is unjustified. The King of Cambodia has abolished Caodaism from his realm and now only tolerates Buddhism and Catholicism. The Mission's attitude has received official approbation. The death of Le-Van Trung in 1935 coincides with the freedom recently granted to this cult by Robin.

The Mission which encouraged the conquest has been, on the whole, a loser by it. If it no longer suffers persecution and has be-

come a great temporal power, the Mission has lost influence—
though now without bitterness—to the administration which has absorbed all but its spiritual functions. Its converts and missionaries
have not increased, and many of its compatriots openly flout its
ideals. From without it is threatened by Communism and Caodaism, and from within by nationalist insubordination. Stalemated
in every direction the Mission's eye has been forced to turn inward,
to care for its own, and to attempt the conversion of primitive
tribes. The native reaction to the Mission has been very realistic.
Around the small nucleus of sincere conversions there has been a
cloud of converts through self-interest. With the decline of Mission
power and the opening of new and more profitable fields the Annamites have turned away from the Mission, and put pressure to bear
on the more powerful administration to win certain concrete aims in
this world. It is even doubtful whether the Mission influence is responsible for the one constructive indigenous religious movement
among the Annamites—Caodaism.

FOOTNOTES

[1] Lefebre, Paul, Faces Faunes (Paris, 1886), p. 54.

[2] De Carné, Louis, Voyage en Indochine (Paris, 1872), pp. 5—6.

[3] Lyautey, H., Lettres du Tonkin et de Madagascar (Paris, 1921),
p. 81.

[4] Vassal, G. M., Mes Trois Ans D'Annam (Paris, 1911), p. 36.

[5] Ajalbert, J., Les Destinées de L'Indochine (Paris, 1901), p. 60.

[6] Pham Quynh. L'Evolution Intellectuelle et Morale des Annamites
(Paris, 1922), p. 15.

[7] Société des Missions-Etrangères; Compte Rendu des Travaux
(Paris, 1907), p. 200.

[8] Monet, P., Les Fauniers (Paris, 1931), p. 116.

[9] Olichon, Mgr., Le Baron de Phat Diem (Poitiers, 1931).

From Agrarian Unrest in Southeast Asia by Erich H. Jocoby. Published by Columbia University Press. Used by Permission.

CHAPTER 5

The American Philippines

The Philippine Islands mark the eastern boundary of Southeast Asia. The archipelago consists of over 7, 000 islands which cover an area in excess of 1, 100 square miles and forms a barrier between the Pacific Ocean and the South China Sea. In the twentieth century, the island of Luzon, and its capitol city, Manila, dominate almost the entire region economically, politically, and culturally; and Manila ranks as one of the most important trade depots in Southeast Asia. Reflecting this importance, vessels flying the flags of all major maritime nations frequent her harbors making Manila, like Hong Kong and Singapore, an important communication center between East and West. Today, the Philippines, with a population which exceeds nineteen million, stands as one of the more important independent states in Southeast Asia.

The early inhabitants of the Philippines came from Malaya and gradually overpowered the indigenous Indonesians. At the time of the Spanish conquest, the social organization of the islands consisted of small units or tribes of varying origin and linguistic backgrounds reflecting both their Malayan and Indonesian heritage. In terms of religious development, they practiced a form of nature worship without benefit or direction from an organized priesthood. Religious mores and traditions originated from ancient superstitions and mystical teachings of long standing. Neither the major Oriental cults nor Islam penetrated the Philippine community to any great extent prior to the European colonization of the islands, The Philippines, as compared to the rest of Southeast Asia, remained primative in terms of culture, religious orientation and political development. This relatively low level of achievement accounts for the importance of the Spanish and American impact on the islands after the sixteenth century, and explains why the Filipino has become the most Western of the peoples of Southeast Asia.

The first major contact between the Filipino and the European came with Magellan's attempt to circumnavigate the world in the 1520's. Once the voyagers touched on the islands, they found themselves involved in a skirmish with the natives, resulting in Magel-

lan's death. After his death the expedition divided into two parts.
One group sailed west in the Victoria. After crossing the Indian
Ocean and coasting along Portuguese Africa the Explorers eventually reached Spain. The second expedition re-crossed the Pacific
Ocean and eventually arrived in Mexico. After this initial contact,
Spain continued to show some interest in this region, but half a
century would pass before actual conquest would be attempted. The
process of subjugating the area remained relatively simple. The
conquerors, armed with both weapons and the cross, came from
Mexico rather than Spain proper. Since Mexican troops actually
accomplished the conquest of the islands, a political union between
the Kingdom of New Spain (Mexico) and the Philippines developed,
which survived until Mexico asserted her independence from Spain
in 1820. In order to avoid the unfortunate aspects of the Spanish
occupation of the new world, the conquistadors received specific
orders not to repeat the bloody exploits that had characterized part
of their conquest of the Americas in the preceding century. These
instructions required that the Spanish armies and the missionaries
ought not destroy the heathen, but rather, offer the natives enlightened colonial rule and Christian guidance. This more humane attitude, combined with the lack of political and religious unity within
the native community, in part, accounted for the relatively simple
conquest of the islands.

Spanish interest in the Philippines involved three basic motives. First, Spain, like most European nations, hoped to participate in the spice trade. However, Spain soon discovered that the
area offered few of the spices demanded by the European community. The second cause for Spanish interest in the islands involved
a general desire to participate in the Oriental trade. Manila, with
its excellent harbor potential and strategic location, quickly developed into a trading depot for exchange of goods between Spain,
China, Mexico, and Japan. Within a century after conquest, Manila
had become a major trading center between the Eastern and Western
worlds. The route of the Spanish-Oriental trade followed a rather
interesting pattern. Technically, the Portuguese barred Spanish
trading in the Philippines by way of Africa. As an alternative, the
Spanish traded by way of Mexico and the Pacific. Each year, the
Manila Galleon sailed between Manila and Acapulco, Mexico. In
Mexico, Oriental goods were exchanged for Spanish merchandise
or Mexican silver dollars. Over the years Mexican silver came
to play a rather important role in the Oriental trade, in that Mexican silver, along with chests of opium, became the medium of
international exchange in the East, serving not only the Spanish but
all who traded in this area. A second important side effect of the
Spanish trading policies in Manila occurred with the gradual growth
of a Chinese community in that city. Once the Spanish had established Manila as an Oriental trade depot, the Chinese flocked to
this area, and over the years, they eventually came to dominate a

significant portion of the economic community in both Manila and the surrounding islands. In addition to their economic contribution to the growth of the Philippines, the Spanish found the Chinese useful as scapegoats for the periodic depressions that occasionally settled upon the islands in the following centuries. This was possible because the Chinese dominated the everyday aspects of the Philippine economy and the Spanish found it highly useful to blame them for the economic problems of the empire. The third and final factor which brought the Spanish to the islands entailed the religious motivation, a factor common to the entire development of the entire Spanish empire. The Iberians hoped to convert the Filipino, and then to use the islands as a base for further conversions in China and Japan. This dream, like the anticipated spice trade, proved illusory. Though the Spanish did succeed in converting the Filipinos, neither the Chinese nor the Japanese opened their doors to the Spanish missionary. Regardless of the intent of the early conquerors of the islands, by 1660, Spain controlled the Philippines. In so doing, she established an empire that would survive for three hundred years, one of the most long lived empires in the East.

The nature of Spanish rule in the Philippines resembled the kind of government she had established in the Americas. Highly autocratic in nature, the government combined the interests of both the church and the state with little opportunity for self expression. The central administration of the colony consisted of three levels or areas of authority, all of which governed the colony in the name of the Spanish Crown. The Governor or Captain General exercised supreme executive power. In theory, he symbolized perfection in every facet of life, while in practice he seldom lived up to this expectation. Though the Governor held a royal appointment, the Viceroy in New Spain (Mexico) served as his immediate superior. Because of the distance between Spain, Mexico, and the Philippines, the Governor remained free from most forms of royal supervision. The office of the Governor carried with it a broad base of power and a clever appointee could exercise considerable influence over the administration of the colony. The position of Bishop of Manila formed the second side to the government of the islands. His authority embraced all aspects of religious life in the colony and the Bishop rivaled the power of the Governor in directing Philippine life. Like the Governor, the chief prelate in the Philippines pursued a relatively independent course of action because of the isolation of the colony from Spain and Mexico. The third branch of the administration was the Audiencia. The Audiencia served as both a supreme court and as an administrative council, which could, in theory, dominate both the offices of Governor and Bishop. Of the three institutions, the Audiencia generally exercised the greatest degree of uninterrupted power. Two factors account for this, first, the Audiencia remained in closer contact with the general population, and secondly, those appointed to the Audiencia held their posi-

133

tions in the colony longer than either the Bishop or the Governor. Below the high offices of state, a collection of local officials attempted to keep order and enforce the laws. Men who occupied these lessor positions frequently used their power for personal gain rather than to serve the crown. Throughout the entire colonial period, all varieties of corruption were associated with these offices. Lower level religious offices also functioned as tools of control. Generally, the image of the lower clergy remained about the same as that of the regional colonial officials. The Spanish intended to establish a comprehensive government for the islands, but in practice there remained a shortage of qualified and honest officials at all levels of government, both church and state, to provide good and efficient government.

The Spanish impact on the Filipino ran far deeper and lasted longer than most other colonial systems in Southeast Asia. As a result of both Spanish, and later American domination of the islands, the Filipino has become the most western of all peoples in Southeast Asia. Several factors account for this remarkable transformation in Philippine life. When the Spanish arrived in the Philippines, they found the level of civilization exceedingly low as compared to most areas in this region. This meant that Spanish culture would basically remain unchallenged after the conquest, and Spain, as the superior could force her values on the natives without competition from a pre-existing civilization. Secondly, Spain established a comprehensive form of government over most of the important islands, particularly the island of Luzon. Despite the weaknesses of this government, it gave to the Philippines a degree of political unity unknown to the islands prior to the conquest. To further this control, only Spanish and highly cooperative native chiefs received appointments to political and religious offices. The appointment procedure ensured Spain that her values and culture would remain the standard for future development and growth. A third method of control came with the re-organization of the land tenure system. In the preconquest era, land was held in common. After Spanish occupation, the crown claimed title to all real property. Eventually the crown redistributed the land to important native rulers, Spanish colonists and to the Church. These royal grants called encomiendas created large estates and gave to the holder of such grants specific rights and obligations over the natives living on the land. Those who held an encomienda had to see to the well-being of the natives, to urge conversion, and to collect tribute for the Crown. Through this process, Spain secured the general adoption of both Catholicism and a degree of Spanish culture. Finally, the role of the Church in perpetuating both culture and religion became extremely important in maintaining Spanish influence within the colony. The Church found the task relatively easy. Islam had not reached the islands in sufficient force to challenge the Christian missionary. Eastern cults had not become important in this area and the relatively unsophisticated native religions could not withstand the pressure of Catholicism and government encouragement. Two factors contributed to easy conversion; government and social pressure made it advantageous for an ambitious person to adopt the new sect, and some of the rites of the new faith paralleled the practices of the natives in the preconquest days. As a result, most natives adopted the basic attitudes and beliefs of the Spanish. In the early years, the depths of understanding of the new cultural and religious values remained shallow, but as time progressed, tradition served to maintain the Western orientation of Philippine life; religiously, politically, and culturally.

The deep impact of Spanish colonialism on the Phillippines stands in marked contrast to the depth of cultural penetration of other colonial systems in Southeast Asia. The French attempted to enforce a policy of cultural assimilation in Indo-China, but they only partially succeeded in making oriental Frenchmen out of the Indo-Chinese. Part of the failure of the French stems from the firmly established Indo-Chinese culture which existed in this region prior to the coming of the European. The Spanish came very close to transforming the Filipino into a semi-Oriental Iberian. In the case of the Spanish they did not have to face the challenge of a well developed civilized community. As for the Dutch and English, their principal interest in Southeast Asia remained primarily economic rather than cultural and religious. Owing to this economic orientation, there are relatively few Oriental Protestants while there are many Catholics in this region and the depth of English and Dutch culture has not proved to be as extensive as the Catholic colonial powers. The legacy of Spanish colonialism has permanently affected the Philippine Islands. Catholicism remains the dominant religious orientation of the people, and many of the cultural values of the Western world have survived into the present age. As for the social and economic impact, the Iberian legacy remains, but this aspect of the Spanish heritage will probably be altered in the future.

During the age of Spanish and American colonial rule in the Philippines, the social and economic orientation of the Philippine community divided into two parts, the very rich and the very poor. This tremendous gulf between the haves and the have-nots has created enormous hardships and divisions within the Philippine society. During the early colonial period the Church, the Spanish colonial settlers, and the co-operative native rulers acquired vast personal estates out of what had formerly been communal property. These giant landholdings or (encomiendas) provided tremendous power and wealth for those fortunate few who owned them, and misery for those who lived, worked and died on these estates. Both Spanish and American colonial law protected the landowner against complaints and problems raised by the peasants on these estates. In the present era, this same land owing system has been preserved by the ruling elite. Stemming from the power given the landlords during the colonial era, a semi-legal tradition called "debt slavery" has arisen. Debt slavery has come to mean that a man and his family cannot leave an estate until his debts have been satisfied. The patron, or landowner, generally acted as creditor to peasants living on his land. The patron willingly lent small amounts of money to the peasants but charged high interest rates which quickly increased the total debt many times. Usually the debt plus interest reached an amount far beyond the ability of the peasant to repay. As a result, the debtor found himself tied to the patron and the estate for life. Two particularly unpleasant aspects to this system of debt slavery are; first, the right of the creditor to transfer a debt from one landlord to another thus forcing a family to move from one area to another without considering his wishes and secondly, a general assumption existed that a son inherited his father's debts, which served to perpetuate the debt slavery system from one generation to another. The Americans encouraged the continuation of the debt slave system by transferring political and legislative power to the very class that profited from the debt slave system. Once this native upper class acquired independent power, they enacted sufficient protective laws to safeguard their favored economic position.

In the nineteenth century, metropolitan Spain failed to adjust to modern European life. Spanish technology, public administration and social concepts failed to respond to the standards of the age. This backward orientation of Spanish life impaired the development of the Philippines during this era. While most areas of Southeast Asia began to respond to some of the benefits of colonial rule, the Philippines remained exceedingly old-fashioned and unreformed. By 1898, the year Spanish rule ended in the islands, this far outpost of Western colonization remained the most unprogressive region in colonial Southeast Asia. Using the field of medicine as an example of the backward nature of late Spanish colonialism, it becomes quite clear how far behind the Philippines were at the turn of the century. Manila, in the 1890's, had greater health problems than any similar city in Southeast Asia. Most of the basic preventitive devices to ensure proper health either did not exist or remained unknown to the native-Spanish population. Polluted water, tainted food, filth, disease, bacteria and most every variety of parasite abounded in the market place, in hospitals, and in the home. This situation existed for both the rich and the poor. The practice of medicine combined ancient European healing arts with luck, religious incantations and native superstition. It is said that if all cures failed, a poultice of three garlic heads in honor of the Holy Trinity might help, and in extreme cases, a poultice of thirty-three heads of garlic in honor of the years Christ remained on earth might be useful. This illustrates the best of native-Spanish medicine. For the wealthy, hospitals did exist, but here, without benefit of a surgeon and a qualified medical staff, the patients would probably die of infections and diseases found in great abundance in these places. At the end of the nineteenth century the annual death rate in Manila equaled the death rate in most tropical cities during plague. The practice of medicine and disease prevention serves as but one example of the quality of Spanish rule in the late nineteenth century. Basically, the empire had outlived itself. From a political point of view, Spanish colonialism in the East lingered near death. Revolutionary activity on the part of the natives, combined with Spanish determination not to grant sufficient reforms to pacify the mounting hostility of the rebels convinced the Filipino of the necessity of severing his ties with Spain. Though revolutionary activity had begun against Spanish control, the final blow to the empire came with the arrival of Commodore Dewey in 1898. The United States and Spain were involved in the Spanish-American War, and as part of the war activities, Commodore Dewey sailed the American Pacific fleet into the Manila Harbor. Agreement between Dewey and the native rebels enabled the Americans to take advantage of Spain's weakness in the Philippines. The combined efforts of the natives and the American fleet terminated Spain's long rule in the Philippines; it also began a new age of colonialism in the East, the age of American imperialism.

American involvement in the Philippines came as a result of the Spanish American War. During the last years of the nineteenth century, the Western world, including the United States, had reached its intellectual peak concerning imperialism and colonialism. The question of empire and trade came to be considered as vital to national existence as standing armies or impressive navies. In extreme cases, empire became synonymous with survival in the age of materialism and world politics. The arguments favoring imperialism dominated the foreign offices of most every Western government from St. Petersburg to Washington and generally the imperialists carried the day. As for the American government, traditionally she had opposed colonialism and had identified with the anti-imperialist community. However, by the 1890's, the fever for empire had even reached Washington. Important political leaders such as Theodore Roosevelt, leading members of Congress, and the more aggressive press, all spoke in favor of American participation in the scramble for empire.

During this period, American imperial interests involved the Caribbean and the China trade in the East. In 1898, the opportunity to enhance American influence and power in both areas came with the sinking of the Maine. The expansionists demanded war with Spain and the liberation of Cuba from Spanish colonialism. Through the combined efforts of the popular press and those who believed in the manifest destiny of the United States, the war with Spain began. Initially the war started in the Caribbean area, but with the activities of Commodore Dewey in the Pacific, American colonial aims reached the Philippines. Dewey, with government approval, and with the aid and support of various rebel groups in the Philippines destroyed Spanish power over the Islands. In mid-1898, American sailors occupied Manila. When news reached Washington that Dewey has been successful, the expansionists believed that their dreams had come true. They argued that the United States had become an Eastern power, and that the occupation and annexation of the Philippines would protect American interests in the East and would also serve as a check upon the policies of those European states which sought to exclude or limit American activities in Southeast Asia and China.

After American occupation of the Islands, the question arose as to whether America should embark on such an extensive colonial venture in the Orient. Business and commercial interests, military and naval experts, and nationalists clamored for annexation. Though many organizations spoke in favor of annexation of the Islands, some groups still opposed colonialism and the abandonment of traditional American isolationism. To convince the anti-imperialist forces, the colonialists had to convince these elements that America had a moral obligation to save the noble savage and to bring the blessings of civilization to this part of the world. President McKinley symbolized the approach used by the expansionists toward the opponents of empire. In an address to a group of Methodists, the President said:

"The truth is I didn't want the Philippines and when they came to us as a gift from the gods, I did not know what to do about them . . . I walked the floor of the White House night after night until midnight; and I am not ashamed to tell you, gentlemen, that I went down on my knees and prayed to Almighty God for light and guidance more than one night.

And one night it came to me this way—I don't know how it was but it came: (1) that we could not give them back to Spain—that would be cowardly and dishonorable; (2) that we could not turn them over to France and Germany—our commercial rivals in the Orient—that would be bad business and discreditable; (3) that we could not leave them to themselves—they were unfit for self-government—and they would soon have anarchy and misrule over there worse than Spain's was; and (4) that there was nothing left for us to do

but to take them all, and to educate the Filipinos, and
uplift and civilize and Christianize them, and by God's
grace do the very best we could by them, as our fellow
men for whom Christ also died."[1]

Though the logic of the above might be open to question, the appeal
of McKinley's statement could not be denied. The Americans could
not turn the Islands over to France, England or Germany; this
would be economically foolish. The return of the Islands to Spain
or to grant the Filipinos independence did not fit the character of
the age. To civilize and Christianize them proved to be adequate
justification to even the most skeptical critic of American political
aims. It is interesting to note that the Filipinos had been subject to
the civilizing mission of the Spanish for almost three hundred years
and in many respects they had done the job fairly well, at least in
exposing many of the natives to the arts of Western civilization.
No one could truthfully say that the Filipinos were uncivilized. As
for Christianizing the natives, the Catholic Church had not been in
the islands for three hundred years for nothing, for the natives
then, as now, are Catholic.

Whatever the justification for expanding American colonial
interests into the Pacific might have been, the Islands became part
of the benefits of victory over the Spanish and the United States now
possessed an empire extending from Cuba in the Caribbean to the
Philippines in Southeast Asia. Once the decision to keep the Islands
had been made, the commitment to improve the life of the native
population and to introduce democratic government into the Philippines characterized the policies of all the forms of colonial governments that dominated the Philippines during the American regime.
This is not to deny the economic advantage as motivation behind
annexation or to deny the strategic value of the Islands to American
military occupation of the Islands, the humanitarian factor took
precedence over the economic and military aspects of American
colonialism.

Between 1898 and 1907, the American military pacified the
Islands and secured control over the Philippines. The government
remained autocratic and oriented toward establishing order under
military leadership. During this pacification period, various misunderstandings arose between the native rebel groups that had
assisted in the fall of Spanish power and the Americans. Native
leaders insisted that Commodore Dewey had promised immediate
independence to the revolutionary leaders. Both Dewey and the
American government denied this charge. Out of this disagreement, and in part because of traditional American policy toward
empire, the two sides eventually agreed that self-government would
be granted to the Filipinos as soon as possible. Furthermore, as
a result of these discussions, a colonial policy emerged which
provided for the gradual transfer of political power to the native

population as soon as the American government deemed it safe and beneficial for the Philippine people. As long as the Republican party dominated the government the general trend toward self rule and independence remained exceedingly slow. However, under the Woodrow Wilson administration, this policy radically changed. President Wilson appointed Francis Harrison Governor General of the Philippines. Harrison shared Wilson's determination to move rapidly toward self-government for the Islands. During the Wilson-Harrison era, the Filipinos' acquired considerable control over the government and made important strides toward self determination. As an example of the Harrison policy over eighty per cent of American civil service positions fell under native control. When the Republicans returned to government in 1920, they reversed this liberalization policy, justifying their attitude on the basis that the previous administration had undermined the quality of government of the Philippines. In order to "restore" good government to the Philippines, Americans once again replaced native civil servants, particularly in positions of authority and power. For the next few years the government imposed a more rigid and authoritarian policy on the Islands. However, the liberal policies of the Harrison administration could not be totally reversed and pressure continued to mount for the establishment of a Philippine Commonwealth. After considerable discussion in Washington, the Commonwealth was created by the Tydings McDuffie Act in the 1930's. In 1946, in keeping with the Philippine Commonwealth Act, the Philippines received complete independence.

American rule in the Philippines lasted for approximately forty-six years. During this period the Americans established two basic goals for the benefit of the natives; to raise the standard of life in the islands and secondly, to prepare the natives for self-government. These two exceedingly ambitious projects became the dominate theme of American colonialism in the Philippines. Though these goals were not fully realized, important steps were taken toward the betterment of Philippine life under American guidance.

Once the Americans assumed control over the Philippines, they found it necessary to introduce a series of reforms which would draw this area into the mainstream of world progress and reform. Spanish colonial officials had not taken the initiative in advancing modern medical techniques, public welfare, education, and land reform. In all of the above areas the Filipino stood woefully behind the rest of Southeast Asia. As a result of this situation, the Americans initiated what might be called a social service revolution into the Philippines.

The first assault against the social problems in the Philippines began with the arrival of American troops in Manila. Sanitation and health measures had to be immediately undertaken to protect both the occupying troops and the natives against the ravages of tropical diseases which traditionally plagued this area. The army established a health commission which attempted to determine what reforms in sanitation and health standards were needed to control disease, to introduce modern health standards, improve medical services for both the American and native residents in Manila, and to begin an educational program to enlighten the population in methods of disease prevention. Under this basic policy, the Army Medical Corps stopped the spread of smallpox, cholera, plague, and dysentery and began the eradication of beri-beri, leprosy, tuberculosis, and various other tropical diseases. Health records immediately reflected the improved standards set by the new rulers of the Islands. For example, deaths from plague at the turn of the century averaged about 500 per year, but within a decade after occupation, the government recorded no deaths from this traditional curse of the tropics. In almost all areas of preventive medicine the first decade of American rule reduced, and in some cases, ended deaths from curable diseases. In addition to the introduction of preventive medcine, hospitals and operating facilities were expanded and improved along with a training program for the natives in modern medical practices.

The most difficult aspect of the preventive medicine program came in the area of educating the population in personal hygiene and the eradication of ancient superstition and unhealthy habits. To accomplish any permanent change in the health standards of rural, and to a lessor degree, urban communities, the native population had to be taught the value of hygiene and standard personal precautionary methods of disease control. This basically involved changing ancient modes of conduct. The native population hesitated to accept any change in their mode of conduct, particularly if foreigners insisted that they conform to new patterns of activity. The Americans, like most all colonial powers, found that the only solution to improve personal health standards involved intensive education to convince the population to abandon their old modes of conduct and to adopt the new and improved methods of disease control. Programs such as this involved vast sums of money, considerable time, and a well-trained force of skilled teachers, preferably native instructors. Both the expense and the shortage of qualified staff limited the educational aspect of the preventive health program.

Public education, like the health program, became another major theme of American rule in the Philippines. During the Spanish era, only a small portion of the colonial elite received any form of education, and the instruction they received remained exceedingly poor. Traditionally, the educational system had been under the control of the Church, but since the Church functioned as a means of suppression and symbolized the unenlightened aspects of Spanish colonial rule, the educational system had become old fashioned and very low in standards of instruction. The Americans introduced

141

modern public education, attempted to raise the level of instruction, and initiated a general program to extend education to the lower classes. Had the Americans been able to achieve their ambition they would have made all Filipinos literate and made available adequate facilities to educate a large percentage of the entire native population. Though the goal of providing facilities to achieve literacy at the lower levels of society may appear modest, it is important to remember that facilities and teachers at the time of occupation literally did not exist, and that the training of teachers and providing adequate facilities required a long period of development and a considerable amount of money. Throughout the entire American colonial era, lack of money, shortages in staff and inadequate facilities remained a constant problem. For example, teachers' salaries remained low, and for those qualified to teach, government employment in large cities or opportunities in business offered far more attractive potential than being a teacher in an isolated rural area. Secondly, the native population, particularly in rural areas, had to be convinced of the value of sending a child to school. In many families the question arose, which had more value, field work or education. In an alarming number of situations, field work took precedence over education. At the higher levels of education, facilities existed to prepare the Filipinos for eventual leadership in business, government, education, engineering and health. Unfortunately, most Filipinos selected professional degrees such as law rather than vocational or scientific degrees. Manila and other cities teemed with an excessive number of lawyers while shortages remained in the other professions. The excessive number of lawyers eventually led to the creation of a class of urban malcontents called the intellectual proletariat; unemployed professionals bitter toward colonial rule because they could not secure employment with the government or in the business community. They generally blamed the colonial government for their misfortune rather than their poor choice in vocations. From this class a deep feeling of bitterness arose concerning colonial rule. Every colonial official came to be viewed as a block to the personal advancement of the unemployed professional. In conclusion, education remained a difficult matter to handle. Cooperation and understanding between the native population and the colonial educators seldom existed, and where progress did occur, those who profited from the educational system frequently turned against the organization that had educated them. Though progress remained exceedingly slow, the Americans did provide a set of standards for later governments to achieve in the realm of public service and education.

Economic and social development during American rule brought few major changes in Philippine life, particularly for the lower classes. When the American arrived in the Philippines, the dominant agricultural pattern involved large estates farmed by a heavily indebted peasant class bound by tradition to the landlord or cacique. The Americans did not effect any major reform in land holdings, and in many cases made it possible for the cacique to expand his estate by using the courts and local government to legally justify their expansion of power. When the American arrived, debt slavery existed on a large scale. When they left in the 1940's, the problem remained even more pressing than it did in 1900. One of the major factors accounting for the increased plight of the peasant came with the growth of self-government under American supervision. First, local government came under the power of the landlord, and later the central administration fell under the domination of the cacique. At both levels politicians and community leaders acquired the necessary power to expand their exploitation of the native population. In terms of rural development, the Americans did extend the rail system and constructed roads into undeveloped areas. However, local politicians quickly gobbled up the new lands and forced the local inhabitants into debt slavery. Laws existed to prevent this kind of social malady, but the enforcement of such laws fell under local self-government and were therefore never used to benefit the lower classes. As for the peasants, they had no knowledge of their rights under the various land reform laws, and where they did know about their rights, local governments prevented them from succeeding against the large landowner. Self-government in rural areas did not prove helpful to the lower classes.

Direct American rule ended in the mid 1930's, with the establishment of the Philippine Commonwealth. Soon after the founding of the Commonwealth, World War II broke out, followed by Japanese invasion and occupation of the Islands. At the conclusion of World War II, the Philippines received complete independence in 1946. With this, direct American involvement in the domestic life of the Philippines ended. The following reading selection presents the problem of government and the role of the United States in preparing the Filipino for democratic self-government. How well the American colonial period prepared the Filipinos for independence and democracy is, in part, answered by the following article by George E. Taylor.

FOOTNOTES

[1]Harry B. Hawes, Philippine Uncertainty, An American Problem, (New York: 1932) p. 144.

THE POLITICAL LEGACY OF THE UNITED STATES *

The Continuing Revolution

A half century of American rule in the Philippines was devoted to the self-imposed task of mothering the national revolution of another people. When the United States granted the Filipinos their independence in 1946, it turned over to them a revolution which they themselves had started and no one else could finish.

While denying to the Filipinos for almost fifty years the main objective of their revolution—political independence—the United States strongly supported other objectives. It imposed the doctrine and practice of the separation of Church and State, insisted on the secularization of education, took away from the friars their local administrative and political power, opened up all careers to Filipinos, improved public health, stimulated the development of the economy, and above all, eventually provided for a constitution based on the same philosophical concepts of natural rights that had inspired the writers of the Malolos Constitution. The Propagandists had demanded that all Filipinos should be permitted to learn Spanish; the Americans insisted that English should be the language of instruction. Instead of representation in the Spanish Cortes, Filipinos were to send delegates to the American Congress. Freedom of the press and other rights, at first denied until American sovereignty was accepted, were soon to be firmly established.

The parallel between measures taken by the United States in the Philippines and the objectives of the Filipino nationalists is not surprising in view of the fact that the Propagandists drew their ideas from the same sources as had the Americans a century before, but the program that the United States carried out was actually more revolutionary than that of the most extreme nationalists. It carried to its logical conclusion the idea of popular sovereignty, which the Propagandists had used more as a stick with which to beat the Spanish administration than as an appeal to the masses. It developed compulsory education for all far beyond anything the Propagandists had in mind. While it did not take away all the friar lands or banish the religious orders as some of the nationalists wished, it began to lay the foundations of a new land title system which was not at all to the liking of some who had supported the revolution. The United States, in a word, tried to shift the internal balance of forces away from oligarchy and in favor of political and social democracy.

Filipinos are still in the process of evaluating the changes that took place under the Americans and of finding out what hap-

*George F. Taylor, The Philippines and the United States: Problems of Partnership, (New York, Frederick A. Prager, for the Council on Foreign Relations, 1964).

pened to their nationalism and which direction, now that they are in control again, the national revolution should take. After the establishment of U.S. sovereignty there was something of a partnership between Filipinos and Americans in carrying out important social and political changes that led to the growth of real bonds of mutual respect between the two peoples. Except for the humiliation of having had to accept foreign rule, the Filipino nationalists acknowledge the fact that the Americans helped them achieve many of the things that they wanted for themselves. But partnership in revolution can exist side by side with a good deal of hostility and political antagonism. This is quite apparent in Teodoro Agoncillo's treatment of the American Occupation:

> In consonance with President McKinley's "Benevolent Assimilation" Proclamation, the United States introduced in the Philippines a regime of democratic partnership under which the Filipinos played the role of junior partner. The policy, while not satisfactory enough from the point of view of the Fillipino nationalist, was nevertheless a decided improvement over that of Spain. Universal education was stressed; public health and welfare was carried to the remote barrios; commerce, industry, and trade were given impetus; basic individual freedoms were respected; means of communication and transportation were greatly improved; and political consciousness was developed through the introduction of American political institutions and practices. Side by side with these positive results of the American Occupation were the negative results: the general economic dependence on the United States, the partial loss of the racial heritage, the continuance of the colonial mentality, and a distorted sense of values. [1]

Mr. Agoncillo's statement represents the views of one large group of Filipino nationalists who are sufficiently honest and objective to see the picture in colors other than black and white.

It is because the program of the American administration was more revolutionary than that of the leaders of the revolt against Spain that so many Filipinos accepted American rule. Some elements of the elite resisted, not unsuccessfully, certain aspects of the American-style revolution, which from their point of view were far too extreme. And for others, the Americans did not go far enough. But for all Filipino nationalists today there is no escaping the fact that it was a foreign power that carried out their revolution for them, and this fact alone affected the quality of Filipino nationalism. [2] No matter which way the Filipino turns for inspiration,

145

for examples, or for concepts about himself, his country, and his future, he has to come to terms with the record of the United States of America in the Philippines.

Growth of a Policy

It was a political fact of the first order that a great power surrendered sovereignty over a colony on its own initiative and not under effective pressure from the colony itself. But so much is made of the granting of independence to the Philippines that it is necessary to put it in the perspective of the American view of colonial responsibilities.

Colonial responsibility began at a time when the United States had no colonial policy and no tradition. Even Charles A. Beard has said that the McKinley school did not openly "adopt the imperialist dogma in the British, French, and German style, although the deed implied the word" and that McKinley took advantage of the popular enthusiasm of the moment over the war with Spain to push his policies. "Yet as the course of events subsequently showed," according to Beard, "the program of the school had not become a national creed rooted in the unshakeable affections of the whole people."[3] The tradition that emerged was thoroughly American in character. The pacification of the islands was not a pleasant undertaking as the Filipinos did not welcome the Americans and fought hard to resist them; some ugly methods were used by both sides. Although civil government began in the pacified areas in July 1901, it was not until July 4, 1902, that the U.S. considered the situation sufficiently well in hand to terminate military government throughout the islands. Pockets of resistance continued to hold out for several more years.

The first recommendations on how to govern came from a commission sent to the Philippines in March 1899 under the chairmanship of President Jacob G. Schurman of Cornell University. While in Manila, Schurman stated that the United States intended to accustom the Filipinos to an ever-increasing measure of self-government, and to encourage them in democratic aspirations, sentiments, and ideals. The commission later suggested a government comprising a U.S. appointed governor-general with an absolute veto, a cabinet of his own choosing, a general advisory council chosen on a limited suffrage, and an independent judiciary. These suggestions had a great deal to do with the decision of important leaders among the Filipinos to come to terms with the United States. Though it thought immediate self-government impractical, the commission made it clear that only by understanding the Filipinos and sympathizing with their aspirations and ideals could the United States govern them well. The commission recommended that the customs duties, the whole taxation system, and Philippine finances should be separate from those of the United States and the government should be self-supporting. Most of these recommendations were accepted, and formed the basis of the instructions to the second commission, sent to the Philippines under the chairmanship of William Howard Taft, who, like Schurman, had not been in favor of their acquisition.

The instructions to the Taft commission, drafted by Elihu Root, were issued in April 1900. Although the occupation began with assurances to the Filipinos that they were to be given a large measure of self-government, it was made clear that this was to be within the confines of a policy of "benevolent assimilation"; neither McKinley nor Taft was in favor of independence. Taft did not exclude the possibility of independence but thought it highly unwise to make premature promises when, in his view, the Filipinos still had so far to go before they could govern themselves. All legislative power was to be transferred to the commission on September 1, 1900, and civil government was to be established with elected officers and with municipal and provincial governments. McKinley instructed the commission to respect the main body of Philippine law and custom but to impose American concepts of the division of power, strong local government, due process, respect for private property, and public education. On June 21, 1901, President McKinley appointed Taft civil governor of the islands, and the system of governors-general continued until the coming of the Commonwealth in 1935. Three Filipinos were added to the commission within a year of its assumption of legislative power, and Filipinos were employed in the whole administrative system. In large measure the United States stayed clear of the temptation to establish a huge, centralized bureaucracy of Americans to run its colony.

After rejecting a bill to promise independence, Congress passed the Cooper bill, the first Philippine Organic Act, in July 1902. This act legalized the organization and functions of the Taft commission and recognized the islands as an unincorporated territory. All persons who were Spanish subjects became citizens of the Philippine Islands if they so wished, and as such they were entitled to the protection of the United States and the Bill of Rights. An elected Philippine lower house (the commission was the upper house) would send two resident commissioners to the United States, and under certain conditions appeals could be made from the Philippine Supreme Court to that of the United States. In other words, the United States appointed the chief executive, the governor-general, and a commission that had both legislative and administrative functions; and the Filipinos elected a lower house, which could block an increase in appropriations but not the continuation of the budget of the previous year. Until 1916 the Filipinos had little positive influence, though they did have a considerable negative one, on the governing of the islands.

The Filipinos acquired even more power over their own affairs as a result of the Jones Act of 1916 and the rapid "Filipinization" policy during the eight years of the Democratic administration. The Republicans in the 1920's tried to undo some of the damage, as they saw it, that had been done to the public services by the steady attrition of American authority and administration, but it was imposible to turn the clock back. Hopes for independence had been raised, but it was not until the early 1930's, when powerful economic pressure groups helped to bring about the passage in 1934 of the Tydings-McDuffie Act, did independence become practical politics in the United States Congress. [4] The act set a definite date for independence; it was to be ten years after the establishment of a Commonwealth Government. With the establishment of this government in 1935, the U. S. Governor-General became High Commissioner. During the Commonwealth period certain duty-free quotas were fixed on Philippine imports into the United States, but after independence, all Philippine products were to be subject to the full U.S. tariff rates on foreign goods. The act limited Filipino immigration into the United States but set no limits on American immigration to the Philippines.

The United States retained the right to maintain military bases in the Philippines after independence. Thus, the strategic considerations that played so large a part in the acquisition of the Philippines were not sacrificed to the economic interests which hoped to gain by cutting off the Philippines from free trade with the United States. The Filipinos wanted their independence so badly that they were willing to pay the price, but the price was high; at the time it looked like economic ruin, bringing in its train political chaos. Writing at the time, Grayson Kirk charged the U.S. government with the betrayal of a national trust, for which, however, no single person or group could be held responsible. "It means, rather, that a great ideal was traduced, less by individual or group malevolence than by the sheer force of circumstances bearing inexorably in a depression-ridden democracy upon harrassed and none too far-sighted public servants." [5] About this event, Charles A. Beard wrote that the neutrality legislation of 1935, coupled with the granting of independence to the Philippines, signified, at least temporarily, "the steep decline of the imperialism sponsored by McKinley, Mahan, Lodge, Hay, and Theodore Roosevelt, and also punctured the universal philanthropy expounded by Woodrow Wilson." [6] From the worst features of the Tydings-McDuffie Act the United States and the Philippines were saved by the cruel accident of Japanese occupation during World War II, but even in the entirely changed circumstances of the postwar world the United States made arrangements with the Philippines of which it has little reason to be proud. It did, however, accept the moral obligation to grant independence, and on July 4, 1946, the Filipinos celebrated their independence amid the ruins of war.

Criteria for Independence

The concept of a self-liquidating colony inevitably raised the question of what conditions would have to be met in order to achieve independence. American colonial experience produced more thought on the criteria by which to judge the capacity of a people to govern itself than on any other aspect of colonial government. Contributing to this debate were the Americans who had kept alive the independence movement in the United States, the Filipino nationalists, who argued their case in Washington and Manila, and American officials and members of Congress. The discussion of criteria was important for several reasons. In the first place, it set the tone in the relations between ruler and ruled and thus probably had something to do with the absence of any violent Filipino efforts to secure independence. In the second place, the discussion made it possible for the Tydings-McDuffie bill to become law in 1934 because all parties to the debate took for granted the eventual granting of independence. It was because the mood of the country in 1934 was for independence that powerful economic interests which wanted to cut the Philippines loose succeeded in getting their way. It is perhaps necessary to make this point because the view is often advanced that the United States deserves no credit for promising independence to the Philippines in the 1930's as the enabling legislation was passed at the bidding of sordid economic interests. Those who hold this view usually charge that President McKinley took the Philippines because of tinsel dreams of empire, of popular support for "manifest destiny," and the missionary enthusiasm of the Protestant churches. Third, the discussion comes back to haunt us as we struggle with the unfriendly charge that legal sovereignty coupled with military and economic dependence is meaningless, that the United States is still an imperialist power and the Philippines a colony. The granting of independence is not, of and by itself, the ultimate political weapon.

The criteria for independence were not objective standards whose achievement could be measured quantitatively, and by the nature of the situation, the United States was judge and jury in its own case. When the decision to grant independence was actually made, many of the arguments used only a few years before to prove that the Philippines was not ready were brushed aside in the rush to protect American agricultural interests by ending free trade between the two countries. Very few of the criteria had been satisfactorily met when independence came in 1946, except possibly the most important one of all: the will of a people to fight and suffer for its right to a separate national existence.

The most important criteria were: the political maturity of the Filipino people, including the level of popular participation in government and the will to be independent; the stability of the political process and of public administration; the viability of the economy; the treatment of minority groups; and the capacity of the Philippines to protect itself. The range of opinion on these criteria was wide indeed, and a few voices were even raised in favor of permanent occupation. Even those who wished to delay independence for the Philippines accepted the assumption that some day, at some time, it would have to be granted. This distinguishing feature of American imperialism is important because it robbed the Filipino nationalist movement of much of the intense anti-Western feeling and fanatical drive found in other colonial countries.

The criterion of political maturity is a particularly difficult one to test. To Governor Taft, for example, the test of self-government was defined by the degree to which the Filipinos had acquired a knowledge of the nature of individual liberty and the processes of constitutional government. In his view the future form of government, whether dominion status, incorporation in the Union, or statehood, could be left for the future to decide. In 1908 he reported to President Roosevelt that it would take at least another generation for the Filipinos to be ready for full self-government.

From the very beginning the United States had assumed that one precondition for independence would be the presence of a mature public opinion, nurtured by public education and by increasing opportunities for Filipinos to participate in the process of government. When this had been achieved, the government would be responsible to the wishes of the people. Such a condition had not been reached by 1930, according to Secretary of State Henry S. Stimson. Independence at that time, he said, would result in either chaos or rule by an oligarchy, and both were inadmissible. But how was one to judge maturity? One view was that a working electoral system was sufficient evidence; another, that maintaining law and order was sufficient. In retrospect it is easier to see now the inevitability of oligarchical rule so long as the suffrage was limited to literate males and the social and economic condition of the mass of the population remained unchanged since Spanish times, except for the spread of formal education. While suffrage was limited in effect to those who had the main stake in society, it worked against the very changes—extension of the suffrage, social mobility, responsiveness to the popular will—that were set as conditions for a healthy and informed public opinion. [7]

How shall an imperial power measure the intensity of the wish for independence on the part of a colonial people? As early American experience has shown, it is the few who are willing to fight and die for freedom, not the many. Intensity of nationalist feeling cannot be measured by counting heads, and President Coolidge vetoed the proposal for a Philippine plebiscite. [8] It could be argued that the bitter struggle of the Philippines against American conquest

150

was in itself sufficient evidence of the desire for independence, and that this was a more significant indication of the popular will than participation in elections or the percentage of literacy or the attitudes of certain members of the elite whose economic interests were bound up with the maintenance of the status quo. The ambivalence of some Filipino leaders toward independence—due to the conflict between their economic interest, either private or national, and the need to associate themselves with the nationalist movement for their own political survival—was used to advantage by the United States when it wished to delay the granting of independence. But when Congress chose to act, these considerations dropped into the background.

If the popular will was a flexible criterion, so was the concept of a stable government. For those who wanted to delay the granting of independence it was natural to set up a model of excellence that would reflect the best in American political institutions, while for those who favored an early separation the standards were much lower. Although President McKinley is on record as favoring due respect for the customs, institutions, and laws of the Filipinos prevailing at the time of conquest, there is no doubt that the weight of his influence, as of his successors and of most governors-general, was on the side of imposing American concepts of political behavior, public administration, rights of the individual, fiscal policy, and public order. It is practically impossible, however, to separate the criteria of stable government from those of a stable economy.

Those who set up the most exacting requirements for stable government stressed the protection of private property, particularly foreign investments, and the regulation of the tariff. They wanted the assurance that there would be no unilateral repudiation of the debts of the previous regime and no sudden change in the conditions of trade to the detriment of American interests. At the same time they argued that a stable economy was a necessary basis for a stable political system.

What is a stable economy? In the case of the Philippines, there was general agreement that it required diversifying the economy and lessening its excessive dependence on that of the United States. Many American officials pointed out that the economic dependence of the Philippines on the United States was a poor basis for political independence, the stated objective of U.S. policy. Colonial policy had tended to consolidate the power of an oligarchy that profited, after 1909, from the free-trade relationship and would be likely to respect, after independence, the rights and privileges of Americans. The same policy had done more, perhaps, to increase than to decrease the gap between rich and poor in the Philippines, and the oligarchy showed little interest in raising the general living standards of the people. If the economic bonds between

151

metropolitan power and colony were broken, if free trade were abandoned, however gradually, then the economic foundations of the existing order would also be shattered. Given the evidence of social pressures, this might lead to a change in political leadership and to different attitudes toward foreign rights and interests in the Philippines and international debts and other obligations. A stable economy—diversified and independent—might not go together with a government friendly to U.S. interests.

It was assumed in the 1930's that all responsibility for the military defense of the Philippines would cease with independence, and the inability of the Philippines to defend itself was used, on occasion, as a reason for delaying the granting of independence. President Hoover vetoed the Hawes-Cutting Bill on these grounds, although it provided (as did the Tydings-McDuffie Act) for the retention by the United States of certain military installations in the Philippines. As a criterion for independence the defense argument is almost meaningless. How can the capacity of a weak country to survive be estimated unless it follows its own policies, makes its own alliances, takes its own chances? As events were to prove, an independent Philippines could hardly have suffered more from foreign aggression than did the Philippines in World War II at a time when it was still under American military protection. The defense argument was actually an argument for the continuation of U.S. military power in the western Pacific, for which there were other good and sufficient reasons. It had little relevance to any estimate of the ability of the Filipinos to take care of themselves. When independence came in 1946, the Filipinos were barely able to take care of internal subversion, let alone external aggression. But just as the acceptance of responsibility for economic aid compensates in some measure for the economic dependence of the Philippines, so do regional defense arrangements compensate somewhat for its military dependence; except that military dependence is even more constricting to the nationalist than is economic. Imperialism is not easy to liquidate.

* * * *

Education as a Means

The introduction of a compulsory system of public education was intended to be the cutting edge of the social and political revolution, the device that would make the difference between a literate oligarchy and an educated democracy. William Howard Taft, who dominated Philippine policy from 1901 to 1913; first as Civil Governor, then as Secretary of War, and finally as President of the United States, thought that the granting of independence should not be considered until the "decidedly ignorant masses" were educated sufficiently to be informed and responsible citizens. Once the United States undertook the task of making the Philippines into a democracy, such a policy was certainly the course of wisdom. But public education by itself, as the Japanese example had shown, does not necessarily lead to democracy. Much depends on what is taught and how it is taught.

In the United States the public school has been more than an academic institution; it has served as a means of molding peoples of diverse origins into a nation; the schools are the melting pots. It was natural to assume that this unique American concept of the school and of the role of education in the building of a nation would be peculiarly appropriate in the Philippines where there were also many peoples of diverse origins, differing in language and religion. The school was a device with the two essential characteristics of an instrument for revolutionary change: organizational continuity and direct access to the sources of ideology. For American purposes in the Philippines both the instrument and the point of attack, which was the values and loyalties of the ordinary Filipino, were well chosen.

A foundation already existed. The Malolos Constitution in 1899 had provided for free and compulsory education entirely under state control and for the elimination of religious instruction from the curriculum. Elementary education under the Spaniards had been largely in the hands of the church, and in spite of directives from Spain to teach the doctrine of the church in Spanish, the friars used the native dialect because they feared that a common language would encourage nationalism. A system of secondary schools and colleges had made it possible for a few Filipinos to learn Spanish and study for the professions, but for most of the population, memorization of the prayers and the Doctrine Cristiana was considered sufficient. Proposed reforms under the Spaniards were never carried out as intended, and, as a result, by 1898 there were 2,167 government-supported primary schools attended by about 200,000 boys and girls out of a total population of seven million. [9]

Although only a small minority of Filipinos received an education, enough had been done to stimulate tremendous interest and to create a demand that could not be satisfied. The Spanish educational system had attained its main objective, the teaching of Christianity, but had not succeeded in preparing the Filipinos to live in the modern world. The revolutionary leaders were ready for the American view of education as the handmaiden of the state, and of the school as the breeder of patriots and the training ground for citizens—though they took for granted the Spanish view that the educated man belonged to a small, privileged group.

It was the reformation of Philippine education that made other changes possible. The separation of church and state, the constitutional commitment to popular sovereignty, acceptance of social mobility, participation in the electoral process—all of these

153

changes depended, in the long run, on the success of popular education. During the American period the rate of literacy increased faster than the increase in population. According to the census of 1948, two years after independence, 59. 8 per cent of the population above ten years of age could read and write in some language or dialect. [10] Literacy in the English language was 37 per cent. When the Philippines acquired their independence more people could speak English than any other language, and with few exceptions English was still the language of instruction, even in the primary grades.

The imposition of the English language in the schools solved some serious problems but created others. It opened up to the Filipinos the world of Western learning and gave them a common language for government, the professions, business, and diplomacy. At the same time the prevalence and prestige of English made it more difficult to develop the use of Tagalog when it was chosen as the national language and impeded the emergence of a truly national literature. American-style curriculum and textbooks introduced the Filipino to a world he did not live in and placed before him traditions, heroes, and events that could never be part of his inner life and experience. This had serious consequences for the national ethos, and it accounted, among other things, for much of the ambivalence of the present day Filipino toward his native and his American heritage. In the long run, however, the Filipinos will make the educational system their own, and cultural pluralism will put the American contribution in perspective.

The most significant and lasting consequence of American educational policy is stated in Article XIV of the Philippine Constitution: "The Government shall establish and maintain a complete and adequate system of public education, and shall provide at least free public primary instruction, and citizenship training to adult citizens." The problem of financing this great undertaking has always been difficult, and at no time has the Constitution been fully implemented, but tremendous efforts have been made in response to the pressures of public opinion. Under the Americans, education became the main route of upward social mobility. While there is no exact way of measuring the social impact of the educational system it is clear that it has helped to bring new social classes into being, that the demand for education continues to be very great, and that, whatever its shortcomings, the educational system is second only to that of Japan among the countries of eastern Asia.

The shortcomings, however, are serious. The public school educational system is not doing the job for which it was intended and for which it is so admirably devised as an institution free from distinctions of class or sectarianism. The main trouble is that the public school system was never extended sufficiently to secondary and higher education. The Filipinos have a large number of college degrees, more per capita than any nation other than the United

States, but this does not reflect a well-ordered educational system. It is estimated that 72 out of 100 students do not reach the sixth grade and only 5 out of 100 complete high school. While there may be enough trained Filipinos for the level of economic development today, there are not enough to furnish the need if economic growth actually takes place as planned.

The quality of education has gone down since World War II for a variety of reasons. Schools and colleges had to be rebuilt. (For instance, the University of the Philippines campus in downtown Manila was completely destroyed during the war.) The United States has given some help in reconstruction, but there is no way of recovering the loss of time, morale, and valuable collections. The salaries of teachers at the universities are so low when compared with opportunities in politics and the professions that it is hard for the University of the Philippines, for example to keep its top faculty. In addition, the quality of education has also been lowered by the growth of large numbers of "diploma mills" on the college level, since the war. Finally, the public education system has been bypassed by the parallel system of church-affiliated schools, many of them excellent academically, but none of them, by definition, performing the essential task that only the public school can carry out. Practically all education beyond the elementary level is either private or parochial; and as it has to be supported from tuition the quality of instruction in fields such as medicine and science, which require expensive equipment, is even worse than it is in the fields of law, government, and the humanities. The only solution for this situation is to revitalize the public school system, but since many members of Congress either own or have shares in the diploma mills or support the parochial schools, this is not likely to be an easy task. Yet the future of Philippine democracy depends, in large measure, upon the quality and quantity of the public educational system.

Closely related to the emphasis on education during the American period was the development of a system of communications along American lines. As a result, the Philippines today is better provided than other Southeast Asian countries with postal, telegraph, telephone, and radio facilities, as well as with newspapers, periodicals, and books. The Philippines has had a free press longer than has Japan. There are important newspapers in the national and other languages, but English dominates the press and most of the literature, even poetry. As with many other things, the greatest concentration of intellectual communication is in the Manila area, where the literacy rate is also highest and where the political and economic decisions are made, just as they were in the Spanish period.

The Political Process

Political tutelage has ranked second only to public education among the important policies of American colonialism. The first step, the enactment of an excellent civil service law, was a bold and direct effort to implant the merit system in public administration and to train a group of professional administrators. "The Patronage or spoils system would prove absolutely fatal to good government in this new Oriental territory," wrote the Schurman Commission; public employment was not for sale to either Americans or Filipinos. At a time when, as Hayden points out, appointments in the British colonial service were handled on a patronage basis and only three states of the Union used the merit system, the United States set about introducing the most advanced concept of public administration in a country that had long been accustomed to corruption in government. American officials thought that without the civil service law and its strict enforcement American government in the islands would be "foredoomed to humiliating failure."[11] Because the Bureau of Civil Service was an independent office directly under the governor-general, it was possible to enforce the regulations with some measure of success. It is generally agreed that the administration of government in the Philippines up to 1913 was remarkably honest and efficient, with 2,777 Americans in the Philippine civil service, a little more than half the total number. When the Democrats took over in 1913 and Governor Harrison speeded the Filipinization of the civil service, the number went down to 29 per cent and by 1921 to 4 per cent. In 1936 there were 160 Americans and 22,555 Filipinos in the civil service, or less than one per cent of the total.[12]

Much that had been achieved in the first fourteen years of American rule was rapidly undermined; these were the only years, in fact, when the United States ruled directly and had sufficient Americans in the field to do so. It was too short a period to achieve a change in the value system of a people unaccustomed to the merit principle in appointments and firmly convinced by their experience with Spain that political connections were essential for advancement and that government service was for personal profit rather than the public welfare. The Filipino concept of corruption differed radically from the American. To the Filipino, that man was corrupt who failed to pay his political debts with the spoils of office or to promote the interests of his kin group. The concept of honest and efficient administration as an end in itself, or as a necessary condition of good government, found little support in theory or in practice. Filipinization of the civil service came before the educational system had had time to inculcate the administrative concepts of the modern state.

The political training of the Filipinos in the responsibilities of national electoral office had begun with the creation of the Philippine Assembly in 1907. To be sure, the United States reserved to itself tremendous powers—Congress could annul any Philippine law on any subject, and the signature of the President was required for all laws dealing with currency, coinage, public land, timber and mining resources, tariff, and immigration. But the Assembly was in a position to have considerable influence over the executive and the civil service, especially after 1913. It was part of the process of political tutelage to encourage the growth of political parties; but one party, the Nacionalista, dominated the Assembly because of its monopoly of the issue of independence. The Assembly was the platform for two important Filipino leaders, Manuel Quezon, who led the Nationalista party from 1922 until his death in 1944, and Sergio Osmeña. These men encouraged Filipino lawmakers to agitate for independence both in the Philippines and in the United States. They used their powers, whenever they were permitted, to dominate the executive branch of government for the remainder of the time that it was in American hands.

The policy for local government laid down by President McKinley was in line with American practice. "The natives of the islands . . . shall be afforded the opportunity to manage their local affairs to the fullest extent of which they are capable . . . In all cases the municipal officers . . . are to be selected by the people." In the distribution of powers among the governments organized by the commission, the instructions read, "the presumption is always to be in favor of the smaller subdivision" so that the central government of the Islands, "following the example of the distribution of powers between the state and the national government of the United States, shall have no direct administration except of matters of purely general concern."[13] There was a clear contradiction between the need for great authority in the hands of the executive arm of government, if it were going to be able to establish the institutions of the modern state, and the instruction to put more authority in the hands of local elected officers.

The Spanish tradition of centralization, combined with the American practice of supervising local government, ensured that there would be no revolutionary growth of local autonomy. Municipal officials were elected by the small propertied class which had the right to vote, but there was no diminution of central government control over finances and the administration of the new public services. The lines of authority ran directly through the executive departments to the president. Local government never became independent of central authority in any real sense. If the executive today carries out administrative functions at the provincial, city, and municipal levels through the departments of finance, agriculture, health, education, public works, justice, and the Office of

Local Government, it is largely because the instructions of President McKinley were not and probably could not have been carried out. It has been suggested that if American supervision had continued longer there might have been sufficient antagonism against it to foster a stronger spirit of independence in local government, but even this possibility ceased in 1916 when American supervision of local government ceased.

The end result of American political direction was an American-type constitution but not an American form of government; the Philippine Republic is a centralized, not a federal government. The unusual concentration of authority in the person and office of the chief executive certainly did not come about by American intention, but resulted from historical factors and the structure of Philippine society. The Filipino looks for the charismatic element in leadership and is accustomed, through personal experience of the patricentric family, to accept authority. The relation between landlord and tenant, the most common of all relationships outside the family, was much more than a contractual affair. It had many of the elements of deference and responsibility that were common within the family. In the Philippines, traditions of individual initiative and responsibility in the political process had to be created as far as the masses were concerned. While it is not true to say that the ideological bases of the Western type of democracy have found no acceptance in the Philippines, they still compete with powerful forces.

The decentralization of government is probably an essential condition for economic progress along the lines decided upon by the Filipinos today. Some steps have been taken in this direction. The Barrio Act of 1960 provides the barrios with a legal personality and official powers to raise taxes, and the office of the Presidential Adviser for Community Development (PACD) stimulates local self-help projects. But much remains to be done if there is going to be a real working democracy in the Philippines. At the very minimum there must be a great improvement in the educational system to provide local leaders, a rapid building of physical communications, the provision of electric power to the barrios for light and for industry, the delegation of greater tax-raising powers to local authorities, and the abolition of the pork barrel system. The public works budget is called the Pork Barrel Bill and it amounts to around 30 percent of the national budget. Each congressman receives a share of these funds and is free to allocate them as he pleases in his own district, but the president controls the disbursement of the money. Obviously such a procedure means that all roads lead to Manila from whence comes all the money for public works projects, both large and small. If there is to be any growth of democracy, responsibility for most of the public works will have to be given to local agencies. And if units of local government had adequate powers, they could improve on what the central government provides for education, and they would have the incentives to better the tax collection system. The character of politics would change, and political parties, perhaps, would cease to be nothing more than coalitions of personal factions and local political bosses.

The Americans have mainly themselves to blame for the failure to build democracy at the grass roots when they had the opportunity to do so. All that they can do now is to encourage those groups and those forces in the Philippines that are moving in the right direction. Unfortunately, it is still an open question whether the Filipinos want a modern democratic political and economic system more than they want their traditional social system. They cannot have both.

FOOTNOTES

[1]Teodoro A. Agoncillo and Oscar W. Alfonso, A Short History of the Filipino People (Quezon City: University of the Philippines, 1960), p. 435.

[2]Same, pp. 293 ff.

[3]Charles A. Beard and Mary R. Beard, The Rise of American Civilization (New York: Macmillan, 1930), p. 374.

[4]Grayson Kirk, Philippine Independence (New York: Farrar & Rinehart, Inc., 1936), pp. 100–101.

[5]Ibid, p. 208.

[6]Charles A. Beard, America in Mid-Passage, V. 1 (New York: Macmillan, 1939), p. 433.

[7]Georges Fischer, Un Cas de Decolonization (Paris: Librairie Generale de Droit et De Jurisprudence, 1960), p. 62 ff.

[8]Annual Report of the Governor-General of the Philippine Islands, 1927 (Manila: Bureau of Printing, 1927), p. 64.

[9]HRAF Handbook, cited, V. 2, p. 752.

[10]Ibid, p. 956.

[11]Hayden, cited, pp. 88–91.

[12]HRAF Handbook, cited, V. 2, p. 967.

[13]Dean C. Worcester, The Philippines; Past and Present, rev. ed. (New York: Macmillan, 1930), pp. 793, 795.

CHAPTER 6

The Chinese

The intent of this study has been to provide an account of foreign influence in Southeast Asia up through the World War II era. Normally, a study of this kind is limited to an examination of Western colonialism. However, during the age of European imperialism, the Chinese added their influence to the growth and modern development of this region. In order to complete the examination of the foreign influences which have dominated this area, some attention must be given to the contribution of the Chinese in Southeast Asia.

China has traditionally been the dominant Oriental power in Eastern affairs. In many respects, the relationship between the nations in Southeast Asia and China have been similar to the association between the Spanish American states and the United States; in that both areas, Southeast Asia and Latin America, have been forced to live under the shadow of a powerful and influential neighbor to the north. China, with its overwhelming size, large population, and power has played a direct role in the growth of many parts of Southeast Asia, and on occasion, it has actually ruled portions of this part of the world. In the pre-Western era, some of the Southeast Asian rulers had to account to the imperial Chinese court for their foreign and domestic policies, and in Indo-China, the Chinese emperors assumed the position of feudal overlord over some of the native princes. Another aspect of Chinese influence in Southeast Asia came during the age of Western colonialism when thousands of Chinese migrated to this area under the protection of the Western colonial governments. This situation occurred throughout the entire European colonial era, but during the nineteenth century, the Chinese came to play a particularly important role in the fringe areas of Asia. These immigrants are called Overseas Chinese. The term Overseas Chinese is not limited just to Southeast Asia, but applies as much to Chinatown in San Francisco as to the Chinese community in Manila and Saigon. With varying degrees of intensity, the question or problem of the Overseas Chinese has become a highly international occurence and has played an important role in the modern development of Southeast Asia.

161

The role of the individual Chinese in Southeast Asia has existed for many centuries. Long before the arrival of the European, Chinese merchants and traders frequented the port cities of most of China's southern neighbors. During the many generations of Chinese interest in this area, the merchant class developed powerful financial contacts within each of the trading centers of this part of the world, and an ability to trade with the native population using local methods of exchange. In the more important trading areas of Malaya, Indonesia, and Indo-China the Chinese gained considerable strength, while in Burma and the Philippines, the Chinese economic and cultural impact remained relatively unimportant prior to European colonization. After the arrival of the European, the role of the Chinese increased in all of the above areas, including Burma and the Philippines.

When the European arrived in Southeast Asia, he found that the native people lived primarily as peasant farmers and had no understanding of European economic concepts and no ability or interest to participate in a money oriented economy. For the average native, his economic life involved barter rather than the exchange or accumulation of money. He paid his taxes in kind, he bartered with his fellow community members and he seldom, if ever, had the opportunity to use or to accumulate money. As for the European, he had no interest in barter as a means of exchange, particularly on a small basis. He preferred to deal in gold or to exchange Western merchandise for Eastern goods on a large scale. Since the native element neither had the training nor the interest to engage in trade in this fashion, the Western colonial trader turned to the only element in Southeast Asian society who could conduct trade in a manner similar to European standards and who understood the native system of barter. This was the Chinese businessman. As European influence grew, the need for an expanded business community capable of understanding a money economy and also willing to barter with the natives created a serious problem which could only be solved by either training the natives to use money as a means of exchange, or by encouraging more European businessmen to migrate to Southeast Asia, or to permit the Chinese to expand their operations. In most instances, the natives refused to alter their traditional economic orientation and European businessmen refused to live in small native communities. This left the Chinese as the only persons capable of trade between the native and the European. In most instances, the Chinese expanded their operations with the blessings of both the colonial governments and the financial interests involved in empire building. In this fashion, the colonial trading firms bridged the gap between themselves and the native farmers by using the services of the Chinese.

By the nineteenth century, the Chinese dominated the role of the middleman between the native and the European. The position of the middleman in a colonial society offered considerable economic reward, and as an added encouragement to those willing to attempt a business venture in the middle sector of the economic life of a colony, the imperial governments gave the enterprising merchant official protection and a safe environment to conduct his activities and good markets for trading. The Chinese, their refined sense of business techniques and their appreciation of the potential offered them by the European, migrated to Southeast Asia hoping to work their way into the business community. A simplified account of the growth of the Overseas Chinese community begins in South China. Life in southern China proved ideal to encourage enterprising peasants to move from this area to the outer fringes of Asia. Merchants and travelers frequenting this area of China provided sufficient accounts of the economic potential that Southeast Asia offered to attract aggressive peasants willing to consider a move from China to this new land of promise. This proved to be particularly attractive since conditions in South China offered few opportunities for economic betterment. As a result, many peasants left their homeland to seek a new and potentially better life in the cities of Southeast Asia. Once they arrived in a metropolitan area, they supported themselves by manual labor, working close to eighteen hours per day, 365 days out of the year. By living very carefully, they could send money back to China or save enough money to attempt a small business venture. In later periods, the Chinese community frequently assisted the potential businessman with loans and sound advice. Either through personal initiative or with the assistance of the Chinese community, they found it possible to establish permanent and successful businesses. Once a degree of success had been achieved, they either sent money home to support their families or brought their families and friends to their newly adopted land. Furthermore, as stories circulated in China how a man could go to Southeast Asia and acquire sufficient money to support parents and family, more and more young Chinese attempted to repeat the cycle. The appeal of economic success and social betterment attracted the more aggressive South Chinese to this region in Asia, and by this means the basis of the large and generally economically powerful Overseas Chinese community in most all parts of Southeast Asia was founded.

The Chinese businessman had many advantages in his newly adopted homeland. When he arrived in the area in which he hoped to settle, he could readily identify with a segment of society which had a long established tradition of economic success, he could obtain a degree of psychological security from his fellow countrymen, and if he showed promise, he might receive financial support in the development of his business enterprise. In many respects, the Chinese formed the same kind of social-economic group that is frequently identified with the Jewish community in most European and American cities during this time. Aside from the support which a Chinese migrant might obtain from his fellow countrymen, the Chinese could also count on a degree of protection and assistance from the European community, since most colonial governments and resident Europeans approved of the activities of the Chinese as middlemen between the native and the European trading companies. As an added inducement to further Chinese economic expansion in Southeast Asia, they found it easy to make money by exploiting the natives. A small Chinese merchandiser sold both the everyday necessities of life and introduced into rural areas new and highly attractive luxury items from Europe and the Orient. Most of these items could be acquired by the Chinese for a very small price but since most peasants had no real concept of the value of these new products, the local merchant always overcharged the native. For an enterprising and aggressive merchant, the childlike peasant provided an excellent opportunity for exploitation. Another side to the economic success of the Chinese community came with money lending. By becoming the local moneylender, the Chinese quickly gained an economic stranglehold over the native population. They willingly lent small amounts of money to the peasants to purchase either necessities or luxury items at highly inflated prices. Credit charges on these purchases frequently exceeded one hundred per cent. To satisfy the ever-mounting debt, the peasant had to sell his crops to the moneylender. The merchant-moneylender paid the lowest possible price for these goods and in turn, marketed them in urban areas at a substantial profit. Throughout most of the nineteenth century, and well into the twentieth century, these activities had the blessing of the colonial governments. In the twilight years of European colonialism, most governments made an attempt to regulate the role of the Chinese. These attempts failed because the Chinese still filled the void between the native and the European economic community. If the Chinese had been either driven out or limited in their activities, most colonial economies would have fallen apart. However, to further protect themselves, the Chinese formed alliances with the European trading firms to assist the Chinese in maintaining their preferential position in Southeast Asia. Once having secured this alliance, the Chinese could count on the strong voice of the European economic interests to defend their role in colonial Southeast Asia. A second condition which helped to maintain the position of the Chinese was the matter of rural credit. Most colonial governments attempted to solve the problem of rural credit, however well intentioned these efforts might have been, European credit schemes generally failed to benefit the small farmer. Three reasons account for this failure. First, the government required security for their loans, and most peasants had no real security to offer and as a result, their loan applications seldom received approval. Secondly, the government generally rejected loan applications because they did not approve of the reasons for the loan. The government favored loans for rural improvement while the native sought loans for marriage feasts or religious celebrations. Finally, the few peasants who had security and a valid reason for a loan understood the complicated procedure to acquire government assistance. Thus the peasant had no where to turn but to the traditional Chinese moneylender who required no security, made no judgements concerning the application, and always kept the process of lending exceedingly simple and uncomplicated. Another attempt to break the power of the Chinese came during the later colonial period when Western governments tried to educate natives to fill the role of the economic middleman. Some natives acquired adequate training to conduct the Chinese type business activities, but once they received sufficient education to replace the Chinese, they refused to return to the rural areas to practice their skills. Owing to this situation even today, a generation after the age of colonialism, the Chinese shopkeeper still remains a powerful and necessary economic force in most areas of Southeast Asia. Even in areas where natives did replace the Chinese, they exploit the simple native in the same fashion that the Chinese did in the past.

A second area of Chinese activity came in the field of urban employment. Again, the Southeast Asian situation provided an excellent opportunity for the Chinese to prosper, or at least to survive, at a better level than they could in South China. Most of the natives in Southeast Asia preferred to live in rural areas. Because of the European need for urban workers, they had to turn to the Chinese labor market. Because of the demand for their services, the Chinese acquired a monopoly over most skilled labor positions and with this monopoly, they developed unions or guilds which excluded native workers seeking employment in the skilled labor force. To maintain their control over the labor market, the Chinese used every tactic available to prevent any form of competition in their fields of activity. By using the general strike, European employers learned that it was advisable to keep native workers out of areas of employment dominated by the well organized and powerful Chinese unions. Since the European business interests and the colonial officials accepted the role of the Chinese in the urban work force as a means of solving the gap between the indifferent attitude of the native to city life and the needs of a growing metropolitan area, the Chinese laborer, like the Chinese businessman, could generally count on the support of the colonial society in their demand to maintain their monopoly of the work force. Today the problem of the Chinese dominated labor force still creates difficulties for the governments of most Southeast Asian nations since the natives lack sufficient training to replace the Chinese in this field of economic activity.

In the nineteenth century, the role of the Chinese in Southeast Asian colonial society remained about the same as that of the Europeans. They lived a clannish existence in urban areas and identified with the Chinese sector of the city. In their home environment, they used Chinese rather than the European or native languages, they practiced their own form of religion, and they maintained a general cultural environment similar to that which they had known in China. Like the European, once they had made an economic success of their activities, they frequently returned to China as a successful retired businessman. From the native point of view, the Chinese and the European functioned in about the same fashion, a temporary resident exploiting both the land and the people. Beginning in the post World War I era, the attitudes of the Chinese began to change. They kept their strong identification with China and her culture, but they began to assume a more permanent position in urban Southeast Asia. Several factors account for this change. Travel by the early 1900's, became cheaper and migrants of the twentieth century generally brought their families to their new residence as soon as possible, where they settled down to raise a family on a permanent basis. Secondly, as the twentieth century progressed, the idea of returning to China gradually became less and less attractive. Domestically, China experienced many internal disruptions which made life in China far less attractive than it had been in the past. For those who had left in the nineteenth century, twentieth century China had little appeal. After the fall of the imperial Chinese government, China changed. Civil wars destroyed an important portion of her traditional culture and society. Most Overseas Chinese did not like the new China and they felt no loyalty toward the new Republic of China. Thirdly, as the Chinese community grew in numbers, the attachment to "Chinatown" proved to be far stronger than the desire to return to home. Finally, many successful merchants and businessmen hated to abandon their businesses to a stranger, preferring to establish their sons in the family business. For those who did not achieve success, they frequently elected to remain in Southeast Asia, rather than to admit failure to family and friends in China. The end result brought forth a change in the Chinese attitude toward their residency in Southeast Asia, a sense of permanency descended on the Overseas Chinese. In an effort to maintain what they believe to be "superior Chinese culture," schools, religious and cultural centers, and newspapers were established to assist in the preservation of their culture. The Chinese made no attempt to become part of the culture of their newly adopted homeland, preferring to remain culturally isolated from the native community.

While the Chinese attempted to establish their culture in Southeast Asia, the Southeast Asians began to experience the impact of nationalism within their society. This growth of native nationalism, combined with their mounting resentment toward the Chinese businessman and laborer, turned the nationalists against the Overseas Chinese. In general, the same factors which produced a reaction against the European colonial system also created a similar feeling toward the Chinese. Nationalists maintained that the European controlled the government and that the Chinese controlled the economy, and as long as these two elements remained, there would be no room for the native to assume direction over either the government or the economic life of their country. Secondly, during the twentieth century more and more natives secured an education which enabled them to compete for important economic and governmental positions. The nationalists insisted that as long as the European and the Chinese dominated the economic and political life of their country, the educated native had no chance of succeeding against these powerful elements in society. By demanding that the foreign elements in their society leave, the nationalists secured the support of the educated elite in furthering the anti-colonial cause. The growth of communism also worked against the Chinese. Communists insisted that colonialism stood for exploitation, and the example of the Chinese served the communists well in damning the entire colonial system in Southeast Asia. Finally, since the European had given both official and unofficial protection to the Chinese, the Chinese came to be looked upon as merely an extension of European rule in Southeast Asia. With the growth of nationalism and the rise of anti-colonialism, the Chinese became a prime target for both the nationalist and the educated elite in attacking the entire system of foreign domination of their particular nation.

As long as the European remained in control of Southeast Asia, the Chinese had protection and the strength of the government behind them. This came to an end with the outbreak of World War II. Japanese occupation of Southeast Asia hit the Chinese population particularly hard. China and Japan were at war during this period, and since the Overseas Chinese identified themselves as Chinese citizens, they automatically became the enemy of the Japanese. The Japanese also attacked the Overseas Chinese because of their strong identification with European colonialism, the existence of which the Japanese hoped to destroy. Finally, during Japanese occupation of Southeast Asia, the Japanese hoped to please the native by attacking both the Westerner and the Chinese. Since most Europeans abandoned Southeast Asia during the Japanese era, this left the Chinese as the prime target of the conquering power. In their attempt to destroy the Chinese, the Japanese found that many native nationalists willingly cooperated with them in this aspect of the occupation. With Japanese encouragement, many native nationalists committed acts of terror against the Chinese community. After World War II, the European colonial governments returned to power, but their attitude toward their restored colonies had changed. Europeans began to turn power over to native leaders, and in so doing, they tended to abandon their Chinese partners to the hostility of the new nationalist leaders. As a further complicating factor for the Chinese, the situation in China no longer afforded them a satisfactory place to return. Communist China, with its anti-capitalist and anti-religious orientation, differed markedly from the highly capitalistic and culturally conservative Overseas Chinese. Since most nationalist governments closed their doors to Chinese migration and since China is hardly an acceptable place to resettle, the Overseas Chinese have become prisoners in their adopted land. As basically unwelcome guests, the Overseas Chinese remain at the mercy of the highly nationalistic governments in Southeast Asia.

The following reading selection by Professor L. A. Mills, presents an overview of the present role of the Chinese in Southeast Asia. Each country is examined in summary form suggesting the Chinese position in Southeast Asia, and the influence they have in this area, both today and in the past.

THE CHINESE *

The Chinese in Transition

The post-war World War I emergence of strongly nationalist states and Mao Tse-tung's victory had profound effects upon the position of the Chinese. These factors are still working themselves out, and it is not possible to foresee what will be the outcome. Nor can one predict what attitude the Chinese themselves will finally adopt. For obvious reasons of expediency they are not talking. It is not possible to generalize about the unexpressed ideas of eight to nine million people who run the gamut from millionaires to penniless laborers, and from the English-speaking and partially anglicized Queen's Chinese of Penang and Malacca through conservative supporters of Chiang Kai-shek to Communist agitators. Still another complication is that the treatment and future prospects of the Chinese are different in every country, so that each must be considered separately. The probability is that they do not know what is the wisest course for them to follow. In most parts of Southeast Asia the assured position which they held before the war has changed very much for the worse, and every course of action has as many uncertainties and disadvantages as it has possible benefits. The likelihood is that their minds are confused and that they cope as best they can with each emergency as it arises without trying to forecast the future or devise a plan of action for years ahead. They seem to be driven by the tide and to follow a policy of one step enough for me. It is unlikely that they are considering whether they can make a bargain with Mao Tse-tung by which they will become his fifth column and in return he will be their protector and promise to respect their economic interests. It is also improbable that they have consciously decided that they will not irrevocably commit themselves to either side in the cold war, but will remain sitting on the fence with a leg on each side until it becomes clear which is going to win. Doubtless they intend to be on the winning side, but to write in these terms is to oversimplify. It is much more likely that they do not see any necessity to choose between West and East. Of course much will depend on how rigorous the anti-Chinese measures are that each government adopts. They might be pushed so far that they are driven over to the side of Mao Tse-tung.

The end of colonial rule deprived the Chinese of their Western protectors. In Thailand and South Viet Nam the governments set up a monopoly of the rice trade which they had largely controlled. Their commercial position was attacked in Indonesia, Cambodia, and Burma by reserving the bulk of the licenses for importing and exporting to nationals. In the Philippines and Indonesia they

*Mills, Lennox A., Southeast Asia Illusion and Reality in Politics and Economics, University of Minnesota Press, Minneapolis. © Copyright 1964 University of Minnesota.

were partially excluded from retail trade. The Chinese showed their usual acumen and ingenuity in evading many of these laws, and so increased the hostility of the new governments. They profited from the incompetence of the new Southeast Asian importers and exporters, they evaded controls by smuggling, and they used their traditional weapon of bribing officials. Almost every government passed regulations to curtail the freedom of the private schools, and sometimes closed them. The unwillingness to give up Chinese citizenship was overridden, and limits on immigration were imposed which sharply reduced the number of entrants. [1] The only exception was Malaya, where the Chinese were too numerous to be attacked, and Tengku Abdul Rahman was able to control the Malays and prevent any unjust discrimination. Elsewhere the Chinese were made to realize that they were an unpopular minority, and that they were not strong enough openly to oppose the new governments. They badly needed a protector and the only possibility was the Communist government at Peking. Its failure, however, to halt the drastic measures taken by Sukarno against their retail trade in 1959 must have made them realize that they could not rely on its help. There were probably two reasons why Peking did not go beyond protests. It did not have the power to compel Sukarno to change his policy. Furthermore, it has been trying hard to cultivate friendly relations with the neutralist states, and success would have been endangered by too vigorous a championing of the Chinese in Indonesia.

Within limits Peking was willing to help, since it wanted the Overseas Chinese to contribute liberally to the party funds and repatriate their money for investment in China. In addition they could be a very useful fifth column. A special government department, the Commission of Overseas Chinese Affairs, was set up in 1949 to protect the interests of Chinese abroad, foster close ties between them and China, and persuade them to send home money on a generous scale. Their pride and affection for China were appealed to, and they were exhorted to help the reconstruction of their fatherland. Copying an old practice of the Kuomintang, intimidation was used to reinforce patriotic appeals. Most of the Chinese emigrants had relatives in China, and they were threatened with reprisals unless handsome remittances were made. An energetic campaign was carried on to persuade Chinese students to come to China for their education, and they were promised scholarships and subsequent employment. The Communist teachers in the private schools acted as recruiting agents. Hundreds of boys and girls accepted deck passages to China provided by the local consul, despite the tears and protests of their parents. They departed "singing and chanting Communist songs and looked for all the world as if they were destined for a New Jerusalem." The governments of Indonesia and the Federation of Malaya passed laws forbidding them ever to return. [2] Propaganda was carried on by radio, books, and newspapers. In the electoral law of 1953 provision was made for the overseas Chinese to elect thirty deputies to the All-China People's Congress. Imitating Chiang Kai-shek, the government insisted that nationality was determined by racial descent, and that once a Chinese always a Chinese. Whenever diplomatic relations were established with one of the new states, the embassy and consulates were used to control the Chinese and support the local branch of the Communist party. As a result of the victory of Mao Tes-tung the Chinese Communist party acquired an overwhelmingly dominant influence over Asian Communism. An elaborate organization was developed with its headquarters in Peking and branches overseas by which the government was able to coordinate and control the branches of the party in Southeast Asia. [3]

The overseas Chinese regarded Peking's mingling of blandishment and threats with confused and contradictory feelings. They realized that they needed protection and that this could come only from Peking. Their leaders at least knew that the outcome of the cold war was uncertain, and they wanted to safeguard themselves against reprisals if Communist dictatorships were set up in Southeast Asia. This was the reason why some wealthy Chinese in Malaya subsidized the Chinese Communist revolt and for some years did little to oppose it, although their own interests were bound up with the success of the British government. The majority were not Communists, and they would suffer economically if the party brought Southeast Asia under its control. It was true that only a minority were wealthy, but even the manual laborers had the ambition to become rich and respected, as many had done before them. The Chinese were well aware of conditions in China, and by 1951 they were beginning to be disillusioned. Their relatives had written them of how the government had seized the remittances which they had sent, and some had been deprived of their land. In 1955, Peking belatedly tried to repair the damage by ordering that families should not be robbed of funds sent them from abroad, and that greater facilities should be given for the investment of money from overseas. The Chinese in Southeast Asia knew of the liquidations and concentration camps in China, the treatment of private business, and the collectivization of the peasants. Their conclusion was that they did not want Communist rule in Southeast Asia but that this was unlikely to take place, at any rate in their lifetime. [4]

Chinese Nationalism

Another factor which has very greatly influenced the Chinese has been the growth of Chinese nationalism since World War II. This appears to be general throughout Southeast Asia. The term "nationalism" is not strictly accurate, for apart from the Communist minority they do not want annexation. Perhaps a more accurate

171

description would be that they are determined to preserve their distinctive language and culture which separate them from the people among whom they live. The majority are unwilling to abandon their Chinese nationality. Along with this goes great sympathy and approval of the Peking government. This attitude is most pronounced among the students and the younger Chinese, but it also affects the older generation including the wealthy business men. It is strongest among the Chinese-speaking, but is gaining ground among those who know a Western language much better than their own. One symptom of it is that a stigma attaches to a Chinese who cannot speak his own vernacular, and some who find themselves in this predicament have belatedly begun to study it. The pro-Peking attitude is compounded of traditional loyalty and affection for China, attachment to Chinese culture, and pride in the much more important position that China has won in the world under Mao Tse-tung. For over a century the Chinese felt bitterly humiliated that they, the world's most civilized people, had been defeated and ordered about by despised Western barbarians. They hoped for a time that Chiang Kai-shek would make the West accept China as a first-class power. His failure in this was one main reason for his loss of support. It is dangerous to generalize because in countries where the government is anti-Communist, as in the Philippines and Thailand, it would be very inexpedient for the local Chinese to show any preference for Mao Tse-tung. The guess might be hazarded however that on the whole Chiang Kai-shek has been written off as a failure.

Mao Tse-tung succeeded where Chiang Kai-shek did not. As the Chinese see it he fought the United States, the strongest of the Western powers, to a standstill, and prevented it from conquering North Korea. With his help Ho Chi Minh defeated the French. Mao Tse-tung made China feared and respected by the West. A government that could accomplish this deserved the sympathy of all Chinese, even though they might not want to come under its control. This point of view is not due to conversion to Communism: it arises from Chinese nationalism. It explains why wealthy business men in Singapore who were not Communists gave dinner parties to celebrate the defeat of General MacArthur at the Yalu river.

> By standing up to the foreign powers in the way it did,
> and by the speed and energy with which it set about
> carrying out its plans, the new regime quickly made it
> clear that it was totally different from anything that had
> been seen in China for well over a century. Here at
> last was a strong central government, seemingly effi-
> cient and free from corruption, which knew its own
> mind and was prepared not only to enforce its will on
> its own people, but to ensure that the New China and
> its people received from other powers the treatment

172

and respect due to equals. No longer would China
tolerate any treatment short of equality . . . either
in her own ports or in foreign lands. [5]

This pro-Peking attitude was one reason why Tengku Abdul Rahman
declared in 1961 that if Communist intervention in Laos led to war
with the West, he would not allow the British to use their military
and air-force bases in the Federation of Malaya to assist the government of Prince Boun Oum. His power was based on the alliance
between U.M.N.O. and M.C.A., and he could not afford to alienate
his Chinese supporters.

Another influence which seems to be affecting the Chinese is
that apparently they are abandoning the hope of returning to China,
and are coming to look upon their country of domicile as their permanent home. Movement to and from China has been interrupted
for a quarter of a century, first by the Japanese invasion, then by
World War II, and after that by Mao Tse-tung's victory. Moreover, the Chinese know that from the economic point of view a return to Communist China would be a change for the worse. A large
number have married and established homes in Southeast Asia, and
a generation is growing up which was born and brought up overseas.
It is likely that they toy with the idea of going home, as a city clerk
may talk of becoming a farmer when he retires, but that this is a
vague dream and not a real intention. Probably their chief desire
is to be let alone so that they can make money without interference,
and preserve their own nationality and culture. On the whole they
seem to have no political ambitions, and are content to let some-
one else govern the country so long as they are left in peace. The
extent to which they approve of a government depends on how far
it protects their special interests. The mass of the Chinese continue to believe that "governments exist to be placated, to be
evaded or to be bought when they are oppressive: to be patiently
obeyed at other times." China was not a democracy, and emigration did not give them democratic ideas.

The Chinese in Indonesia

Prior to 1941 the Chinese triple monopoly of retail shopkeep-
ing, produce-buying, and money-lending had aroused a latent resentment among the peasantry which could flare into violence when
stimulated by local Indonesian leaders. The small middle class
was consciously hostile, and one purpose of Sarekat Islam, a political party which was founded about 1910, was to liberate the
Indonesians from economic dependence on the Chinese. Nationalism and support of the Kuomintang party were strong among the
large majority of the Peranakans (Chinese born in the East Indies)
as well as newcomers from China. The Chinese private schools
which were established in large numbers from about 1900 onwards

173

were strongly nationalist in their teachings. These was the same deadlock as elsewhere over dual nationality, the Dutch government claiming under jus soli that all Chinese born in the Indies were Dutch subjects, while China insisted under jus sanguinis that they were Chinese citizens. [6]

The Chinese suffered severely in life and property during the Japanese occupation and the ensuing revolt against Dutch rule. In many parts of Java they were robbed and killed by peasants or guerillas of Sukarno's army. The peasants repudiated their debts to the moneylenders, who incurred heavy financial losses. The attitude of the Chinese community during the revolt increased the illwill of the Indonesians. A minority profited greatly, some by supplying the Dutch armies and others by running the Dutch blockade and bringing much needed goods to Sukarno's soldiers. The majority tried to remain neutral and carry on business as usual, following their traditional policy of taking no part in politics. They did not especially like the Dutch, but they tended to feel that a return of colonial rule was the best guarantee of a restoration of the pre-war security of life and property. Very few were active and loyal supporters of the Indonesian Republic, and after the war was over the gulf between the Indonesians and the Chinese was perhaps wider than it had been in 1941. [7]

The government of the republic wished to solve the problem of dual nationality, and in 1949 Chinese who had been born in Indonesia were automatically given Indonesian citizenship unless within two years they rejected it and declared themselves citizens of China. This offer encountered two obstacles. China still insisted on citizenship by jus sanguinis, and the Chinese in Indonesia were unwilling to give up their Chinese nationality. Even when they accepted Indonesian citizenship there was reason to suspect that they did so only from motives of expediency. In 1954 Chou En-lai announced that China was willing to settle the question of dual nationality, and a treaty was negotiated which was signed at the Bandung Conference of Afro-Asian states in 1955 and ratified in 1960. It did not apply to Chinese who had rejected Indonesian citizenship, nor to those born in China who were never naturalized as Dutch subjects. These groups were recognized as Chinese citizens, and were given no further choice in the matter. The agreement was confined to those of Chinese descent born in Indonesia who had accepted Indonesian citizenship. Within two years they were required again to choose whether they wished to be Chinese or Indonesian citizens. Those who failed to do so would automatically acquire the nationality of their forefathers. They would become Indonesian citizens "when his or her father's side is of Indonesian descent," and Chinese when the father's side of the family was Chinese. In future all children born in Indonesia of alien Chinese parents would have Chinese citizenship. The treaty did not provide for voluntary naturalization, either of immigrants or of their children born in Indonesia. However, for the first time China abandoned her traditional claim that all persons of Chinese descent remained Chinese citizens even when they acquired another citizenship. In 1958 Indonesia passed a law which provided that aliens who were over twenty-one, who had lived there for five years, and who could speak the language, could apply for citizenship. It was estimated that the number of Chinese in Indonesia was around 2, 100, 000, of whom about 1, 500, 000 had been born there and 600, 000 were immigrants. The majority were merchants, small manufacturers or rubber-estate owners, and only a minority were laborers. It was believed that something like forty to forty-five per cent of the total number were Chinese citizens. [8]

Chinese private schools numbered about a thousand and were believed to have between 250, 000 and 300, 000 pupils. Most of the teachers were alien Chinese, and the emphasis was on Chinese studies although the Indonesian language was taught. Communist influence was strong, and more young Chinese from Indonesia went to China to complete their education than from any other part of Southeast Asia. The government looked upon the schools with disfavor and made some attempts to control the curriculum. The teachers evaded them as far as they could, and some schools were closed. [9]

Economic discrimination of increasing severity was enforced against the aliens and also those who had accepted Indonesian citizenship. Apart from the long-standing dislike of them the government wished to create a class of Indonesian business men and oust the Chinese. It used its control of import licenses and the allocation of bank loans and foreign exchange to reduce the Chinese share of foreign trade. An ordinance was issued that the only way in which a Chinese firm could avoid the discrimination was by forming a partnership with native Indonesian business men and turning over fifty per cent of the capital and profits to them. The regulation applied whether the owners were aliens or Indonesian citizens. Some firms complied with the order, some accepted Indonesian partners at least in name, and a good many got their import licenses and foreign exchange by bribery. Chinese were also prevented to a large extent from establishing new industries which required imports of foreign machinery. [10]

In 1959 Sukarno forbade Chinese retail trade in rural areas and ordered that the businesses be closed and the owners moved to the towns by January 1, 1960. The decree seems to have been pretty generally enforced in Java at any rate. The protests of the Peking government were rejected, and the Chinese were given an object lesson of its failure to protect them. Sukarno's attempt to replace them by Indonesian cooperatives did not succeed, and the result was chaos and confusion in the rural retail trade. A large number especially of the younger men left Indonesia, many going to China. They discovered that government restrictions forbade them to take with them the proceeds from the sale of their property.

The Chinese have a growing sense of insecurity and alarm. They feel that accepting Indonesian citizenship has been no safeguard against discrimination, and they know that many Indonesians including officials look upon all Chinese as undesirable aliens. There seems to be little wholehearted loyalty to the government of Indonesia, and most of those who became Indonesian citizens did so from motives of self-interest. The majority would like to avoid taking part in politics and attend to their own business affairs, but they realize increasingly that their economic prospects are precarious. As to the attitude toward China, a large part of the Chinese are nationalist though not Communist and therefore sympathetic toward the Peking government and proud of its successes. There are conflicting opinions as to whether the Indonesian Communist party is financed by the Chinese community or the Soviet and Chinese embassies. A dwindling minority still adhere to Chiang Kai-shek, and a much larger number of those who are interested in politics support Mao Tse-tung. [11] Chinese Communist propaganda has been carried on vigorously, and the discriminatory policy of the Indonesian government has intensified the effect of nationalism in making many of the Chinese look toward Peking. If Sukarno continues to antagonize the Chinese the number responding favorably to Communist propaganda will grow, with the qualification that they realize that Peking cannot protect them at present.

The Philippines

No reliable statistics exist of the number of Chinese. The one certain fact is that far more than the legal annual quota of fifty enter by giving bribes or being smuggled in from Borneo. The average Filipino estimate of the total number which tends to magnify the "menace" is over 600,000, while the Chinese, who prefer to minimize it, give a figure of under 350,000. The Chinese have been strongly entrenched in the retail trade as well as in importing and exporting, wholesaling, manufacturing, and money-lending. Discriminatory legislation has wholly or partly excluded them from various fields of business such as foreign trade, but even here their share was still 13.2 per cent in 1957. In retail trade they accounted for 46 per cent of the sales in 1951, or in other words less than two per cent of the population handled nearly half the retail business. There is a strong suspicion that the published figures are most likely a gross understatement. Chinese ownership is often concealed by using a Filipino man of straw as the nominal owner, by transferring assets to a Filipino wife, or by obtaining Filipino citizenship. For a Chinese to become naturalized, however, is very expensive and difficult even when he has been born in the Philippines. [12]

The Chinese are strongly disliked as alien exploiters, and there is a long history of legislation against them. The earliest was the Bookkeeping Act which required Chinese businesses to translate their accounts into English, Spanish, or Tagalog (the official national language). The result was a dual set of books—an official statement for the Bureau of Internal Revenue and a private record of actual business. When the Philippine Commonwealth was established, the constitution excluded Chinese from owning land, developing natural resources, or operating public utilities. Many Chinese dealt with these restrictions by the methods mentioned in the preceding paragraph. The government tried to force the Chinese out of the rice trade by setting up a corporation to buy, sell, and refine rice, and thus break the large measure of control which the Chinese had over the industry. Other laws imposed restrictions such as forbidding aliens (principally Chinese) from entering certain occupations.

The public demand for laws limiting Chinese economic rights was widespread and persistent, and politicians found it profitable in two ways. To advocate further restrictions was sure to be popular, and it was equally certain that the proposer would be well paid by the Chinese to abandon his proposals. The threat to introduce anti-Chinese legislation in order to be bribed to abandon it is a widespread and lucrative method of raising funds. The necessity of giving bribes has become a normal operating expense of Chinese business men, and according to Professor Appleton almost amounts to "unofficial and unregistered taxation." They also contribute to political parties so liberally that they are the chief source of funds for both sides.

The heaviest blow suffered by the Chinese was the Retail Trade Nationalization Act of 1954. It provided that no person who was not a citizen of the Philippines, and no partnership or corporation the capital of which was not wholly owned by Philippine citizens might take part in retail trade after May 15, 1954. Aliens engaged in retail business prior to this date might continue until their death or retirement, but their heirs must close it down within six months. Corporations and partnerships must liquidate within ten years of the passage of the law. The majority of the Chinese merchants were aliens owing to the expense and difficulty of becoming naturalized. They controlled 46 per cent at least of the retail trade, and the purpose of the law was to eliminate them, although in a less confiscatory fashion than Sukarno's decree of 1959.

Professor Appleton investigated the manner in which the bill became law, and his account was illuminating. It

was passed by the Philippine Senate in the closing hours of its 1954 session, under unusual circum-

stances. Leading representatives of the Chinese community appealed to influential Congressmen who had received substantial Chinese financial aid in their cam-
paigns and were assured that the bill would not pass.
Due to "politics," however, including an attempt by a
Congressman to extort money from Chinese leaders
in return for a promise to block its enactment, the bill
was brought to a vote and passed, because many Congressmen feared that opposing it would not only be unpopular but might lead to charges that they had accepted
bribes . . . Many of the Chinese interviewed expressed
resentment against Magsaysay's "betrayal" after the
generous financial backing Chinese had given his campaign. [13]

Some abandoned retail trade for other occupations, while others
transferred their capital through the black market to Hong Kong. A
large number made Filipino dummies or their common-law wives
the nominal owners, while many fell back on their traditional solution of bribery. The law apparently failed to break the Chinese
"economic stranglehold" of retail trade. Professor Appleton concluded that, faced by the public insistence on anti-Chinese legislation

only a very courageous (or very well bribed) Filipino
politician would venture to introduce significant mod-
ifications in favor of the Chinese. . . . For the fact
of the matter is that "the Chinese Issue" is being used
by demagogic Philippine politicians . . . to divert public attention from more fundamental economic issues,
such as the polarization of wealth, mass unemployment,
official corruption and retarded industrial development. [14]

So far the government's attempts to create a class of Filipino business men which can compete successfully with the Chinese have
been only moderately successful.

There are about a hundred and fifty Chinese elementary and
secondary schools with around fifty thousand pupils. Until 1957 the
curriculum was dictated by Chiang Kai-shek's Department of Education, and the subjects and text books were substantially the same
as those on Formosa. In 1957 control was taken over by the Philippine Department of Education, but there seems to be a lack of Chinese-speaking inspectors for adequate supervision. The curriculum
includes Philippine as well as Chinese subjects, but there is a subtle
differentiation. "Our" country is China and "foreign" is Philippine
history. The schools help to maintain the community's Chinese
cultural identity to a remarkable degree. For the most part they
staunchly support Chiang Kai-shek, but there is evidence that some

of the teachers are sympathetic to Communism. Many Filipinos would like to close the schools, although their right to exist is guaranteed in the treaty negotiated between the governments of Chiang Kai-shek and the Philippines.

The Chinese community insists that it is loyal to Chiang Kai-shek, and it is impossible to determine how much support there is for the Peking government. The Huk revolt made the Philippine government uncompromisingly hostile to Communism, and the party was declared illegal in 1957. If in addition a Communist were a Chinese the offense would be aggravated, and he would be immediately deported. The community realizes that it dare not give its Filipino enemies an opportunity to attack it, and all the leading institutions such as the Federation of Chinese Chambers of Commerce and the schools seem to be solidly pro-Kuomintang. The government has diplomatic relations with Chiang Kai-shek but none with Peking. Trade with China is forbidden, although some commodities from there are smuggled in. The Philippine intelligence service estimated in 1958 that there were about two thousand Chinese and nine thousand Filipino members of the Communist party, and at least thirty thousand Chinese who were potential Communist supporters. Professor Appleton came to the conclusion that it was impossible to discover how far the community genuinely supported Chiang Kai-shek. On the whole it had a strong sense of the superiority of Chinese culture and wanted to preserve its separate identity and not be assimilated, although there was some intermarriage. Most Philippine Chinese including those who were naturalized were Chinese first and Filipino second, and their attitude was strengthened by the government's hostile policy. As a protector Chiang Kai-shek had been a failure, for he had not been able to prevent the passage of the Retail Trade Act. As business men the Chinese did not favor Communism and some at least were genuinely loyal to Chiang Kai-shek. But if Mao Tse-tung were able to prove himself a more effective protector, it was widely believed that this would be the determining factor with most of the Chinese in deciding their political alignment. . . .

South Viet Nam

Eighty-five per cent of the Chinese in French Indo-China were in Cochin China (now part of South Viet Nam) and Cambodia. There was a considerable amount of intermarriage with women of the country because male immigrants outnumbered female. Neither the French government nor the peoples of Indo-China welcomed the Chinese. Immigration was restricted, and heavy taxes were imposed on them. They were predominantly engaged in retail trade and produce-buying which they combined with usury. They took advantage of the improvidence and indolence of the peasants, who were chronically in need of money, and were disliked for their exploitation and at the same time admired for their superior ability. They controlled the purchase, milling, and export of rice, and owned saw mills and most of the sugar refineries. 15

After the French defeat in 1954 most of the Chinese in North Viet Nam fled to the south. They were estimated to number over 950, 000, and to control eighty per cent of the retail and particularly the rice trade. Ngo Dinh Diem was determined to bring them under his authority, since he was afraid that they would support the Peking government and become a dangerous fifth column. In 1956 he issued a decree that all Chinese born in the country were Vietnamese citizens, and those born in China could be naturalized. Another ordinance required their private schools to conform with the regulations of the Department of Education. This meant that Vietnamese must be the language of instruction and the schools must be controlled by Vietnamese and not Chinese teachers. The president forbade alien Chinese to be retail shopkeepers or engage in the rice trade. These decrees struck at two of their most cherished possessions, their separate Chinese identity and their principal source of livelihood. The Chinese retaliated with a boycott, and the inexperience of the Vietnamese who tried to replace them in trade brought about a condition approaching economic paralysis. Chinese merchants in Hong Kong and Singapore helped by boycotting the trade of South Viet Nam. In 1959 both sides agreed to compromise: Chinese in increasing numbers took out Vietnamese citizenship, and alien traders resumed possession of their businesses but transferred fifty-one per cent of the shares to their sons who had been born in Viet Nam and were technically Vietnamese citizens. The quarrel over the schools was settled, at least for the time being, by the Chinese agreement to add the Vietnamese language to the curriculum. It would not be surprising if eventually South Viet Nam adopted the same educational policy as Thailand. The Peking government does not appear to have much influence, and there is a cultural link between the two peoples which encourages the hope that eventually their antagonism may be ended by assimilation.

Cambodia has some two hundred fifty thousand Chinese and trade is largely in their hands. The government is trying to break their monopoly of the rice trade and has debarred them from some occupations. They are believed to favor the Peking government, and Cambodia has forbidden them to engage in political action.

The Federation of Malaya

The policy adopted by the government of the Federation might best be described as incorporation. The size of the Chinese community makes impossible the discrimination practiced in Indonesia and the Philippines, and it is also alien to the tolerance and shrewd farsightedness that have distinguished Tengku Abdul Rahman. The

180

result of discrimination would be civil war and the destruction of Malaya's prosperity. Assimilation is equally impossible, given the refusal of Malays and Chinese to consider intermarriage. The only hope for the future is that the two communities preserve their separate identity yet at the same time develop a realization that both are Malayans and that they must work together harmoniously. To help bring this about the leaders of the Alliance government agreed that the Malays and Chinese should have substantially equal rights, with some minor reservations that favored the former. There were no restrictions on the economic rights of the Chinese, but the Malays were given preferential quotas for licenses to operate certain businesses such as road haulage. A special government department was set up to carry out rural development projects and assist Malays in establishing small businesses. The requirements for citizenship were made so liberal that the bulk of the alien Chinese living in the Federation could become naturalized. The requirement that applicants must have some knowledge of Malay was waived for one year in order to accommodate the large number who had never troubled to learn the language. The Malays insisted that all aliens who became naturalized must swear allegiance to the Federation and renounce all other loyalties. This rejected the demand of some of the Chinese that they be allowed to retain their Chinese citizenship and have dual nationality. All those born in the Federation after its establishment in 1957 would be citizens by right of birth, thus satisfying the Chinese demand for jus soli. The government refused to give Chinese equal status with Malay and English as official languages. Malays retained their existing preferential quota of four to one in appointments to the administrative service.

The Chinese kept their private schools, and continued to teach their own language and culture. The reasonable requirement was laid down that they must also use Malay or English as the principal medium of instruction and emphasize the Malayan aspects of their curriculum, so that their pupils would no longer be "China-conscious to a degree . . . that limits their consciousness of being a part of Malaya." In return the schools were offered the important inducement that grants at uniform rates would be paid to all of them which conformed to the government's education policy. Those which did not would be refused assistance. The plan was a reasonable compromise, but part of the teachers condemned it as an attack on Chinese culture. They demanded the grant but insisted on teaching whatever they liked. The government's policy was condemned by extreme nationalists of both races, and the complexity of the Federation's problem makes prediction impossible. At bottom the Malays are afraid of political and economic domination by the Chinese, while many of the latter are unwilling to make concessions to a people whom they regard as inferiors.

FOOTNOTES

[1]V. Thompson and R. Adloff, Minority Problems in Southeast Asia (Stanford, 1955), pp. 5—8.

[2]Daily Telegraph, March 8, 1953.

[3]Thompson and Adloff, Minority Problems in Southeast Asia, pp. 11—13. R. H. Fifield, The Diplomacy of Southeast Asia: 1945—1958 (New York, 1958), pp. 288—290.

[4]Thompson and Adloff, Minority Problems in Southeast Asia, pp. 9—10. Royal Institute of International Affairs, Collective Defence in South East Asia (London and New York, 1956), p. 87.

[5]Kennedy, op. cit., p. 380.

[6]D. E. Willmott, The National Status of the Chinese in Indonesia (Ithaca, N.Y., 1956), pp. 2—15.

[7]Ibid., pp. 16—21. Kahin, ed., Major Governments of Asia, pp. 518—519.

[8]Thompson and Adloff, Minority Problems in Southeast Asia, p. 49. Willmott, op. cit., pp. 25, 33—50.

[9]Ibid., pp. 58—59. Thompson and Adloff, Minority Problems in Southeast Asia, pp. 52—53.

[10]Willmott, op. cit., pp. 53—54, 60—61. Far Eastern Survey, XXIV, 9, September 1955, p. 133.

[11]Willmott, op. cit., pp. 65—73.

[12]Much of the material for this section comes from a long and detailed report by Professor Sheldon Appleton, based upon an investigation which he carried out in the Philippines. Parts of his findings were published in Pacific Affairs, XXXII, 4, December 1959, pp. 376—391, and The Journal of Asian Studies, XIX, 2, February 1960, pp. 151—161.

[13]Journal of Asian Studies, XIX, 2, February 1960, pp. 157—158.

[14]Ibid., pp. 160—161.

[15]C. Robequain, tr. Isabel Ward, The Economic Development of French Indo-China (London and New York, 1944), pp. 37—41. V. Thompson, French Indo-China (New York, 1937), pp. 167—169.

CHAPTER 7

The End of the Colonial Era

There is no precise moment when colonialism ceased to exist in Southeast Asia. Certainly the traditional governments are gone, but the heritage of Western imperialism remains. Local economies are still tied to European and American business interests, cultural links between East and West dominate much of this region, and finally, the social alterations introduced by the West continue to play an important role in the composition of Southeast Asian society. Though the impact of the colonial era lingers on, the beginning of the end of European political domination of Southeast Asia originates, in part, with the rise of Japan as a major factor in Asian and world affairs.

The Japanese have both directly and indirectly influenced the growth of modern Asia. Located far to the north and preferring an isolated existence throughout most of her early history, this small Asian nation did not actively participate in early Southeast Asian history and also managed to avoid direct involvement in the mainstream of colonial politics in Asia during the early age of imperialism. In the nineteenth century the increased activity of the European in Asia brought the Japanese into closer contact with the West, but even with the growing involvement of Europe in Asia, the Japanese managed to maintain their independence and relative detachment from the colonial experience. By the beginning of the twentieth century, Japan began to change. She abandoned her traditional isolationism and gradually emerged as an important part of the Asian world. With this change in internal policy and national attitude, Japan became more aggressive in Asian politics. She now sought economic and political ties with the West, she initiated her own concepts of imperialism, and she began to assert a degree of leadership in Asian affairs. One of the first indications that she had emerged on the world political scene came in the last years of the nineteenth century when England and Japan concluded a mutual defense treaty. This treaty gave to Japan international recognition as an Asian power and the rather unique position as an Asian ally with the foremost naval power of the West, England. In 1905, Japan took a further step toward world involvement by defeating both the Russian army and navy. This victory, plus her successful attacks against China, gained for Japan an opportunity to emerge as the new leader in Asian politics, a chance to expand her empire, and to enhance her prestige in Europe, America and Asia. In Southeast Asia, the impact of the Russo-Japanese War had particular importance, in that never before had a European state been defeated by an Asian power. The significance of Japan's victory was further enhanced by the failure of the nationalists to appreciate the tremendous difference between the Russian military machine and the might of the Western colonial powers. Nationalists, believing that all European powers were the same, decided that if one European nation could be defeated, all Western nations could now be attacked and destroyed as colonial rulers in the East. In effect, Japan's victory over Russia fanned the flames of Asian nationalism and also gave to Japan the opportunity to assume a stronger position as the leader of anti-colonialism in Southeast Asia and the leader in general Asian affairs. During World War I, Japan's image in Asia received a second boost through her alliance with the victorious allied powers and the general recognition by the West that Japan ranked as one of the world leaders. In this part of the world, prestige is exceedingly important, and Japan had now acquired an important reputation as a major force in both Asian and world affairs. An additional factor to increase Japan's role in the East came with the gradual decline of China as a dominate force in Asia. In the nineteenth century, China suffered a series of military and diplomatic losses which eventually resulted in European domination of a considerable portion of Chinese life. In the twentieth century, the old imperial government gave way to the Chinese Republic which was soon followed by civil war and destruction of China's prestige. In the eyes of the Southeast Asian, China no longer deserved her traditional position of leadership and with this loss, Japan was now looked upon as the new leader. As for the Japanese, their prestige continued to climb during the inter-war years. Japan became a major critic of the West, she emerged as an economic competitor with the West for Asian markets, she continued to expand her empire at the expense of China, and she openly damned Western imperialism in Southeast Asia. The fact that Japan had become the leader of Oriental criticism of the West, combined with her victories over China and her growing economic power, served to convince most Asian nationalists that the West was on the decline and that the age of colonialism would soon die. Many also believed that the death of colonialism would come about with the help of Japan.

World War II brought even greater Japanese involvement in Southeast Asian affairs. Between 1940 and 1945, Japan embarked on a massive empire-building program which resulted in the overthrow of all colonial governments in Southeast Asia. Many nationalists applauded the arrival of the Japanese as the beginning of a new age of independence and self-determination. However, the five years of Japanese rule in Southeast Asia produced a long series of alterations in most every nationalist movement in colonial Southeast Asia. In the beginning, many nationalists lent their support to the Japanese invasion, but, within a relatively short time most native leaders realized that Japan's Greater East Asia Co-prosperity Sphere meant little more than exchanging Western imperialism for Eastern colonialism. With this realization, most nationalists adopted either a neutral attitude toward the Japanese or openly assisted the European in destroying Japan's power in the east. The nationalists adopted this attitude because they found that the Japanese were particularly harsh military overlords and that they had no real intention of assisting the peoples of Southeast Asia in obtaining their independence. As World War II came to an end, the Japanese sought to prevent the return of Western colonial rule by establishing semi-independent governments in Southeast Asia. These new governments received military aid from Japan and acquired a renewed determination to resist the return of European domination. Though these governments failed to maintain their independence, the taste of political freedom and power made the nationalists even more determined to see the end of Western domination of Southeast Asia. After the restoration of European power in this region, some nationalists turned to guerilla warfare, others looked to Russia for assistance against the West, and others attempted to negotiate with the West to end colonial rule in their country. Though the means to acquire independence differed, all nationalists sought to either destroy or undermine traditional Western colonialism in Southeast Asia.

At the conclusion of World War II, the West did manage to restore colonial rule in Southeast Asia. But, by 1945, world opinion had turned against imperialism. The broad acceptance of the concept of self-determination of all peoples, the growth of socialism and communism with its anti-colonial orientation, the determination of the United States to impose its anti-colonial policies on the free world, and the general discouragement with empire in Western Europe served the interests of the Asian nationalists well and also forced most Western colonial governments to recognize that the age of colonialism had come to an end. Reform of the colonial system was not sufficient; complete independence became the demand of all anti-colonial forces in Europe, Asia and America. By 1960, the defenders of colonialism bowed to world opinion, and in so doing, one of the major war aims of the Japanese was realized; Southeast Asia had acquired its political independence. Traditional Western colonialism had become a part of the historical past.